Peace in World History

In *Peace in World History,* Peter N. Stearns examines the ideas of peace that have existed throughout history, and how societies have sought to put them into practice. Beginning with the status of peace in early hunter-gatherer and agricultural societies, and continuing through the present day, the narrative gives students a clear view of the ways people across the world have understood and striven to achieve peace throughout history. Topics covered include:

- comparison of the *Pax Romana* and *Pax Sinica* of Rome and China
- concepts of peace in Buddhism, Christianity, and Islam, and their historical impact
- the place of peace in the periods of expanding empires
- the emergence, starting in the nineteenth century, of both formal schemes to promote peace and increasingly destructive technologies for warfare.

Moving away from the view of history as a series of military conflicts, *Peace in World History* offers a new way of looking at world history by focusing on peace. Showing how concepts of peace have evolved over time even as they have been challenged by war and conflict, this lively and engaging narrative enables students to consider peace as a human possibility.

Peter N. Stearns is Provost and a Professor of History at George Mason University.

Themes in World History

Series editor: Peter N. Stearns

The *Themes in World History* series offers focused treatment of a range of human experiences and institutions in the world history context. The purpose is to provide serious, if brief, discussions of important topics as additions to textbook coverage and document collections. The treatments will allow students to probe particular facets of the human story in greater depth than textbook coverage allows, and to gain a fuller sense of historians' analytical methods and debates in the process. Each topic is handled over time – allowing discussions of changes and continuities. Each topic is assessed in terms of a range of different societies and religions – allowing comparisons of relevant similarities and differences. Each book in the series helps readers deal with world history in action, evaluating global contexts as they work through some of the key components of human society and human life.

Peace in World History

Peter N. Stearns

Routledge
Taylor & Francis Group

NEW YORK AND LONDON

First published 2014
by Routledge
711 Third Avenue, New York, NY 10017

And by Routledge
2 Park Square, Milton Park, Abingdon, Oxon OX14 4RN

Routledge is an imprint of the Taylor & Francis Group, an informa business

© 2014 Taylor & Francis

Library of Congress Cataloging-in-Publication Data
Stearns, Peter N.
  Peace in world history / Peter N Stearns.—First edition.
  pages cm.—(Themes in world history)
  Includes bibliographical references and index.
  1. World history. 2. Peace. I. Title.
  D62.S74 2014
  303.6'6—dc23
  2013042311

ISBN: 978–0–415–71660–4 (hbk)
ISBN: 978–0–415–71661–1 (pbk)
ISBN: 978–1–315–87959–8 (ebk)

Typeset in Times New Roman
by Swales & Willis Ltd, Exeter, Devon

For Holden Jack, and a life of peace

Contents

Acknowledgments

Christina Regelski provided invaluable research assistance for this book. Laura Bell went beyond the call of duty in readying the manuscript. My wife, Donna Kidd, encouraged the project from concept stage onward. I always appreciate the support of the Routledge series editor, Kimberly Guinta. Interaction with many faculty in George Mason's School of Conflict Analysis and Resolution has educated me in many ways. I'm grateful to Kevin Avruch for his interest and guidance. My admiration also goes to Dr. Daisaku Ikeda, and the inspiration his ideas on peace have provided.

Introduction

World history has not been kind to peace, either in human experience or in scholarship. While all sorts of people in many different societies and time periods have craved peace, a successful devotion to peace is not usually as dramatic a goal as the pursuit of war. Most societies spend more time not at war than in war, but this statement is complicated by the extent to which wars may be planned or prepared during apparently peaceful interludes; and, as we will discuss, it is certainly a rare moment in modern human history when a significant war is not occurring somewhere. That's true today, and it has been true in the past.

It's also true that – in contrast to at least some other historical subjects – it's impossible to paint a historical picture that suggests clear progress toward peace, despite some important efforts, at various points in time, in that direction. We will see that there is a serious contention that right now, over the past 20 years, that the rate of global conflicts has been declining, and we have to assess this claim and whether it suggests a new stage in human affairs. But certainly that past century has been a century of bloodshed, as people have learned how to kill each other in larger numbers than ever before. Here too, the study of peace may seem to go against the standard tide of history.

Certainly historians have not for the most part treated peace kindly. There are far more studies of war than of peace. Survey histories, in most national and regional traditions, spend more time on war. The same is now true of the growing field of world history; to take a crude measure, it's the rare index in a major textbook that lists peace as a topic at all. Of course there are countercurrents. A beginning has been made in writing historical studies of peace, and certainly specific moments – a major treaty, the emergence of organizations devoted to peace – have their place. As a genre, peace study is gaining ground, and historical background normally plays a role here. Still, there's little doubt that most people, at least in our society, think of history more in terms of war than of peace, and most history students gain little systematic knowledge about peace as a topic.

At the popular level, the history of war can seem almost an obsession, particularly among American males: to fill the hours of the History Channel on television, if World War II had not occurred, it would have had to be invented.

Military history is surpassed only by personal family history as a topic in the discipline, among the public in the United States.

Yet there is a history of peace. Knowing something about this history broadens our understanding of the past, and that is arguably a desirable goal. Exploring the history of peace may also expand our sense of options in the present and future. We will see in later chapters that many Americans and American leaders have played an important role, for more than half a century, in assumptions about the normalcy of military preparations and activities. We tend to look askance at societies that are not prepared for war, both now and in the past. But there are other vantage points, and an exploration of peace as a historical topic can contribute to a more expansive sense of human options.

The goal of this book is to contribute further to an understanding of peace as an element in the historical experience of human beings and also, without unduly editorializing, to use history to promote more self-conscious thinking about peace as a human possibility.

The topic is huge. There are at least three kinds of peace: there's a personal or group quest for calm and tranquility. There's an effort to establish a larger society that is not wracked by excessive strife or violence. And there is, finally, the attempt, conscious or unconscious, to minimize the possibility of war. This book deals primarily with this final meaning. The quest for personal tranquility may of course relate to commitments to discourage war, but the goals may also separate: some people are so bent on personal calm that they actually ignore some of the larger conditions of violence around them and have little or no impact on that violence. Many societies are eminently successful in reducing internal unrest but continue to maintain aggressive roles toward the world at large. Indeed, war or the threat of war are sometimes used as deliberate distractions from internal disorder – this was a factor, for example, in the willingness of several belligerents to go to what turned out to be a disastrous war in 1914. Different types of peace, in other words, are complexly related.

Even the focus on efforts to avoid formal war must have several facets. We will be particularly interested, in this book, in ideas about peace – in individuals and movements that saw peace as an important, achievable goal; but also in arrangements that have attempted to reduce the possibility of war. Anti-war arrangements may flow from formal thinking about peace – the two main aspects of our topic may be linked. But arrangements may flow as well from more pragmatic circumstances. The history of peace can involve deliberate attempts to minimize, even eliminate military organizations. There have certainly been many arguments, at various points in world history, that real peace and military capacity are ultimately incompatible. But peace has also resulted at times from the existence (as well as the careful guidance) of strong military organizations. Again, even a brief overview of peace in world history must embrace many different facets.

Dealing with peace as a recurrent theme in world history provides a fresh perspective, but it also links to familiar aspects of world history in several ways. At least some of the standard periods in world history turn out to be relevant categories for the history of peace as well. The advent and spread of major world religions, for example, which seized center stage in world history after the classical period, clearly encouraged some new thinking and new organizational efforts on the peace front. The long nineteenth century, with the rise of industrial societies and the spread of new ideas, generated terrible new capacities for war, but it also saw the spread of some novel thinking and international experiments toward more systematic peace. The contemporary period in world history also ushered in important peace innovations, including a new current of formal pacifism. Again, use of major world history periods must not suggest some pattern of progress across time, but it does allow a connection between certain types of general change, in religion or in international contacts, and the quest for peace.

Assessment of peace in world history unquestionably involves some of the same comparative building blocks that other types of analysis in the field encourage. Some societies have traditionally valued war more than others have, though of course the comparative situation can change over time as well. Some cultural and political traditions are more conducive to discussions of peace than others. Again, no large, complex society has yet managed to generate a formula for durable peace, but comparison clearly highlights some different propensities at various points in time including today.

Some people and some societies don't like peace. Some value it, at least implicitly, but have little idea how to express relevant goals and scant notion of how peace might be pursued. Some, finally, at various points in world history have articulated peace goals or introduced new arrangements designed to encourage peace, or both. The story is an important part of the human record and deserves more attention than it often receives. The story also remains significant today, both in capturing unexpected varieties in approaches to war and peace among major societies and in reminding us that there may be more options than some of us – accustomed to frequent war or threat of war – may imagine. A history of peace may challenge some assumptions; it might also prove liberating. Without evading often harsh reality, we don't need to think of the human experience only in terms of the next big conflict waiting to happen.

* * * * *

Our discussion will proceed in terms of major chronological periods. The first chapter discusses the status of peace in hunting and gathering and early agricultural societies and civilizations. The discussion will raise three fundamental issues. First, not surprisingly, we don't know as much about early societies, in this and many other respects, as we would like. But second, it's clear from the outset that a great deal of variety prevailed. Some societies – and we know this both from archeological records and from the experience of more recent hunting and gathering groups – were remarkably peaceful, sometimes quite intentionally. Others emerged in a situation where war was more common and where, probably, a culture supportive of war developed. There may have been greater variety concerning peace among early societies than there is today, though the theme certainly persists even in the heavily armed contemporary world. Putting the point starkly: some early societies had gods or goddesses of peace, others did not, sometimes favoring instead the more famous inclination to venerate warlike divinities. From considering variety, finally, comes perhaps the most fundamental point, which is whether the experience of early societies suggests a basic human proclivity for war and violence, such that peace efforts always go against the grain of human nature; or whether human nature itself is more nuanced and complicated. Our first chapter hardly resolves this basic issue, but at the least we can indicate some of the factors involved. How much does the variety of approaches toward peace developed in early societies reflect ambiguities in the human makeup, as opposed to particular local contexts or maybe sheer accidents of leadership?

Chapter 2 turns to the great classical civilizations, and particularly China and the Mediterranean. Did the development of more elaborate governments and cultures contribute to new approaches to peace? Do more elaborate historical records help us trace explicit types of thinking about peace, or was this a development still in the future? The emergence of the great Roman Empire generated the term *Pax Romana*, or Roman peace, which suggests some relationship between new political and military structures and peace goals. Historians have also invented a corresponding term, "Chinese peace," or *Pax Sinica*, to capture the fact that this great empire, also, endeavored to protect internal peace and security. There are two opportunities here: first, assessing the classical period overall in terms of changes in conceiving and implementing peace, compared to earlier societies including the river-valley civilizations; and second, comparing the two greatest empires, China and Rome, which turned out to generate some interesting differences in leading ideas about peace and war.

Chapter 3 also focuses on developments that began in the classical period, but under the distinctive aegis of Buddhism and its initial context in India. The Emperor Ashoka in India, during the period of the Mauryan dynasty, is the first great world-historical figure to be associated clearly with a devotion to peace. We know that he came to this devotion after a more characteristic engagement with war. The experience of war sickened him and facilitated his conversion to Buddhism, still a new reform religion in South Asia. Ashoka's own peace policies are not recorded in detail, but his promotion of Buddhism as a missionary religion allows exploration of this particular religious strain and its recurrent role in a quest for peace, first in parts of Southern and Eastern Asia, but more recently on an even wider scale. Exploring the Buddhist approaches to peace, and their limitations, will take us well beyond the classical period, but the classical origins form the clear starting point.

The advent of the other two great world religions, Christianity and Islam, as the classical civilizations began to crumble, takes us into the next relevant world history period – from the sixth century CE onward. Both of these religions, along with their predecessor in Judaism, developed important new thinking about peace, both on this earth and in the heavenly afterlife, and some practical measures toward its achievement. Both generated new communities of peace, and some larger peace movements that would dot subsequent world history. But both also encouraged explicit military activity, so the overall impact on peace was at the least extremely complex. Comparing the two religions from the standpoint of peace – and including other religious traditions and policies in the same comparative mix – helps address the question of where the postclassical period sits in a larger history of peace. New ingredients were unquestionably added, though probably not as decisively as in the case of Buddhism, but new regional differences also emerged. The postclassical period also embraces a century and a half of Mongol dominance over much of Eurasia. The dominance was created by military force, but it did generate a period of relative peace that requires some assessment.

Chapter 5 turns to the early modern period, from the fifteenth to the eighteenth centuries. The basic shape of the period was remote from peace: the centuries were defined by the growing use of guns and cannon, by new European colonies created in part by gunnery, and by the formation of a series of new Asian and Eurasian empires also established by force. The "age of the gunpowder empires" is not an inaccurate description. Peace, and thinking about peace, unquestionably retreated in many of the world's regions, while on the seas new capacities for naval warfare extended the reach of violent conflict. Against the grain, however, a few more positive developments deserve exploration. In Europe, for example, innovative attempts at peacemaking surfaced in the seventeenth century, after decades of religious strife. The Asian empires also experimented with negotiated settlements though with mixed results.

The new period that opened in the later eighteenth century, extending until World War I, introduced several new ingredients into the history of peace – though they hardly pulled in the same direction. Beginning in Western Europe, though ultimately extending to other areas, the ideas associated with the Enlightenment provided unprecedented support to the idea of progress on this earth. Enlightenment figures envisaged gains ranging from greater life expectancy to new levels of scientific understanding. At times, as well, they included new possibilities of peace in their vision. After all, if humankind was really going to move forward, one could hardly avoid some measures that would reduce the scourge of war. Along with new thinking, however, came the new kinds of weaponry associated ultimately with the industrial revolution. The killing potential of war expanded steadily. This development could, of course, be combined with new ideas, to produce more formal efforts to limit war or its damage; innovations here emerged particularly in the second half of the nineteenth century. But there was no easy harmony: ideas and realities increasingly clashed, and while this was not an entirely new phenomenon it took on new dimensions from this point forward. Finally, the potential for conflict became increasingly global, partly because of new technologies, partly thanks to the extension of European imperialism. Europe's growing military reach, and its brief but vivid superiority in military hardware, posed new problems for many different regions, and here too reactions could include some novel thinking

about peace. By the end of the nineteenth century, the result of this complicated mix of trends included some unprecedented efforts to discuss innovations aimed at limiting war – innovations that included new attempts to set up
international measures for conciliation or directly to address the possibility of
limiting armaments. And when many regions heralded the dawn of a new century, in 1900, hopes that greater levels of peace could be achieved were high
on the wish lists.

And of course optimism and experiment came crashing down in 1914, with
the largest and at least in some ways the most horrible war the world had experienced to that point.

Chapter 7 picks up the pieces after World War I, covering the short but
intense decades from that point until 1945. We know in retrospect that the three
decades after 1914 operated under a huge cloud, with growing possibilities for
conflict, new ideologies like fascism that elevated the glories of war, and the
steady expansion of military weaponry. The short period born in war would
end in another war, which means that from the standpoint of the history of
peace the decades were first and foremost a time of failure.

But there were some promising innovations as well, extending some of the
thinking and initiatives that had emerged in the nineteenth century. Though
they proved abortive, in some cases surprisingly naïve, they deserve more
attention than they usually gain in world history coverage. Precisely because
World War I had clashed so horribly with previous optimism, efforts emerged
during and particularly immediately after the war to seek remediation. Formal
pacifism, elaborate attempts at arms limitation, the establishment of the League
of Nations as a means of reducing the potential for international conflict – all
these were the fruit of reactions to the 1914 conflict, the attempt to make this a
war which might end war. In other settings, additional efforts emerged, particularly the experiments with nonviolence as a means of effecting change. Here, in
sum, were important new components in the elusive history of peace.

Finally, for these troubled decades, as war clouds mounted in the late 1930s
a misguided attempt at conciliation, as British and French leaders met then
Nazi dictator Hitler in Munich, gave compromise a bad name, and echoes of
this failure would persist for many decades thereafter – a further though fascinating complication in the contemporary story of peace.

The final section of the book deals with developments since 1945. The goal
is both to connect earlier patterns – the larger world history of peace – with
recent changes and continuities, but also to provide a slightly more detailed
history of the contemporary period itself.

Chapter 8 deals with the immediate results of World War II and the emerging Cold War. The formation of the United Nations involved a concerted
effort to redress some of the mistakes of the interwar years, by creating a body
with greater capacity to control conflict. While the results have certainly not
measured up to expectations, the role of the UN not only in advocating for
peace, but actively intervening in certain situations, deserves emphasis. With
the defeat of fascism, outright ideological advocacy of war clearly declined.

New efforts in international law, bringing certain leaders to trial as "war criminals" also sought to drive home new responsibilities for peaceful behavior. And while the Cold War immensely complicated many of these efforts, and clearly promoted the growth of military establishments in many countries, the competing coalitions in fact showed some restraint. Further, the new danger of nuclear weaponry – another product of World War II – created a certain degree of circumspection, and ultimately active efforts to negotiate reductions in the most menacing armament levels. Overall, then, the framework for peace in the decades after 1945 involved several important innovations, some obvious new threats and tensions, but ultimately a greater level of restraint than some observers, seeing the Cold War unfold so soon after World War II, would have predicted. The balance sheet is complex. Finally, this chapter takes up some larger forces, from globalization itself to the spread of consumer societies, that must also be considered from the standpoint of contemporary frameworks for peace.

Within this context, Chapter 9 addresses regional patterns of peace and war during the same postwar decades. A number of nations ventured new leadership toward peace, even though formal pacifism, discredited by the failure to prevent World War II, probably declined. Several former colonies, a number of Latin American countries, and a number of movements based in Germany and Japan sought to limit particular conflicts and more broadly to promote greater attention to peaceful goals. Against this, however, and not only because of the Cold War dynamic but also many regional rivalries, military commitments and reactions gained ground in many regions, including the United States. Some of the demilitarized societies, most notably Japan, faced new pressures to modify their stance under assumptions that "normal" states needed protections beyond vows of peace. Regional comparisons during the later twentieth century suggest some dramatically different approaches to the prevention or limitation of conflict, with explicit interest in peace sometimes overshadowed by tactical responses.

Chapter 10, the final main segment, pulls this contemporary history into the present, assessing the current status of peace efforts, including the emergence of more formal scholarship on peace and on conflict resolution. Religious leadership, including the Catholic papacy, regained interest in promoting peace. And there were particular moments – for example, in the anti-Vietnam protests during the 1960s, when advocacy for peace gained ground in other societies. New moves toward considerable demilitarization spread to additional regions, such as parts of Africa, New Zealand, and additional portions of Latin America. Dramatic optimism would be misplaced. But there was some belief that new forms of conflict control were paying off. It would be grandiose and misleading to see the contemporary scene as some culmination of a historical movement toward peace. But at many points in history, but most obviously during recent decades, there have been attempts to learn from past tragedies, to avoid some of the mistakes that have thwarted peace before. Is there a history to learn, and can people agree on what it is?

An Epilogue relates the highlights of the larger record of peace history into current perspective, along with some thoughts about peace possibilities for the future. The future is always a matter of conjecture, of course. But peace professionals currently hope that there will be opportunities beyond what has yet been achieved, and it's worth at least a moment to consider their voice.

*   *   *   *   *

There is a recurrent, complicated, often disappointing account of peace ideas and peace efforts that runs from the early human experience to the present day, a history of great ideals and innovative proclamations that inevitably end in ruins. Unquestionably, assessing the history of peace frequently highlights limitation and failure. But the same history also captures some soaring ideals and imaginative practical efforts. It provides an active backdrop to thinking about the subject in the contemporary world – to making sure that explicit attention to a goal of peace is not buried under the barrage of bad news that so frequently assails us from many quarters. The history of peace is not the story of definitively conquering the darker sides of human nature, but it is not an insignificant story either – and it is not just a study in failure. As always, the historian must argue, we have a better chance of building a successful future if we know the foundations built in the past.

Further reading

Adolf, Antony. *Peace: A World History*. Cambridge: Polity Press, 2009.

Barash, D., ed. *Approaches to Peace: A Reader in Peace Studies*. New York: Oxford University Press, 1999.

Boulding, E. *Cultures of Peace: The Hidden Side of History*. Syracuse, NY: Syracuse University Press, 2000.

Cortright, David. *Peace: A History of Movements and Ideas*. Cambridge: Cambridge University Press, 2008.

Dietrich, C. Wolfgang. *Interpretations of Peace in History and Culture*. New York: Palgrave Macmillan, 2012.

Megoran, Nick. "War *and* Peace? An Agenda for Peace Research and Practice in Geography." *Political Geography* 30 (2011): 178–89.

Samaddar, R., ed. *Peace Studies: An Introduction to the Concept, Scope and Themes*. Newberry Park, CA: Sage, 2004.

Weinberg, A. and L., eds. *Instead of Violence: Writings by the Great Advocates of Peace and Nonviolence throughout History*. Boston, MA: Grossman, 1963.

On peacebuilding

Smith, David J. "How Studying Peace Building Can Be a Tool for Global Education." Available online at http://chronicle.com/blogs/worldwise/how-studying-peace-building-can-be-a-tool-for-global-education/32667 (accessed August 1, 2013).

Zelizer, Craig. *Integrated Peacebuilding: Innovative Approaches to Transforming Conflict*. Boulder, CO: Westview Press, 2013.

1 Peace and early human societies

The early phases of the human experience, stretching over a long span of time, raise a number of questions about peace and about precedents established that might extend into more recent centuries. There is the issue of human nature, as the species emerged and evolved. Were early people more or less peaceful than their modern counterparts? What kinds of arrangements did hunters-gatherers establish to minimize collective violence? Motives and opportunities for war may have increased with the advent of agriculture. But agriculture flourished far more abundantly with peace, and peasant farmers may have found new reasons and some new techniques to reduce their vulnerability to war. Topics under the heading: agriculture and peace, thus follow questions about the early species and peace. The initial civilizations, usually along major rivers, raise a fresh set of challenges for peace, from about 3500 BCE onward. But they also created new opportunities to articulate peace goals. Each phase of the early human experience thus offers its own questions about peace as a priority and a possibility. Each phase also harbors variety, requiring comparisons of different peace capacities and intentions depending on the particular society involved, another anticipation of complexities still with us today.

The early record is not always easy to determine or interpret, as evidence is scattered. But one point does emerge: from early times to the present there has been no simple evolution from warlike to peaceful, or vice versa. Humans have long grappled with options, and of course they still do.

A hunting and gathering species

The debate begins here: is the human species naturally warlike, or is peace more natural or at least equally natural? The evidence is mixed, the disagreements sharp. But the actual historical record of early humans suggest that, whatever one's views of basic human nature, frequent warfare was not a common goal or experience, and a large minority of societies were actually quite peaceful. Here too, the picture is mixed, but not as bleak – from a peace standpoint – as is often imagined.

The dilemmas are not new. Philosophers have discussed this aspect of human nature, in many different societies, for a long time. Some, like the Legalists in

China or Thomas Hobbes in seventeenth-century Britain, have seen humans as naturally disorderly, ready to do violence against their fellows, unless restrained by some superior force such as a powerful state. Others have taken a more optimistic view, compatible with the notion that people may usually seek peace.

The discussion is no mere abstraction. Contemporary peace prospects are clearly related to views of human nature – though one can always argue that even a naturally violent species can and should learn new behaviors. A United Nations offshoot convened a scholarly meeting in 1989, in Seville, Spain, and issued the following as part of the Seville Statement on Violence: "It is scientifically incorrect to say that war or any other violent behavior is genetically programmed into our human nature ... or that war is caused by 'instinct' or any single motivation." Is this hopeful statement accurate? Is it compatible with actual human experience?

The problem of biology

Developments in nineteenth-century science, or more properly perverse popularizations of nineteenth-century science, generated a wider sense that war, rather than peace, is the natural human condition. Charles Darwin's great discovery of the process of evolution involves the concept of natural selection, in which members of a species would compete and struggle, with the superior individuals coming out on top (the genetics aspect was discovered later). "Survival of the fittest" was the slogan that emerged from this concept in the hands of popularizers, and this in turn could suggest a basic biological propensity for war, particularly in species capable of more deliberate planning and organization – such as human beings. War here would be a "filtering mechanism" and an absolutely standard behavior. Ideas of this sort encouraged a view of primitive man as inherently warlike, engaging in recurrent combat to gain greater access to food resources, to seize available females – the aggressive apparatus that long attached to concepts of the cave man.

And it does seem to be true that human beings are among the only species that routinely organize groups to try to kill other adults in the same species. Chimpanzees also engage in war, though it is not clear how often this occurs. Two or three chimp wars have been studied by contemporary observers. In these wars, groups of young males deliberately raid the territory of another group, retreating if they encounter large numbers of the enemy but beating more isolated males to death; females are usually spared but their offspring are eaten. The results of these wars can be the acquisition of more territory for the home group, improving food resources and therefore encouraging population growth. Primatologists argue as to whether the chimp warriors "know" the reasons for their action – that is, are capable of this kind of goal orientation along with their clear capacity for some group planning – or whether the males are simply naturally aggressive.

For our purposes, the bigger question is how chimpanzee behavior relates to that of humans. Some contend that the two species derive from a common ancestor, and therefore inherit similar propensities for aggressive violence and war as well as the capacity to plan. But others point to entirely peaceful primate species – also close relatives – to dispute the connection. There's even an interesting argument that humans, as opposed to chimps, developed a "sociability gene" as part of the later evolution of *Homo sapiens sapiens*, about 80,000 years ago, that actually restrains humans and prompts them to seek mechanisms to reduce disputes and normally restrain violent impulses. Put male chimps on a 13-hour flight, this argument goes, and they will be trying to kill each other well before the plane lands; but do the same for people, and violence rarely results given superior human sociability impulses. More broadly, sympathy for other people and a desire to help others in distress seem natural parts of the human condition, suggesting at least the importance of complexity and options in human responses.

In other words, debates about basic biology do not resolve the question of innate human propensities for peace or for war, though on balance they probably incline toward the side of more natural aggression. Obviously, even if humans are not naturally peaceful, they can learn the behavior, using different cultural norms and institutional mechanisms to "escape" their inherent tendencies. And even if war once served a purpose in evolution, this does not mean that modern war, with its destructive technologies, continues to operate in that fashion. For human beings also have the capacity to work for peace, to develop personal and social mechanisms to reduce conflict, and this, too, can serve basic biological purposes. The "fittest" who survive are not necessarily always the most aggressive, but often those who learn arrangements that reduce exposure to violence. One scholar has suggested that we test the idea of "survival of the peaceful," as not only a more desirable but a more accurate description of what has worked best in human history.

Hunting and gathering societies

Evidence from the earliest forms of human societies, all based on hunting and gathering activities, advances the debate about human tendencies, but it does not definitively resolve it. Many hunting and gathering societies engaged in forms of war, but some never did and many remained peaceful most of the time. Here too, evidence points both ways, in terms of the arguments about natural aggressiveness, though in some ways the available data highlights a greater normal interest in peace than the more abstract discussions of human nature suggest.

Two factors complicate this discussion of the early human experience. In the first place, records are limited. We have no evidence about what people actually thought about peace or war, or how conscious they were of peace as a desirable option. We build data about early societies either from archeological remains, including examination of human skeletons from the period, from the behaviors of hunting and gathering groups that operate still today, or in some combination.

The second complexity flows from the nature of hunting and gathering groups. They were small, with limited resources and relatively simple technologies. This means that their capacities for war were in many ways constrained: the fact that wars were not too common may suggest peaceful motives but may also flow from limited capacities. Hunting bands did not have the resources to support a specialized military apparatus – so the relative absence of war may not prove much about motivations. Thus while armies depend on the advent of agriculture and civilization – the first known organized army dates from about 5,000 years ago – this does not mean that informal groups (particularly of young men) could not practice collective violence that was in fact a form of war. Similarly, we know that early human groups did not pay much attention to the development of weaponry. But this was part of a general lack of technological sophistication, and further, since tools used in hunting could also serve in violence against other humans the claim may be fairly hollow. Finally, while we will see that very little killing occurred even when early skirmishes did break out, even low levels of violent death could have a devastating effect given the small size of the hunting bands; some claim that higher percentages of early humans died in wars, at least in some regions, than is now the case (the contemporary figure is about 5 percent).

With all the qualifications, however, it looks like the long history of early humans was often quite peaceful. Hunting and gathering groups moved around a lot, so that if war threatened some would just pack up and leave. Similarly, additional resource needs could sometimes be met by migration, rather than fights over territorial control. The striking fact is that death by violence is suggested in only 4 of 110 fossil sites left by early humans. There's a huge chronological gap between the long record of hunting and gathering activity and the first definite sign of war.

In fragile hunting and gathering economies, war could be dangerously disruptive. Whatever aggressive sentiments humans – and, particularly, young males – naturally possess could be taken out in hunting. Early societies often developed explicit mechanisms to promote peace – more than war-avoidance was at play here: there was clearly a positive if implicit concept of peace. Bands of hunters and gatherers frequently exchanged gifts, expressly to provide alternatives to conflict. Joint feasts and other rituals developed to promote harmony. Formal opportunities for intermarriage often supported peaceful relations among neighboring bands, creating practical connections whereby groups could share resources.

Some hunter-gatherer societies went beyond the common conflict-prevention arrangements, to develop an explicit and positive concept of peace. An example that has survived to the present day involves the Utku Inuit group in the Canadian Arctic, many of whose characteristics are shared by other Inuit peoples. Though a hunting people, accustomed to administering death, the Utku believe deeply in nonviolence toward people. While killing game excites them, they react with horror to the idea of aggression against other humans. They lack even a word for anger in their language, and while they encounter conflicts they express feelings with great care, and if a sense of hostility becomes too strong the angry party simply walks away. Great emphasis is placed on warmth within family and community. Children's games are organized to foster positive emotions and to subdue aggression. Interestingly, and possibly because of the expectation of tight emotional control and fear of offending others, suicide rates are fairly high, but acts of interpersonal violence are rare, and formal warfare unknown.

The Semai, an indigenous people in Malaysia, offer a second example of deliberate and successful devotion to peace, in a so-called primitive society (though in this case, some agriculture supplements hunting). The Semai work hard to avoid anger and violence, emphasizing sharing and caution instead. A popular saying holds that "dispute holds more danger than a tiger." Individuals suspected of fomenting quarrels are shamed in front of others, but if an actual dispute breaks out the group emphasizes settlement rather than blame. Village meetings work to resolve any conflicts, with the local leaders emphasizing the importance of group solidarity and peace. Disputants get to present their case, but the assumption is that the decision of the meeting will resolve any problems and restore emotional control: Semai belief in their own pacifism provides basic guidelines. As with the Utku, though with different specifics, the Semai carefully raise children to learn that anger wins no response; youngsters who get in a fight are simply pulled away by adults and sent home in shame.

There are obvious problems in generalizing from examples of this sort. They are unusual, involving (for whatever reason; causation is hard to determine) extraordinary levels of emotional socialization and control. At the least, they demonstrate that human societies can consistently avoid war and remain quite intentionally devoted to peace. They contribute, thus, to the complex debate about "natural" human impulses. On the other hand, there is no basis for claiming that societies of this sort were the norm in hunting and gathering settings. Far more typical, though involving some of the same tactics and motives as with the Utku or Semai, were various, though less extreme, peace-promoting strategies:

- Many early societies featured a divinity devoted to peace. Sometimes they had a god of war as well, but in many cases peace predominated in the polytheistic spectrum. Thus the Lakota Indians, though not systematically nonviolent, devote great attention to the goddess Wohpe, devoted to peace. The daughter of Wi and the Moon, when Wohpe visited earth she gave the Sioux Indians a pipe as a symbol of peace (and correspondingly, passing the pipe in the group, and even sharing it with strangers, became an important ritual designed to promote solidarity). Wohpe represented peace, harmony, and meditation. Her presence as a divinity helped support the importance of reducing conflict and underpinned practices designed to prevent or end disputes.
- While the practice of ritual meals was common, as a means of promoting positive social bonds, some groups placed particular emphasis on the intentional strategy involved. The leader of a New Zealand tribe in the nine-

teenth century was quoted to the effect that feasts "have many times been the means of keeping peace between us, and may be of service again."

* Games between groups could also serve to reduce conflict. Early in the twentieth century an Australian tribe promoted a practice called *makarata*, or ceremonial peacekeeping fights, in which individuals were allowed to express aggression as a means of releasing anger and restoring peace.

Some anthropologists, surveying practices of this sort among so-called primitive peoples, argue that peace is in fact the basic human norm, the standard goal of hunting and gathering societies; war, in this view, is a learned behavior, a later product of history, and can therefore in principle be unlearned.

Other evidence, however, is somewhat less encouraging, though not entirely contradictory. A careful survey of current hunting and gathering societies, with conditions similar to the forms that had characterized the early human experience, suggests that about 30 percent rarely or never go to war. Some have military apparatus and capacity, but do not use it; others, as we have seen, are even more conscientiously devoted to peace. Included in this percentage are groups so averse to war that they simply try to flee if confronted with aggression. On the other hand, some of the remaining 70 percent not only participate in war but do so very frequently, in many cases at least once a year. Their wars are usually brief skirmishes, usually raids or ambushes, lasting at most a few days and involving low death rates (though again, even these can devastate a small human band). Motives – apart from a possibly "natural" aggression – seem to emphasize seizing goods and resources, more than any idea of conquest.

This type of evidence is obviously hard to interpret. It certainly suggests that examples like the Utku are not only strange by contemporary American standards, where anger control is not practiced nearly so systematically, but are also atypical even in a hunting and gathering context. It's the variety that is striking: some settings and some cultures really do manage to avoid war, but others do the opposite, in some cases making frequent if minor war essentially a social norm. Whatever one's conclusions about human nature in the abstract, it seems that in actual fact – in lived experience, in the original types of societies – it can go either way. It can generate systematic and successful inculcation of peace; but it can also sustain war. Peaceful hunting and gathering groups may be on the decline in contemporary conditions, where encroachments of settled societies limit opportunities to flee and create greater competition for available space; so the 30–70 split between peace and war may be a bit misleading. But it certainly seems that peace and war are social options, as against any idea that human nature inevitably pushes to a single approach.

So finally, what does available archeological evidence tell us about the actual history of war, and how does this fit with the complicated picture we have assembled up to now? This is the final test to undertake, and yet here too the evidence is murky. Here's what we know for sure: the oldest record of injuries caused by warfare – based on skeletons of people clearly killed by weapons, in some kind of mass violence – dates from about 14,000 years ago, in the Sudan region of northeast Africa. Archeologists wonder if regional climate change at that point forced different kinds of hunting and gathering groups into contact with each other, searching for newly scarce resources, thus prompting this first definite war situation.

But wars may have occurred before this, yet simply did not leave distinct traces. We know that people were violently killed before this point, by stones or spears, but these acts were usually individual fights, not more general wars. Yet more collective deaths could have happened, with the skeletons long since vanished and the weapons, indistinguishable from those used in hunting, gone as well. One student of early wars argues that the average hunting and gathering group probably warred once every century, through mounting or reacting to some kind of raid, with groups in more densely populated regions experiencing war more frequently. Small, local wars could have resulted from efforts to seize food or expand the range for hunting (though durable seizures of territory were rare), or as revenge for a violent act or insult by another group. Yet it is vital to remember that inhibitions against war were also considerable: many groups preferred flight to fight, and the various rituals designed to promote harmony were also extensive. Whether this suggests some kind of positive idea of peace, or simply common-sense tactics to minimize disruption cannot be determined – any more than the actual frequency of war.

Even relations between different human species, notably *Homo sapiens sapiens* and Neanderthals, may have been less warlike than once imagined. Earlier notions that the newer species had simply killed off older rivals are now yielding to a realization that the two groups often coexisted for long periods and time and even intermarried. War was not, among our presumably primitive ancestors, the normal answer.

Granting all the complexities of available evidence, it seems likely that the long period of early human history was marked by occasional war, possibly not very often, while some groups more systematically attempted to avoid conflict altogether. Warlike incidents were usually short-lived and small in scale, though effects on individual hunting and gathering groups – themselves small – might be considerable – one reason that some such groups might have developed more explicit thinking about peace. On the big issue – is war or peace the more natural human condition? – the evidence is inconclusive. But against some images of caveman ferocity, what we know about the early human experience suggests that peace was, frequently, a real and often preferred option.

The impact of agriculture

With the Neolithic revolution and the advent of agriculture, from 9000 BCE onward, a much clearer sense of patterns begins to emerge. Wars almost certainly became more likely. Strategies to maintain peace had to alter in consequence. We still lack any explicit information about peace goals, but we can infer that clearer divisions opened up over orientations toward peace or war. While change was significant, older techniques survived as well, including efforts to use exchanges of goods as a means of avoiding conflict. Change itself was gradual: much of the evidence for greater warfare comes after agriculture had been established for centuries, not from the earliest days.

Surviving traces of human activity become more abundant with the advent of early agriculture. There are far more archeological remains, including remains that suggest interpersonal violence. But better data are not the main point. There were a number of reasons that war, in fact, became more prominent.

Most obviously, agricultural settlements took shape, usually, in fixed locations, and as they piled up stocks of food and often some other goods they were tempting targets for human predators – sometimes including neighboring hunting and gathering groups that might resent, even fear, this new way of life. Villages and, later, small cities represented a kind of accumulated wealth that pre-agricultural economies had not developed, and as a result deliberate raids took on a new purpose. For the peasant farmers themselves, fleeing – as a peaceful response – was far less feasible, for so much invested labor would now have to be abandoned. Finally, with agriculture population size increased, creating greater potential for competition for space and resources simply because of this additional pressure. For various reasons, then, conflict became more likely.

Agriculture also encouraged the emergence of new technologies, including military technologies and specializations. We have seen that hunting and gathering societies introduced hunting equipment, such as spears, that could also be used against peoples but it was only with agriculture that human societies had the resources to support more explicit weapons development. Stone maces were probably the first such product. These consisted of a rounded stone hitting surface attached to a wooden handle through a drilled shaft hole. It had no use other than as a weapon, either to attack other people or to finish off wounded opponents. Surviving primitive maces have been discovered from the early Neolithic period onward, and they became steadily more common over time. Other innovations included sharper spears, and by the later Neolithic period the development of protective body armor emerged.

Around 4000 BCE, horses began to be domesticated, initially in central Asia. Here was another major development in military potential, and for many centuries mounted warriors would be able to terrorize agricultural peoples with their size and maneuverability.

Agricultural resources also permitted various forms of specialization. While most people – at least 80 percent of the population, in most agricultural economies – had to farm, there was a new margin for other activities. Military specialization was one result – initially introduced, in some cases, to provide protection against attacks from hunter-gatherer groups. But while military specialists probably originated for defensive reasons, they probably increased the frequency of war, since they had obvious self-interest in demonstrating their own prowess and importance. Some Neolithic communities began to bury a certain percentage of their populations with weapons such as battleaxes – a clear sign of the growing importance both of military equipment and of a class of men identified by their military commitment.

Not surprisingly, skeletal evidence of death in war becomes much more abundant with the advent of agriculture. Mass graves with people killed in war have been found in a number of early agricultural areas. Not infrequently, raiders overwhelmed a village, chasing its inhabitants away but then attacking the slower stragglers, disproportionately young children and the mothers who were trying to protect them. Most of the victims of these wars, whether fleeing or fighting, died from head wounds, skulls crushed by blows from a mace or stone axe. Warfare was becoming more sophisticated and institutionalized – one of several unintended consequences of agriculture. Even cave paintings from the Neolithic age occasionally depicted soldiers bearing bows and arrows or spears, arrayed against each other in battle.

Yet, as war advanced, so did efforts at peace; indeed, consciousness of peace may have increased simply because of the obvious new threats. Even amid agriculture, there are regions and periods when war was unknown or at least rare. Clearly, some Neolithic societies were able to solve conflicts without recourse to war. Peace options, building on earlier techniques and goals, did not disappear.

Indeed, an important argument has been offered about the importance of prolonged peace in developing agricultural economies in the first place. Anthropologist Keith Otterbein notes what a long time it took to figure out how to domesticate plants, and how essential peace would have been in the process. He sees violent raids decreasing in the Middle East as hunting became more difficult and people began to concentrate on the conversion to planting and harvesting. He identifies one large farming community in the Euphrates valley, with over 6,000 residents, which enjoyed at least a thousand years of peace. He speculates that similar conditions must have prevailed as agriculture spread to Egypt or as it later, separately, arose in Central America. And he contends, further, that early states, emerging in agricultural societies, arose in conditions of peace, and with dedication to peace, rather than a new commitment to war.

Otterbein admits that raids and wars occurred in some parts of the Neolithic world: he simply denies that agriculture is somehow automatically connected to an increase in violence and, even more, he argues, that at least for a time, in places where agriculture first developed, even the reverse was true: violence had to decrease for this initially fragile new economy to take root. This kind of debate, about connections or lack of connection between agriculture and war, though less well developed than the human nature discussion, has important implications for world history not only in the Neolithic period but beyond. Many agricultural societies may have had a legacy of peace to which they could refer even when some of the conditions for greater military activity complicated the situation.

There is no question that peace and farming maintained important connections. Indeed, peace goals on the part of agricultural peoples clearly spurred innovations of their own. Most peasant farmers, men as well as women, probably preferred peace. Agricultural societies generated warriors and military recruits (whether willing or reluctant), but for most of the population war itself was an unwanted imposition. Here was a conundrum that began with agriculture and would persist through the many centuries that describe the long agricultural period of human history. Peasants were not trained for war, and had every reason to prefer protection from war's onslaughts on their families and their land. They did not control larger policy decisions, as agricultural societies became more complex; here, military specialists or their supporters often had an edge. And we have no way of knowing how conscious peasants were of peace as an explicit goal or condition.

Many earlier tactics designed to promote peace were retained or revived in peasant villages. Gift exchange, even with neighboring hunters and gatherers, was one of the strongest initial motives for trade, not for direct economic gain so much as for conciliation. Intermarriage among leading families helped preserve good relations between neighboring villages, through the family bonds that resulted.

Innovative strategies emerged as well, suggesting both new resources and new needs in seeking peace. Some villages and even more small agricultural cities began to invest in walls or other fortifications that might protect them from invasion and thus preserve peace at least on a local basis. The earliest example of local fortifications comes from the Middle East, around 7500 BCE. The small city of Jericho was protected by a deep ditch, backed by a stone wall that at some points was over ten feet tall. The fortification was recognition of the possibility of war, but it also testified to the preference for avoiding it. Enclosures were particularly important in protecting domesticated animals, one of the obvious targets for outside raids. Not surprisingly, defensive enclosures have also been found in the ruins of early Chinese villages. To be sure, not all peasant communities could afford this recourse – the agricultural world remained vulnerable to attack – but the hope to provide greater security without overt conflict was widespread.

Communities that built walls invested massive amounts of labor, showing the seriousness of the threat of war but also the hope that attacks might be deterred with little or no actual fighting. Of course some military effort might join in. Jericho's walls were dotted with a few towers, from which defenders might mount guard and, if necessary, wield weapons. So there is no claim the walls signified an undiluted devotion to peace, or even a specific consciousness of peace as an ideal – quite apart from the fact that determined attackers often penetrated the enclosures and brought war within them. But walled towns, which became commonplace throughout the agricultural world, signified the ongoing effort to provide alternatives to war. They help explain, in fact, why some regions usually managed to preserve peace, even in an age in which the potential for military effort and military goals clearly increased.

Civilizations

The final stage in the assessment of the early human experience with peace involves the advent of more complex societies, often called civilizations, in which cities and formal governments played a growing role. The greater organization of civilizations, beginning with Sumerian civilization in the Middle East around 3500 BCE, enhanced opportunities for military activity, by extending many of the relevant features of agricultural societies more generally. Formal states maintained armies, and more sophisticated trading economies produced the means to sustain additional military specialization. And civilizations, with their larger cities, provided even more attractive targets for invasion than had the earlier agricultural communities. A cursory survey of many of the early civilizations, perhaps particularly in the Middle East where recurrent invasion was seemingly unavoidable, clearly calls attention to the importance of military activity. Civilization and war might seem to go hand in hand.

But civilizations also could generate new apparatus for peace, and also more explicit discussion of peace as a desirable social good. The important linkage between peace and agricultural prosperity also helped define many early civilizations. The fact was that, with civilization, divisions among human societies became even clearer than before, with preferences for peace vying with goals of military expansion. Further, with the more abundant records that civilizations generated, beginning with writing itself, the process of tracing the options of peace and war becomes easier to document.

Finally, early civilizations were not carbon copies of each other, even though all involved some common developments such as the emergence of formal states, the rise of larger cities, and the importance of writing. Some civilizations, through some combination of environment and deliberate goals, were more peaceful than others, and this becomes part of this final portion of the early human experience as well. Egypt generated clearer and more consistent commitments to peace than did its neighbors in the Middle East, adding to the complexity of the assessment of this aspect of the civilizing process.

Sumerian civilization, the world's first, in the fertile Tigris-Euphrates valley, developed a strong commitment to peace, another sign that early states and war were not indissolubly linked, even in the recurrently contentious Middle East. The oldest mosaic thus far discovered, for example, from the city of Ur, pictured a vigorous war scene with armed soldiers and war chariots, but this was matched by a clear peace scene, with banquets and leisure activities clearly highlighting the benefits the social calm brings to a civilization. It was Sumer also that applied writing to the production of inter-group agreements, including agreements among rival cities, designed to spell out mutual obligations in keeping the peace. From Babylonia, a successor civilization in the same region, came the world's first written epic, the *Gilgamesh*, which emphasized the role of war in leading to the downfall of great leaders but also the capacity of peace to avert disasters both natural and man-made. Peace was a clear cultural aspiration and a motivation for innovative measures to promote group harmony.

But war often came; even in *Gilgamesh*, the hero does not learn the lessons available, and war ensues. In real life, reliance on irrigation for farming created new frictions among cities along the great rivers of the Middle East, while also promoting a level of urban prosperity that could attract raiders.

Succeeding empires formed, sometimes on the basis of new invasions but almost always with a goal of military expansion. At their height the empires could offer regional stability, but a primary commitment to peace rarely endured.

The war-prone framework in the Middle East, during the early civilization period, was also reflected in the major new religion launched toward the period's end. The Jewish religion, which offered such vital innovations in the areas of monotheism and ethics, largely accepted the inevitability of war, with blood-soaked passages dotting the early religious literature – including the books that would ultimately comprise the Old Testament of the Bible. Passages such as I Samuel 19:8 were common: "And there was war again, and David went out and fought with the Philistines, and made a great slaughter among them, so that they fled before him." The religion offered some alternative visions, to be sure, which we will take up in a fuller exploration of the Middle Eastern religions, in Chapter 4; but on the surface, early Judaism easily incorporated the military experience of the region.

Egypt, in northeastern Africa, presented a different case. Its concentration along a single river may have promoted stability and reduced the problem of recurrent invasions – again, different environments play an important role in determining potentials for war or peace. The Egyptian religion placed strong emphasis on the importance of peace, as ordained by the gods, with the rulers (pharaohs) entrusted with this charge. The pharaohs' absolute political power was justified by this commitment to maintain peace and stability. Egypt may have been the first case where peace was seen as a religious imperative.

This culture was facilitated by actual Egyptian history, for the unification of Egypt along the Nile seems to have involved more negotiation and conciliation than uses of force, as different regional units worked out agreements to mutual advantage. Early government records are filled with praises of peace. Thus a work designed to educate government figures urged openness to the concerns of the people: "If you are a leader of peace, listen to the discourse of the petitioners." Armies were valued for their role in keeping or reestablishing peace, and this quality was celebrated more than tales of stirring victories. While periods of disruption dot the long span of Egyptian history, long stretches of peace did indeed prevail.

The same approach characterized Egyptian foreign policy in most instances. The pharaohs worked to create buffer zones between their kingdom and outside powers, sending diplomats and merchants into the zones to display their peaceful intentions. There was no emphasis on frequent warfare. Letters to the leaders of potentially rival powers frequently referred to harmony: "Know that in the true condition of peace and fraternity in which I now am with the great King of Khatti, I will abide therein for all eternity." (Khatti were a maritime people from the Mediterranean coast of the Middle East, who had periodically attacked Egypt.) The Egyptian queen followed up with a similar letter to her counterpart among the Khatti people, again referring to a "situation of true peace and fraternity" between the Pharaoh and the Khatti king, "his brother."

The Egyptians translated this approach into a formal alliance with a far more powerful neighbor, the Hittites, when both the Egyptians and their rivals faced the rise of a common enemy, the expanding Assyrian Empire, to the north. Here, a battle did set the stage for peacemaking, in 1285 BCE, but the ensuing agreement, not only ending the war but establishing a positive alliance, is the first record we have of formal international policy based on a mutual desire for peace. Again, the reference was to a "real peace and real fraternity" between the two rulers, "forever." "And the children's children" would be pledged to maintain the some "position of fraternity and peace," "and hostilities shall exist no more between them ever." One historian has described this arrangement as the result of an explicit understanding of the advantages of harmony over conflict.

It's important not to overdo: the Egyptians did use war as an instrument of policy, though more commonly against African than against Middle Eastern neighbors. And a peacemaking approach was not always effective even when employed: Egyptian leaders may at times have neglected to keep up military strength, which created vulnerabilities to invasion from the outside – though more commonly late in the Empire's history than during the centuries of peak success. For all the complexities Egypt does stand as an early case in which geography – the consolidation of territory along the Nile – and a cultural openness to peace created some real alternative to the more aggressive patterns of the empires that rose and fell in the Middle East during the same time period.

It may be, finally, that one other early civilization needs to be added to a peace list. The civilization that arose in the Indus River valley, in what is now Pakistan, may also have been largely free from conflict. Harappan civilization did not represent war in its art, and there is not much archeological evidence of weaponry. Many cities had walls, to be sure, though it is not clear whether these served to provide defense or to protect against flooding. Religious beliefs may have emphasized a Mother Goddess, which is turn could have served as a divine sponsor of peace. The fact is that we don't know a lot about this important society, including how much evidence of conflict may simply have disappeared. But a commitment to peace may have been a component – and if so, might also have provided some basis for beliefs that would surface in later civilizations in India.

* * * * *

Early human history, from the advent of the species to the river-valley civilizations, clearly presents a mixed picture. This complexity stands out far more clearly than any sweeping statement. The species had both violent and peaceful proclivities, and accordingly different hunting and gathering societies emphasized peaceful relations to greater or lesser degrees. Agriculture introduced new complications for peace, but also new needs and opportunities: again, there was no single formula. The same clearly applied to the early civilizations. The advent of formal states definitely created new military specializations, but some rulers and cultures could nevertheless opt primarily for peaceful approaches. Contrary to the views of some political scientists, war and the state are not automatically linked, either early on or more recently. Despite some temptations toward generalizations about human nature, or the requirements of agriculture, or the nature of civilization as a form of human organization, the varied legacy is what stands out. Subsequent societies would have diverse precedents to choose from, as they forged their own balance between war and peace.

Further reading

Aureli, Filippo, Colleem M. Schaffner, Jan Verpooten, Kathryn Slater, and Gabriel Ramos-Fernandex. "Raiding Parties of Male Spider Monkeys: Insights into Human Warfare?" *American Journal of Physical Anthropology* 131.4 (2006): 486–97.

Bigelow, R. *The Dawn Warriors: Man's Evolution towards Peace*. Boston, MA: Little, Brown, 1969.

Christensen, Jonas. "Warfare in the European Neolithic." *Acta Archaeologica* 75.2 (2004): 129–56.

Crook, Paul. *Darwinism, War and History: The Debate over the Biology of War from the "Origin of Species" to the First World War*. Cambridge: Cambridge University Press, 1994.

Kelly, Raymond C. *Warless Societies and the Origins of War*. Ann Arbor, MI: University of Michigan Press, 2000.

Mitscherlich, M. *The Peaceable Sex: On Aggression in Women and Men*. New York: Fromm, 1987.

Otterbein, Keith F. "Warfare and Its Relationship to the Origins of Agriculture." *Current Anthropology* 52.2 (2011): 267–8.

On early civilizations

Pollack, Susan and Reinhard Bernbeck, eds. *Archaeologies of the Middle East: Critical Perspectives*. Malden, MA: Blackwell Publishing. 2005.

Westing, Arthur H. "Research Communication: War as Human Endeavor: The High-Fatality Wars of the Twentieth Century." *Journal of Peace Research* 19.3 (1982): 261–70.

Wilkinson, Toby A. H. *Early Dynastic Egypt*. London and New York: Routledge, 1999.

Wright, Rita. *The Ancient Indus: Urbanism, Economy and Society*. New York: Cambridge University Press, 2010.

On biblical references to peace

Chester, Andrew. "The Concept of Peace in the Old Testament." *Theology* 92.750 (1989): 466–81.

Leiter, David. *Neglected Voices: Peace in the Old Testament*. Scottdale, PA: Herald Press, 2007.

Trimm, Charles. "Recent Research on Warfare in the Old Testament." *Currents in Biblical Research* 10.2 (2012): 171–216.

2 The great empires

Peace in Rome and China

After around 700 BCE, the patterns of the early civilizations gave way to what most historians call the classical era of world history, which in turn lasted essentially for the next thousand years. The major classical civilizations ultimately extended over larger territories than their antecedents had done – the whole of China, for example, instead of the northern regional kingdom that had initially formed along the Yellow River. The classical civilizations also began to generate institutional and cultural traditions that would leave a prolonged legacy, with traces visible still today.

Civilization expansion meant wars, among other things. The classical civilizations built stronger states than most of their predecessors had done, capable of operating over the new domains. They built larger military forces, and extended war – for example, violating traditions in earlier agricultural societies by fighting even in harvest seasons. But stronger states could also work for peace – internally for sure, and at times externally as well. The Roman Empire, one of the leading products of the classical age in the Mediterranean, became famous for the security it established for many residents – the vaunted *Pax Romana*, or Roman peace. The Chinese Empire under the Han dynasty, comparably impressive, has been given a matching label by historians, the *Pax Sinica*. New ideas about peace and war emerged in both these great regions, along with the actual political and military arrangements, and both affected later societies as well. Attitudes and expectations toward peace, in other words, formed part of the legacy of the classical period.

In this chapter we take up the experiences of the Mediterranean and China, saving for the following chapter the patterns established in India, the third main classical center, where somewhat more elaborate ideas about peace may have emerged. For China and the Mediterranean, military ventures are more likely to command historical attention than commitments to restraint, despite the brave noises about Roman or Chinese peace. This was the period, after all, when a Chinese author wrote one of the great treatises on the nature of war, when Roman emperors celebrated their reigns with imposing columns decorated with battle scenes, and when the famous Roman legions provided the muscle for imperial growth and defense. Yet peace was a theme as well, if less often emphasized in historical memory.

Several questions emerge. First, and most obviously: what ideas and initiatives about peace could coexist with new military capacities and priorities? But second – here echoing a theme already discussed for the early civilization period: what were the main variations between the Mediterranean and Chinese traditions, as both societies took fuller shape in the final centuries before the Common Era? And finally, were enduring legacies created, that would influence or constrain approaches to peace, in these regions and beyond, in later periods? We can look back on the classical period in China, for example, for its formative role in creating the Confucian value system or the emphasis on state bureaucracy, with their durable impact on the Chinese experience well beyond the classical centuries themselves; was there a comparably resilient stance toward peace and war? And was there a lasting Roman heritage as well, and if so did it contrast with the Chinese pattern?

Classical China

Between about 700 BCE and the fall of the Han dynasty in the second century CE, China built a large empire from a series of often-competing regional states, pushed its territories outward, and contended recurrently with invasions, particularly from the nomadic peoples of central Asia. Obviously, this history – as with all the classical empires – involved recurrent warfare and careful attention to military institutions and policies on the part of the imperial government.

Yet China approached its military issues with some restraint, and embraced a considerable commitment to peace. Major cultural movements and key policy initiatives both reflected a desire at least to limit military ventures and at best to build toward a harmonious society. The result, arguably, was a distinctive mixture, in which serious peace interests surfaced recurrently and in which Chinese contributions to military strategy reflected a clear sense that war must not become an end in itself.

The Chinese approach may have had roots early in the region's history. Chinese historians during the classical period itself, and more tentatively historians since that time, have argued that initial Chinese societies already placed strong emphasis on peace and harmony. An historical account from the second century BCE thus contends that peace was central to Chinese origins. In truth, very little precise information is available about developments before the Zhou dynasty, so peace claims have to be taken with a grain a salt, but the fact that the idea surfaced at the least suggests some interesting and possibly influential perceptions in the classical period itself. Strong beliefs in the importance of aligning earthly affairs with the heavens reflected deep commitments to natural harmonies, and an assumption that societies that properly managed this balance would be orderly and peaceful.

And there may have been some practical reasons for a strong Chinese interest in peace, beyond the conditions common to agricultural societies. Parts of what would become China depended heavily on rice growing. More than the grains common to the Middle East and Europe, rice requires an unusual amount of coordination in planting and harvesting, including management of irrigated fields – and these elements were obviously vulnerable to collective violence, which could not only spoil a crop but destroy the delicate balance of the rice fields themselves, in which so much community labor had been invested. The Chinese themselves may have been actively aware of these connections, as when Confucius later wrote that "from agriculture social harmony and peace arise." It is also true that China, compared to other large societies, had relatively little need for goods produced in other regions. There were a few exceptions: supplies of horses, for example, depended initially on imports from central Asia, and Chinese interest in the animals ran high. Generally, however, intense needs were limited, in an exceptionally fertile agricultural society with excellent mineral resources. This might have affected attitudes toward peace as well. It is important not to overdo this line of argument: we know in fact that many early regional Chinese kings were quite warlike, not that different from their warrior counterparts in the Middle East or India; some data suggest a level of military commitment far greater than in comparably early civilizations in Egypt or Harappa. We simply can't venture a definitive comparative statement about early China's experience of peace, beyond some possible hypotheses.

Certainly the early historical accounts, though clearly fictional at least in part, asserted both divine and human sponsorship for peace. Demigods who ruled at first carefully preserved harmony – among themselves, and among humans, the heavens and earth. The first human rulers – the legendary Five Emperors who succeeded the gods – did war occasionally, but they also worked to prevent violence and resolve the conflicts that did occur; peace was not forgotten. Thus later commentary on the emperors contended that "only in case of necessity will sage rulers undertake military action," since war disrupts the economy and causes popular discontent. Again, whatever the factual basis – and it is incomplete at best, a sense of precedent was established in the histories of early times that could inspire later leaders to assume the importance of maintaining peace.

And the same values may help explain why, when regional warfare did become endemic under the Zhou dynasty, persuasive voices quickly called for political and cultural alternatives, in the process creating enduring values that could often tame or prevent excessive military ambition. The Zhou group took power around 1122 BCE, and for a time successfully claimed a divine mandate to provide peace and prosperity – the origin of the famous idea that the Chinese emperors were "Sons of Heaven." Early Zhou leaders managed to expand their territories, but ultimately a combination of deteriorating rule and nomadic attacks led to a series of internal wars among regional leaders – a period aptly labeled the "Warring States."

This was the framework for several major cultural responses, beginning in the sixth century BCE, all aimed at providing a firmer basis for peace, a shared goal that spurred a number of different specific approaches. There was the so-called Mohist School, which urged the importance of open debate as a means of reducing conflict and building agreement, hoping that mutual persuasion would establish an orderly peace. The founder, Mozi, argued that universal love could eliminate both external and internal violence. Invasions would cease, along with crime. "So when there is universal love in the world it will be orderly"; compassion would replace aggression, and all would be well. Mohists became peace advocates in a time of war, in practice trying to develop ways to defend their communities without fighting. Government repression ultimately did the Mohists in, but their existence demonstrates the early and diverse roots of peace advocacy.

Far more durably important were the Daoists, founders of a new religion that claimed to trace origins back to the peace of the Five Emperors and an older Chinese esteem for balance and harmony. Led initially by Laozi, Daoists advocated harmony at both individual and social levels. Focusing on the Way, or Dao, the religion urged the development of balance, which would leave individuals with inner peace but alignment with society as well. As a later text urged, "The correct Dao creates no threat … It is useful to individuals and it is also useful to the whole country. Attaining it, an individual will succeed. Attaining it, a country will be at peace." Violence should be shunned, and committed Daoists should simply stay away from conflict: inaction could become a positive virtue. The religion more clearly emphasized inner purity and serenity than positive social measures to preserve peace, but its long popularity in China testified to the ongoing desire for personal harmony regardless of larger social complexities.

A third ideological strand also sought peace, but on quite a different basis: Legalism was the last major political theory to develop during China's classical period. It emphasized the importance of a strong state and dominant laws in disciplining unruly human nature to create "the direction most favorable to … the public peace." This was the cultural underpinning of a powerful emperor who unified China in the third century and ended the period of Warring States, but primarily on the basis of force. Peace was a genuine goal for the Legalists as well, and their thinking would continue to influence the Chinese state even in later centuries; but it had strong military overtones in defense of authority.

Ultimately Confucianism was by far the most significant cultural effort to establish an alternative to the chaos of regional warfare. One of the first ideologies to emerge as the Zhou order collapsed – Confucius lived from the mid-sixth century to 479 BCE, it would become predominant during the Han dynasty, when imperial rule did in fact promote considerable stability over a wide territory and a long span of time. Confucius claimed to be capturing the earlier themes of Chinese culture, including the quest for harmony and a previous period of pervasive peace, but it was his synthesis that established the most characteristic features of Chinese political culture, features that would be exported widely to other parts of East Asia. And while a quest for peace was not quite at the core of Confucianism, it was a clear goal under a larger heading of harmonious relations at all levels of society.

The Confucian approach rested on the idea that through training and appropriate hierarchy, people could master any bad impulses and contribute to an orderly society. Order began in the family, with children's obedience to parents, wives to husbands, and extended to a similar set of loyalties and mutual obligations in the state. "When families are harmonious, states become orderly. And when states are orderly, there is peace in the world." This was not an elaborate disquisition on peace, and it focused more on internal stability than on tactics to deal with external threat. But the valuation was clear: a good society, with good rulers, would seek and attain peace. Most Confucians believed that war might be justified under certain circumstances – for example, in response to clear attack – but they were equally clear that the option was undesirable and that core conditions had to be met.

The orientation inspired further comment by key followers, in subsequent centuries. Mencius for example, writing in the fourth century BCE, regarded those who engaged in war as subhuman, proposing that they be punished by death for the harm they caused. There was no such thing as a just war. Nonviolence was an integral part of ethics, in this rendering of Confucianism, though this turned out to be an extreme view. It remained true, however, that Confucianism, as it gained growing acceptance in China and spread to other parts in East Asia, became one of the clearest forces for peace in this period of world history, and arguably beyond.

The flowering of discussions about peace, in reaction to the warfare associated with the decline of the Zhou dynasty, was a distinctive moment, not only in Chinese history but in the experience of most major societies. Seldom would peace gain this kind of concerted attention. To be sure, the approaches varied widely, from Daoist passive withdrawal and emphasis on inner harmony, to Legalist reliance on state authority, to Confucian promptings toward self-control and mutual loyalties. There was no firm agreement on the most desirable approach, or on the extent to which war should be systematically renounced. On the other hand, the varied voices could be combined in practice: intellectuals might practice elements of Daoism to achieve greater personal balance, while relying on Confucian self-restraint plus an element of Legalist authority to keep the peace in society at large. The variety in fact confirmed the wide interest in peaceful goals, and the role this interest played in shaping durable elements of Chinese culture.

Peace advocacy had its challengers, to be sure, even at the level of ideas. The final centuries of the Zhou dynasty also saw the production of one of the most famous military treatises of all time, the *Art of War*, by an author widely known as Sun Tzu. In 13 chapters, this masterful work outlined a host of elements of military strategy, with great emphasis on wearing down and deceiving any enemy. Surprise attacks and lightning moves combined with discussions of how to encounter even superior forces. Military leaders gained advice on how to win the loyalty of troops. The whole exercise assumed the importance of military preparations, and the resultant treatise would ultimately be widely studied not only by Chinese officials but by military strategists in the West and elsewhere. Even here, however, a marked preference for peace showed through, if more as a matter of superior tactics than as a social ideals. "The supreme art of war is to subdue the enemy without fighting." Clever posturing and intimidation beat outright battle whenever possible: only inferior warriors "go to war first" and they are doomed to defeat. "Supreme excellence consists of breaking the enemy's existence without fighting." There was no glory in war, and indeed "there is no instance of a country having benefited from prolonged warfare." And if outright conflict becomes unavoidable, try to minimize it, among other things by leaving escape routes to enemies so they will not prolong a fight out of desperation. "To win one hundred victories in one hundred battles is not the acme of skill. To subdue the enemy without fighting is the acme of skill." Arguably, even in considering war Chinese culture highlighted a role, and an ultimate preference, for peace.

Culture – even cultural systems accepted in principle by political leaders – is not of course the whole of reality. The Chinese state hardly committed to peace as systematically as the various political theorists advocated. The unification of the Empire, following the ultimate collapse of the Zhou dynasty, was accomplished by force of arms, and while the later Han dynasty – one of China's most successful regimes – worked hard on pacification, military expansion continued on the fringes of the core territory.

It was revealing, nevertheless, that the Han named their capital city Chang'an, or Perpetual Peace. Several other policies suggested that a preference for peace was not entirely rhetorical. Han rulers also put a great deal of energy into conciliating potential enemies, rather than investing in military defense alone. Expeditions were sent into central Asia, where the most obvious threats to the Empire lay, offering nomadic rulers gifts of silk and other items in return for pledges of harmony. One historian has argued that no regime, before or since, ever made such an effort to offer gifts to neighbors, making the whole system a major component of diplomatic policy. Marriages with foreign leaders also cemented good relations, as Chinese princesses were pledged to tribal leaders (often to their great personal dismay, as the loneliness and strangeness of central Asia surrounded them after childhoods in the sophistication of the imperial court).

A preference for peace, or at least a desire to reduce the need to counter military attack, also underwrote one of the most famous Chinese strategies, the construction of a great wall to deter invasions from nomads to the north. Chinese kingdoms gained the technical capacity to build regional walls during the Warring States period – translating for kingdoms the defensive, war-avoidance tactics that many agricultural cities had pioneered. Following the unification of the Chinese Empire the new ruler now applied this capacity to defense of the northern frontier, using combinations of great stones and mounds of earth to construct effective barriers. Hundreds of thousands, perhaps millions of workers were employed in this process – a huge investment in minimizing military risk. This was not the Great Wall so widely celebrated today: that was a creation of later emperors only 500 years ago. But the goals were shared, in trying to limit the need for war.

Small wonder that a Han official, proud of the regime's achievements, boasted that "now all under heaven is in peace and harmony."

Ultimately, of course, peace was not preserved, and at least limited military engagements cropped up periodically even at the height of the *Pax Sinica*, under the Han dynasty. Finally, in the third century CE, a weakening government was not able to hold the line against internal unrest and external, nomadic invasion. The Han Empire collapsed, and over three centuries of division and recurrent warfare ensued.

This final failure aside, the big questions about peace in classical China involve the extent of links between aspirations in theory and actual policy formulation – complicated further by the divisions in the approaches aiming at peace. Did real Chinese rulers and their advisers really take peace goals seriously? We know they did not commit consistently: intentional war was frequently an instrument of policy, even under the Han. Was there, nevertheless, a somewhat distinctive consciousness of peace, that showed up not only symbolically, in a city name, but in some of the strategic choices the government preferred? Not an easy question to answer, but at least a possibility.

And if possible, then another set of questions for later on: to what extent did the peace interests in Chinese culture carry forward, to subsequent time periods after the Empire was reconstituted; and were actual policies affected by the culture, by earlier political precedents, or both? In 2010, for example, a Chinese businessman established a Confucius Peace Prize, seeking to "promote world peace from an Eastern perspective." The effort was controversial: China was reacting to a Nobel Peace Prize award to a human rights advocate it regarded as a disruptive criminal, and the prize did not gain much international traction. More serious is the claim that for long stretches of time, between the sixth and the eighteenth centuries, China was responsible for a "long peace," in which it actively promoted peaceful relations with neighboring Confucian societies – Korea, Japan, and to an extent Vietnam – on grounds of shared Confucian commitments.

Again, the questions about a distinctive Chinese approach and about its durability are tough ones – perhaps particularly at a point, early in the twenty-first century, when many people profess to worry about a rise in Chinese militarism. Yet the experience of classical China lends validity to the inquiry. Chinese interest in peace may have established a somewhat unusual trajectory.

Distinctiveness is obviously also a comparative claim. We turn now to patterns in the classical Mediterranean, where ultimately an empire would emerge approximately the same size as China's. The process of expansion and efforts at integrating larger territory produced many similarities between the two classical giants. But where did an interest in peace fall in this comparative scale?

Greece and Rome

Big comparisons are risky, and certainly deserve careful critical assessment. But here's the claim, for the classical period. On the whole, the civilization that arose in the Mediterranean, based first in Greece and then in Rome, developed less systematic commitment to the possibility, and perhaps even the desirability, of peace than was true in classical China. To be sure, the Mediterranean produced no classic statement of war, to compare to the work of Sun Tzu; and the *Pax Romana* was an important development and precedent. But war played a greater role in life and in thought in this classical civilization than was true at the other end of Asia.

Greek and Roman societies, closely intertwined though not identical, serve as the seedbed for ideas and historical memories for several subsequent civilizations, particularly those that would emerge in Western but also in Eastern Europe; though there was influence in the Middle East and North Africa as well. So the comparative assessment may involve more than the classical period itself, another reason to examine it critically.

Even if the comparative claim is correct, of course, it will also be important to acknowledge several major developments, in thought and in statecraft, involving peace, in both Greece and Rome. Some similarities to China also emerge, another complexity to take into account.

Greek society, developing from about 800 BCE onward, harbored some real or imagined recollections of a peaceful past that paralleled some of the historical assertions in China. An epic by Hesiod, from about 700 BCE, claimed an original Golden Age for humanity, in which the world was aligned with the gods and peace prevailed. This was succeeded, however, by periods of war. Hesiod hoped that peace might be restored, through commitments to virtue and justice – "peace, the nurse of children, is abroad in the land" – but the time of secure peace has passed. Here, perhaps, was a subtle contrast with the ways Chinese thinkers evoked the past in hopes of future restoration.

Greek city states fought frequently, with each other and with foreign opponents – possibly more than the early regional kings in China did, though there is no way to be sure. This did not eclipse ideas of peace. The great Homeric story of the Trojan War included many condemnations of the damage caused by war. At one point the great god Zeus blasts the god of war: "Most hateful to me are you of all gods ... for ever is strife dear to thee, and wars and fighting." After the Trojan War the hero Odysseus struggled with its consequences, hoping that "the mutual goodwill of the days of old will be restored, and ... peace and plenty prevail."

Greek religion certainly featured attention to peace as well as to war. The goddess Eirene, one of three sisters who evolved from an initial focus on agricultural prosperity, was the personification of peace, though different parts of Greece valued her differently. She was often pictured carrying an olive branch, and sometimes was portrayed destroying weapons. Important peace settlements in Greece might be commemorated with sacrifices to Eirene, or statues or altars in her honor. Hesiod, in his early work, also played up the importance of Eirene, linking peace with human harmony and (again a similarity with Chinese thinking) the value of political order. The god of war was far more visible and important, but not uncontested in the pantheon.

Greek dramatists, and particularly Aristophanes late in the fifth century BCE, also discussed peace. Aristophanes in fact wrote an explicitly anti-war play, simply called *Peace*, in a lull in a bitter battle between Athens and Sparta in 422. The play featured gods' disgust with the Greeks for their refusal of peace, with only the god Hermes, who amused himself by destroying several cities, keeping peace captive. A Greek hero frees Peace, and brings prosperity back to the farming population. The connection between war and the harmful destruction of harvests emerged strongly in the play; at one point, the damage to fruit trees from war is compared to the whipping scars on the back of a slave.

Against this, many Greek writers dealt admiringly with military exploits and heroes, and Heraclitus, a philosopher-scientist, indeed declared that "war is the father of all things," in that it causes change.

Actual Greek history generated peace precedents as well. Greek city states collaborated to preserve certain holy shrines as well as to sponsor the periodic Olympic Games, and this coordination generated pledges of peace that though temporary or limited had real impact. Offenders risked attack from the majority of the states acting as allies. Both Athens and Sparta – the leading states – periodically sponsored alliances in which member states pledged peaceful relations as well as mutual assistance against any outside aggressor. The leagues sometimes resulted from military conquests by the sponsors. But the great powers might also restrain themselves – Sparta, notoriously, limited its attack on an enemy so that the smaller entity could be a valid participant in a subsequent peace agreement. Greek states also periodically exchanged ambassadors, designed to limit misunderstandings. And Greek politicians periodically bragged about their achievements of peace. Thus Athenian spokesmen, later in the fifth century, talked of decades of prosperity, political order, and "peace with all the world." These various ideas and developments might be important precedents for later societies, at least indirectly.

But Greek states often warred. Even when they sought peace among themselves they tended to view non-Greek territories – and non-Greeks were called barbarians – as fair game. Here again a possible contrast with China emerges, where a similar concept of barbarians, though lively, did not prevent more careful overtures in the interests of peace. Greece itself began to decline after a brutal war between Athens and Sparta. Periodically, during this Peloponnesian struggle, truces were negotiated, but these were not pledges of peace but rather pauses while each side organized for further conflict.

The great Greek philosophers certainly considered peace, but it was not a particularly clear focus in the legacy they established. Socrates talked of the importance of rational debate, and perhaps (as some enthusiastic historians have attempted) this can be stretched into relevance for peace, but the connection is fragile. In one debate Socrates did, however, conclude that war and political misdeeds stemmed from similar, and undesirable, causes. Plato, writing far more directly about politics, focused less on war and peace than might be expected, dealing far more with the importance of solid political arrangements and political virtue. He did damn tyrants, among other things because they always sought war as a means of justifying and consolidating their power. And his philosopher kings were presumed to use their wisdom, among other things, to weigh the importance of peace. Plato emphasized the significance of thinking about peace, writing about how it could form as a construct in the human mind, but correspondingly suggested that its achievement might be difficult.

Finally Aristotle wrote ambivalently about war and peace. He argued that human society "needs war in order that we can live in peace." He saw peace not merely as the absence of war, but also the commitment to political virtue – possibly another indication of the greater Greek interest in political conduct than in peace per se. And when Aristotle offered advice to rulers, as in his *Rhetoric*, he urged them to study war carefully: a good ruler must know the military capacity of his own society and of those around it. This study would be vital "in order that peace be maintained with those societies stronger than his own." But also, revealingly, identification of other neighbors was equally important "in order that he can make war or not" against those who are weaker. As in so much of actual Greek history, peace here became more a tactic than a goal.

Unsurprisingly, in this context, Alexander the Great, the conqueror who succeeded the classic Greek period, devoted himself to war. He rejected explicit peace overtures from the Persian emperor, Darius III, because he valued complete conquest. His Empire, to be sure, temporarily reduced fighting among vital regional states, but the respite proved temporary.

Rome, rising as a republic as Greece reached its apogee and then declined, based much on war and its famed military apparatus. Of course the Roman state periodically formed alliances as it began to gain power in the Italian peninsula, pledging peace and mutual protection, but for the most part these were temporary arrangements suspended as soon as further conquest became possible. The leagues could, to be sure, generate high-sounding rhetoric: "Let there be peace among the Romans and all the Latin cities as long as the heavens and the earth shall remain where they are. Let them not make war upon one another … let them assist one another when warred upon."

For the most part, however, the Roman republic grew through war, providing peace to its enemies only after they were defeated and accepted Roman supremacy. And sometimes not even then: in the great wars against Carthage, the African city state, the Romans ultimately decided that the whole city must be destroyed, its agricultural fields ruined by salt, so that it could never again generate threat or competition.

Rome also suffered from periodic internal disorder, which could (as in Greece) focus attention more on internal stability than on peaceful relations more broadly. Thus Polybius, a historian in the second century BCE, wrote that "peace is a blessing for which we pray to all the gods; we submit to every suffering in order to attain it." But he was really talking about an end to internal discord, not a cessation of external war.

The later republic did generate a statesman, Cicero, who wrote more broadly about peace, though he too focused even more strongly on internal politics and political virtue. Coining the term "peace with honor," Cicero made a clear distinction between just and unjust wars. "Those wars are unjust which are undertaken without provocation. For only a war waged for revenge or defense can be actually just ... No war is considered just unless it has been proclaimed or declared, or unless reparation has first been demanded." This idea would prove both powerful and durable, at least as a statement of principle, though of course as a basis for peace it can also be criticized. How would Cicero decide whether or not a war was just?

And there were other voices for peace, particularly as the Roman republic became increasingly disorderly during the second and first centuries BCE. Seneca blasted his fellow Romans as "mad": "we check manslaughter and isolated murders, but what of war and the much vaunted crime of slaughtering whole peoples?" Philosophers in the Stoic school wrote of the importance of domestic harmony and peace among states. One writer, Marcus Varro, even undertook a history of peace, probably the first of its kind.

Then came the Roman Empire and the upstart rule of Augustus. Seeking popularity, and clearly building on the ideas about peace that had surfaced in the later republic, the new emperor immediately began talking about the importance of peace and his ability to deliver. *Pax Augusta* became the first iteration of what was later called the *Pax Romana*. The goddess Pax, the personification of political peace, gained massive government patronage. Augustus had a huge arch built to honor Pax (and later emperors would dedicate temples in her name, as their Chinese counterparts had named a city). An annual April festival brought worship to Pax. It remained unclear whether Pax meant primarily internal order (which the early Empire did assure) or whether it had much to do with external warfare (which continued, as the Empire pressed further expansion). Poets began writing hymns in praise of peace. Ovid claimed that soldiers now carried weapons only to deter armed aggressors, and one later emperor even talked of a future time in which "soldiers would no longer be necessary."

The actual strategy of Augustus and his best successors involved a strong emphasis on internal order along with a steady stream of external wars designed both to provide new rewards (including supplies of slaves) and to keep invaders out. Soldiers were distracted for a time from internal meddling through the prospect of booty abroad. This was peace of a sort, and observers could praise the Pax Augusta, "which has spread to the regions of the east and of the west ... and preserves every corner of the world safe from the fear of brigandage." Emperors who periodically built new temples dedicated to peace sought to preserve the vision, though more imperial effort by far went into the construction of columns commemorating battles and victories.

As in Han China, of course, the imperial strategy ultimately collapsed. Military intervention in internal affairs increased, and external invaders pressed in as well. Rome was in fact more vulnerable than China when territorial expansion ceased, because the Empire depended far more directly on the spoils of war to keep internal peace. And as the vaunted Roman peace collapsed, ordinary people quickly withdrew their loyalties, seeking local protection or turning to religious solace that might at least promise peace in an afterlife.

The classical legacy

Both China and the Mediterranean contributed to the story of peace in world history, even as war seemed clearly more prominent at least in the Mediterranean case. Ideas about peace, from Confucius or Cicero, would last, and would be used in later discussions of peace and war. Specific mechanisms, like the Chinese use of emissaries and gift exchanges to distract potential invaders or the formation of regional peace agreements in the Mediterranean, would recur. Possibly – again to extend the risky comparison – the Chinese legacy toward peace was somewhat greater, as in the later idea of peace among fellow Confucian states; this requires some careful assessment of later developments in both regions. But one point was shared: both Han China and Rome created claims and images of extensive peace and security that could be recalled by subsequent societies and that could generate new aspirations. Whether these recollections would generate much actual effort, indeed whether they could rival the memory of military greatness, is worth considering as the later history of peace attempts unfolded.

Further reading

Gichon, Mordechai. Foreword to *The Military History of Ancient Israel*, by Richard A. Gabriel. Westport, CT: Praeger, 2003, xi–xix.

On Greece and Rome

Berens, E. M. *Myths and Legends of Ancient Greece and Rome*. ebook. Project Gutenberg, 2007. Available online at www.gutenberg.org/files/22381/22381-h/22381-h.htm.
Compton-Engle, Gwendolyn. "Aristophanes Peace 1265–1304: Food, Poetry and the Comic Genre." *Classical Philology* 94.3 (1999): 324–9.
Galtung, Johan. "Social Cosmology and the Concept of Peace." *Journal of Peace Research* 18.2 (1981): 183–99.
Hanson, Victor Davison. *Warfare and Agriculture in Classical Greece*. ebook. Berkeley, CA: University of California Press, 1998.
Price, Simon and Emily Kearns, eds. *The Oxford Dictionary of Classical Myth and Religion*. Oxford: Oxford University Press, 2003.
Raaflaub, Kurt A. "Conceptualizing and Theorizing Peace in Ancient Greece." *Transactions of the American Philological Association* 139.2 (2009): 225–50.
Woolf, Greg. "Roman Peace." In Rich, John and Graham Shipley, eds., *War and Society in the Roman World*. London: Routledge, 1993, 171–94.

On China

Yates, Robin D. S. "Making War and Making Peace in Early China." In Raaflaub, Kurt A., ed., *War and Peace in the Ancient World*. Malden, MA: Blackwell Publishing, 2007, pp. 34–52.
Zhou, Dingxin. "The Mandate of Heaven and Performance Legitimation in Historical and Contemporary China." *American Behavioral Scientist* 53.3 (2009): 416–33.

3 Peace in the Buddhist tradition

Beginning in the classical period, important innovations occurred in religious beliefs and structures, in several different regions. The rise of Judaism launched a new religious tradition in parts of the Middle East that would later contribute to Christianity and to Islam – subjects of the next chapter. In South Asia, Hinduism took increasingly clear shape, evolving from an earlier polytheistic religion brought in by Indo-European migrants and invaders. The emergence of Hinduism also formed the context for the rise of Buddhism, a religion that would play a distinctively important role in the history of piece.

This chapter focuses on Hinduism and particularly Buddhism in the cultural and political evolution of South Asia and beyond. But it also begins the process of considering the impact of more complex religions on peace and war more generally.

We have seen how various early polytheistic religions could play a role in the status of peace in different societies. Some polytheistic pantheons inclined heavily toward gods of war, others featured more clearly a divine sponsorship for peace. Early Chinese beliefs about the harmony of the heavens and the desirably peaceful balance this suggested on earth had a strong religious component.

But the rise of more complex religions, some of them with strong missionary impulses, introduced additional elements. These larger religions could contribute three approaches to ideas and practices concerning peace:

- First, they could introduce new reasons for war. Conflicts that were justified in terms of defending the faith became much more common. More broadly still, religious beliefs that claimed a distinctive monopoly on truth and God's guidance could see military action against nonbelievers as a true obligation. Religion could, in other words, motivate wars designed to protect but also wars of aggression. A subset of this category could involve direct military clashes between advocates of different religious affiliations, each side believing it was fighting for a divinely sanctioned purpose. (Later chapters will show that for the last 1,500 years, peace commitments have almost always been associated with an embrace of religious tolerance. But amid various religions all claiming the truth, tolerance was sometimes hard to come by.)

- But the new religions could also claim divine sponsorship of peace, and most of them clearly offered a new vision of peace in an afterlife that could have earthly implications as well. This was the second point. The image of eternal peace, whether in a heaven or in some merger with the divine essence, was truly innovative, and it arguably placed a new level of emphasis on peace as a desirable goal. This could extend to efforts to create more peaceful conditions on earth, as consistent with divine intentions.
- Third, however, the new religions could prompt some people to seek a personal spirituality, intensely meaningful, that would distract from involvement with larger social issues, including wider conflicts; peace could be sought for individuals and small communities regardless of surrounding commitments to militarism. If I as an individual can carve out a peaceful life of prayer and meditation for myself, why worry about what was going on in society at large? Even more broadly, if peace could be expected after life's end, was that not a sufficient promise? Why bother worrying about peace during the testing time here on earth?

The three strands could coexist, obviously complicating the impacts of the new religious impulses on the world at large. Contradictions abounded, which is why most of the great world religions had such mixed results where peace was concerned. By the same token a variety of individuals and groups, from soldiers to peace advocates, could find a home within the same religion, however uneasily.

All major religions harbor varied strands and internal tensions. Ambiguities about peace certainly reflect this complexity, making it dangerous to generalize too readily about any basic patterns. By the same token, religious emphases could change over time, a process that continues to this day. It is essential to explore directly.

Finally, of course, even the powerful new religions did not have full social control. They had to interact with other voices – sometimes various religious minorities and certainly an array of social groups, often including military organizations. Relationships between religion and the state varied, depending on various factors; but it was quite common for religious leaders to feel they had to offer some compromises to government officials in order to coexist, common as well for government leaders to try to override or coopt religious beliefs. Even aside from complexities within a religion itself, this factor could further affect the religious relationship to peace.

* * * * *

The creative religious scene in South Asia during the classical period offers the first opportunity to sort out initial versions of the new religious complexity, which would have implications for peace – in many parts of Asia, and ultimately even globally – in later periods as well. We turn to the framework created by Hinduism and Buddhism.

Hinduism

The Hindu religion developed gradually in India, from a more conventional polytheistic faith imported by Indo-Europeans migrants and invaders. No single text underpinned the religion, which meant that there were many opportunities for widely varying approaches to subjects such as peace and war. Early sagas supported a fairly militant stance, characteristic of many polytheistic religions that highlight the role of war and the importance of military virtues. Among other things, early versions of Hinduism (often called Brahmanism, to distinguish from the later, more mature faith) placed warrior groups at the top of the social pyramid; only later would they drop to second, behind the priestly caste. But later Hindu texts noted not only a clear interest in peace, but a particular commitment to nonviolence that could have wide implications. Indian rulers, in turn, made various uses of Hinduism in their own policies.

One of the strongest principles that ultimately emerged in Hinduism was the idea of *ahimsa*, or "non-injury" – a belief that harming another being would have dire consequences. The idea initially arose in opposition to an older religious practice of animal sacrifice, but obviously it could impact approaches to human violence as well. It was widely discussed by Hindu priests and scholars – the Brahmans – during the centuries between 500 and 200 BCE, as Indian culture began taking clearer shape. The idea of *ahimsa* proved expansive as well, turning in some later versions of Hinduism into a belief not just in non-harm, but in positive, universal love.

But early Hinduism could also continue to praise war, and the impact of religious ritual in war. This was one way the priests could make themselves useful to actual rulers, but more broadly war could be seen as a duty that could preserve or restore order and power. Even more explicitly, the early religion saw Indra as a creator god but also god of war, who could bring success in battle to kings who had the right approach to the gods and to rituals in their honor. There was little discussion, in the early centuries, of what constituted a just war, though later on Hindu thinkers talked of wars that were necessary to restore peace and harmony, as opposed to wars that were sinful. Sinful wars, in this later view, would have dire consequences in the relationship between humans and the divine order.

After 500 BCE, more complex versions of Hinduism, in the later written epics, introduced the idea of *ahimsa* but also the desirability of a positive love for all humanity. All humans contain an element of the divine and so should be treated as part of a common human family.

Still later epics dealt with the great moral tensions involved in war. On the one hand, peace should be a prime goal. "Peace is preferable to war. Who, having a choice, would prefer to fight?" "Slaughter is never praised. It can never do any good." "Righteousness should include harmony and love for all human beings." On the other hand, again, war might be needed to preserve the state and proper social order, and even to protect the vulnerable. Hinduism continued to support the caste system, which in turn stressed the duty to serve well the functions of the caste. With military caste still second in rank, just below the priests, this could involve extensive comment on the ethical obligation to fight well. Moral duty for soldiers would obviously include the duty to obey orders and defeat the enemy. To be sure, unfair or unjust uses of violence would be punished, with the individual relegated to a lower status in the next life. But war for appropriate goals could be positively virtuous. Killing could be a necessary part of virtuous duty, though it should be performed dispassionately. One famous Hindu story even showed that killing members of one's own family, if part of duty in a righteous war, could be a just act. In this passage the god Krishna exhorted an individual to "fight like a warrior," which some have interpreted as a clear religious call to arms. By stressing the temporary quality of life, amid larger cycles of existence and renewal, Hinduism could also reduce moral tensions around killing in war.

By the end of the classical period, as Hinduism recovered in India from the rise of Buddhism, rulers continued to invoke divine support for victory in war. Artistic renderings highlighted warriors whose death in war, following the legitimate orders of a king, allowed them to rise directly to heaven.

But Hinduism and its legacy could never be pinned down to a single formula, and the nonviolence theme added a spiritual aspect to the inevitable complexity of any major religion on the subject of peace and war. In the postclassical period many Hindu priests and philosophers returned to the theme of universal love. A major movement in the twelfth century CE, the *Veerashaiva bhakti* group, organized explicitly around nonviolence toward all living beings and the primacy of peace.

Buddhism

The early period

Buddhism arose in India in the sixth and fifth centuries BCE, inspired by the teachings of Siddhartha Gautama. The new religion sought to reform Hinduism in several ways. It wanted to replace the power of priests with individual piety and meditation. It rejected Hinduism's elaborate rituals, on the same grounds. It attacked the caste system, and stressed the divine essence in all humans. Buddhism gained ground in India for several centuries, but ultimately receded in favor in part because secular rulers preferred the options available in Hinduism including the greater support for war. But Buddhism spread widely in Southeast and East Asia, where its main emphases, including a more consistent appreciation of peace, would have deep influence.

Buddhism preserved many Hindu principles, including the idea of reincarnation. It built strongly on the Hindu ideas of peace and nonviolence, if anything strengthening the emphasis on *ahimsa* and giving the whole approach a higher priority. Not for original Buddhism the balance between peace and the importance of a just war or pleasing a righteous ruler. Attack on the caste system meant among other things release from the notion that one group of people – a military elite – would have special obligations to display valor in war. Ethical obligations were now uniform across humanity, and this included the injunctions toward nonviolence.

The message of peace was, as a result, unusually pure, matched, in the history of major religions, only by the preachings of the early Christians some centuries later. Thus Buddha was reported to have said, "Of death all are afraid/ Having made oneself the example, One should neither slay nor cause to slay." Another precept warned that anyone who hurt another being, would get no spiritual reward. Correspondingly, Buddhist monastic principles – and Buddhism led to the formation of many monastic groups – required immediate expulsion of any monk or nun who killed another human being.

While Buddhism disdained all worldly achievements and pleasures, terming them "miseries" and urging dissociation from the distractions of this life and attention to spiritual elevation, it displayed particular sympathy for the sufferings of humanity. It sought to provide a religion of love and benevolence. It saw violence as the result of a belief that things of this world are worth striving for, that there is something permanent in this phase of existence – in other words, as the distorted result of misplaced priorities.

The Buddhist Path toward righteousness and an end to suffering stressed the centrality of nonviolence. "Abstention from killing is merit," but "destruction of living beings is demerit." Opportunities for spiritual advancement in reincarnation would be deeply affected by peaceful behavior: to have a positive rebirth, a person must avoid cruelty and seek the wellbeing of all living things. The whole universe should be conceived and treated in terms of kindness. War is a moral failure, and those who kill are endangering their future by committing the most serious act of immorality.

As Buddhism expanded, for example into East Asia, texts continued the basic emphasis, as in statements that a Buddhist "must not hate any being and cannot kill a living creature even in thought." Early texts also tried to apply the basic ideals more directly to actual conduct, urging Buddhist kings to live up to the ideals of nonviolence, with ten main duties that included striving for peace and ruling with nonviolent benevolence.

There were, as historians have later argued, some ambiguities even in these seemingly clear prescriptions. A tension existed, for example, around the Buddhist commitment to *ahimsa*: did this really include a concern for other people or rather a means of keeping one's own mind pure, as part of spiritual self-cultivation. Would a good Buddhist try actively to restrain violence in others, or was personal purity the main goal?

Another complexity involved the great variety of Buddhist groups and specific beliefs. A host of different interpretations of Buddhism arose, particularly as the religion began to expand geographically. It became increasingly difficult, as a result, to define consistent Buddhist ideals, and this could obviously color Buddhist commitments to peace goals in practice.

Still, the principles of early Buddhism were rarely entirely lost, and the potential not just for preferences for peace but for more active advocacy was a key part of this continuity. A key stage in the maturation of Buddhism as a world religion, launching the faith on an explicit missionary path, involved the reign of the emperor Ashoka, in India. It was Ashoka also who came to represent, symbolically and possibly in actual fact, the way Buddhist principles could be applied to politics, with a devotion to peace central to the application.

Ashoka

Ashoka came to power around 265 BCE, in India's Mauryan dynasty that extended over a substantial part of the south Asian subcontinent. The new emperor, grandson to the dynasty's founder Chandragupta, initially maintained policies common to the maintenance and expansion of empires throughout the classical period, policies that assumed the centrality of war. Chandragupta, indeed, had been so engaged in conflict that he rarely slept in the same place two nights running, for fear of enemy attack. Ashoka seemed to be cut from the same mold, amassing huge armies to extend the boundaries of his domains. He may indeed have been unusually cruel in his youth, torturing some of his prisoners directly.

Fairly early on, however, Ashoka converted to Buddhism. Whether as cause or result, he also began to experience growing revulsion at military slaughter. In one war, for example, up to 100,000 troops were killed, and Ashoka was reported to be sickened by the result. This was the point at which connections between Buddhism and peace received a real boost in practice. For, as example and symbol alike, Ashoka's regime came to suggest how Buddhist principles might inspire a set of real policies, beyond the promptings so widely distributed in the early Buddhist texts.

To be sure, we know far less about Ashoka's pacifism than would be desirable, if we are to claim him as one of the first principled pacifist regimes in world history. Records are scanty. The emperor crafted some edicts that were carved in stone, and preserved by Buddhist monks, but much of what we know about diplomatic and military policy comes from oral tradition, an inherently unreliable source. Far more is known about Ashoka's other reforms, including welfare measures, undertaken with Buddhist guidance, than about his implementation of peace. And Ashoka's motives – like those of so many rulers, may have been mixed. His adoption of Buddhism might have been, in part, an attempt to win greater popular support for his regime, in contrast to the cost and sacrifice of a more active military direction. Or he may have hoped, again through Buddhist pacifism, to reduce pretexts for internal violence. He might have sought directly to undercut Hindu officials who posed a barrier to his power, finding Buddhist monks more reliable in his service. Obviously, it is impossible to sort out underlying goals with any precision.

Still, the portrait of Ashoka as a devoted convert to Buddhism, and to peace, seems accurate in broad outline, even if other factors mixed in. Oral tradition holds that Ashoka was deeply impressed by one of his prisoners of war, a Buddhist, who seemed immune to the sufferings his guards tried to impose on him. Inspired, so the story goes, Ashoka converted and then began to see his military policies with new eyes, becoming appalled at the violence his wars were causing.

Ultimately, the emperor fully embraced Buddhist principles of nonviolence, while making Buddhism his official religion. The result was three decades of peace, as well as a major effort to spread the faith through peaceful missionary effort. The morality Ashoka now began to advocate urged tolerance, ethical action, and abstention from war. He did not completely disband his army, but he did end wars of conquest. Chroniclers hailed him as a *cukkovatti*, a universal monarch who restored order and harmony, in the face of greed.

One of his edicts drove home his new-found pacifism. "One conquering king felt remorse, for when an independent country is conquered, the slaughter, the death, and the deportation of people is extremely grievous – and all those who dwell there suffer violence, murder, and separation from their loved ones. The participation of all men in suffering weighs heavily on the mind of the king." Ethical conduct, in contrast, consisted of "many good deeds, kindness, liberality, truthfulness and purity."

According to the oral tradition, these sentiments were not just rhetorical. Ashoka sent emissaries to the Middle East, to the successors of Alexander the Great, urging peace in hopes that his own commitments would spread – though there is no evidence they had much impact on Alexander's military heirs.

There is no question that Ashoka actively supported missionary efforts in Sri Lanka and Southeast Asia, that began to spread Buddhism widely in these regions. It was a revealing sign of his priorities for peace that at the same time Ashoka continued to tolerate other religions, including Hinduism. Nor was there any suggestion that missionary persuasion should be accompanied by any military force – a contrast with some other religions, at the time and later on, where conquest in the name of truth often struggled with preferences for peace.

The same pacifism applied to divisions within Buddhism itself. Ashoka sponsored several conferences that sought to work out disagreements over doctrine, an effort that continued after the emperor's death. The effort failed, in that different strands remained. But, again in contrast with the experience of several other religions, no overt conflict resulted. Buddhists usually accepted internal disagreement without violence – again, a strong suggestion that pacifism was more than skin deep.

Ashoka's policies did not, however, directly survive his death. A bitter quarrel over his succession ended the reign of peace, and quickly split the Mauryan Empire into separate, often warring kingdoms.

But a powerful legacy did remain, that could affect Hindus as well as Buddhists later on. Ashoka's name was long honored not only in India (even as Hinduism regained its majority status), but in Tibet, China and other Buddhist areas. The legacy would be actively invoked in the twentieth century, by Mohandas Gandhi's policy of nonviolent resistance to British imperial rule. His name, even today, symbolically graces efforts at peace and social welfare, in the United States and elsewhere.

More explicitly, Ashoka or at least his legend set a model for Buddhist kings in many parts of Southeast Asia in the classical and postclassical centuries, where he was regarded as a paradigm of ethical rule. A number of monarchs sought to replicate his charity and compassion. The association with Ashoka's memory surfaced in many regional kingdoms in Sri Lanka, Burma and Thailand into the fifteenth century. King Dutthagamani, in Sri Lanka, in the first century BCE, thus sincerely repented of acts of war used in conquering the island, seeking then to restore order by peaceful means while claiming divine inspiration for his monarchy. Other rulers, similarly, turned from initial commitment to war, justified by a need to restore order, to a commitment to Buddhist principles of nonviolence and welfare, sometimes proclaiming themselves Buddhist saints in the process.

Thus a Chinese Emperor Wen, in the sixth century CE, again initially reliant on military force to establish his regime, talked later in Buddhist terms of his "universal monarchy." "We spread the ideals of the ultimately benevolent one [Buddha] with a hundred victories and a hundred battles. We promote the practice of the ten Buddhist virtues. Therefore we guard weapons of war as having become like incense and flowers (presented as offerings to the Buddha) and the fields of this visible world forever identical with the Buddhist land."

Obviously, Ashoka's example had its limits, and regional kings might claim his mantle as a gloss over military oppression; actual commitments to peace, as opposed to sweet words, undoubtedly varied. The Emperor Wen shows how Ashokan principles might even be stretched to justify war, or even more commonly simply come into play as a backup ideology once a successful string of wars had yielded initial results. But the existence of Ashoka as example was in itself unusual: few other religious traditions had a practical illustration of this sort, however limited its actual impact.

Buddhism in practice

Well after Ashoka, and as Buddhism became better established in key parts of Southeast and East Asia, further tests of the impact on peace emerged. The results further qualified any oversimple claims about the legacy of early Buddhism's clear pacifist principles or the Ashokan symbolism. Probably inevitably, as Buddhism spread and especially as it was adopted by a wider range of rulers and states, reality became more complex.

The process was similar to the experience of other religions in some respects; comparison with Christianity will be particularly fruitful. People adopt a religion sincerely, but then blend its commitments with other motivations and experiences. Some, seeing a religion's success, even more crudely seek to twist it to other, even contradictory purposes. Buddhism, again, became clearly involved in the resultant compromises and dilemmas, as the commitment to nonviolence could be greatly diluted. The question – like all our key questions, a difficult one to answer – is whether, on balance, Buddhist pacifism suffered a bit less than would be true in other religious histories.

There's no question, however, that Buddhism could and did serve, in some circumstances, not only to tolerate violence but even to justify it. The experience illustrates the wider proposition that no large religion – as opposed to more committed but smaller sects – has ever managed to subdue the military impulse entirely.

We have already noted several features of Buddhism that could contribute to compromise, however unintended. The Buddhist disdain for this world, and the quest for personal piety, might extend to ignoring large social issues such as war, in favor of the quest for individual meditation or the isolation of a Buddhist monastery. The divisions within Buddhism could weaken a religious response to a military state, and occasionally – despite the Ashokan precedent – could lead to violent conflict directly.

An array of examples show how early Buddhist ideals could be tested. We have already met King Dutthagamani in Sri Lanka. The pious king initially carried a relic of the Buddha on his spear, in resisting invaders from India – in battle in which he was joined by Buddhist monks. The king claimed that Buddhist saints assured him that while his armies had killed thousands, only one-and-a-half humans had died, because the invaders were so evil that they were on par with animals. A fighting tradition persisted in Sri Lankan Buddhism that has lasted to the present day, actively invoked in recent fighting against a Tamil minority. The argument was and is that battles to keep order and preserve Buddhism (in this case, from possible Hindu attack) legitimized violence.

Buddhist monks recurrently fought for the Chinese emperor, for example at the beginning of the Tang dynasty in the seventh century CE, and later on battled invading Mongols under a banner bearing the command, "subdue demons." Korean monks also recurrently fought invaders. Tibetan Buddhist documents included "spells for destroying enemy armies," and there were even claims that assassins targeting enemy forces might be regarded as saints.

As Buddhism spread in Japan, it frequently became embroiled in conflict. Early on, in the sixth–seventh centuries, different ethnic groups adopted different forms of Buddhism, which then became pretexts or outright motivations for conflict in the name of claimed religious truth – though ethnic hatreds were probably more important beneath the surface. Battles between sects also emerged later on, into the sixteenth century. This is perhaps the most striking exception to the general pattern of Buddhist tolerance. As in other religious conflicts, the result was not only violence, but explicit religious justifications for violence. One group, fighting to the death in their temple against another Buddhist group, insisted that "the mercy of Buddha should be recompensed even by pounding flesh to pieces. One's obligation to the Teacher should be recompensed even by smashing bones to bits." This was the kind of argument that facilitated a belief that enemies were not really human, but some kind of demon and therefore not within the normal ethical sphere. Less bombastically, one Buddhist group might proclaim a rival sect as "full of deception … Nothing they say can be trusted" – in which violent attack might be fully justified. In certain circumstances, in other words, Buddhist leaders might endorse the idea of a holy war, though without this precise terminology.

Most commonly, of course, Buddhist thinkers, and even more commonly kings who claimed to be faithful Buddhists, argued simply that defense of order and the state, even by violence, was fully compatible with the ethical obligations of the faith. Much later, in the nineteenth and twentieth centuries, many Buddhists would rally to the nationalist appeals of the modern Japanese state, again arguing that service to the state – even, in this case, in imperialist expansion – was compatible with pious ethics. Thus a Japanese Buddhist tract promised "to protect the kings (together with their families and country)" if they professed a true faith and made appropriate religious offerings. Implicitly, though with less formal discussion than would occur in Christianity or Islam, Buddhists often moved toward a belief that some wars were just, and therefore did not fall under the usual ban on violence. In one famous passage, a Korean ruler invoked Buddhism as part of his defense against Chinese invaders, and was rewarded by storms that destroyed the invading force: not surprisingly, he was convinced as a result that Buddhist divinity was on his side all along.

Claims persist, as part of contemporary Buddhism, that this important religion has served as an alternative to the more common Western proclivity to war. It seems clear that, from a historical standpoint, this argument is at the least too facile. Buddhism in Japan expanded as the country suffered through the frequent regional warfare and the parallel devotion to the military samurai who were associated with feudalism (a situation that can be compared to European Christianity during a comparable feudal period). And while many wars occurred resulted from military leaders who simply ignored or violated Buddhist promptings, the religion itself could be part of the conflict.

Buddhist peace claims, however, were not forgotten. They could be revived in fairly pure form, or combined with other approaches. A Japanese Buddhist in the eighth century thus talked about the importance of warriors who would defend the king, while noting specifically the importance of the king's own commitment to proper, peaceful ethics and invoking associations with the memory of Ashoka.

In the thirteenth century, to take another but even more complicated example, Nicheren, a Japanese Buddhist leader, tried to defend a particular version of Buddhism, and to argue that the Japanese state should commit to the result. Here, he suggested a relationship between state and religion more similar to Islamic or later Christian approaches, than to standard Buddhism. But what might have been a simple invocation of the need for military action in defense of religious truth proved more nuanced, as Nicheren tried to combine his effort with Buddhist peace goals. In this vein, he explicitly argued that "the Visitor asks if one must kill in order to eliminate those who slander Buddhist ethics, as suggested by some of the passages cited previously. [But] the Visitor replied to the effect that it is prohibited to punish those who slander the ethical code." At the same time, somewhat confusingly, Nicheren contended that if the correct

version of Buddhism were adopted, but only then, "the world will be a p**
place." Otherwise all sorts of disasters will occur. "Now surely the peace of **
world and the stability of the nation are sought by both ruler and subject and
desired by all inhabitants of the country." But Nicheren's commitment to one
particular form of Buddhism, and his goal of state support for what he called
the Buddhist Law, added a less familiar qualification to this plea for peace. A
believer might be somewhat confused as to what to do about the kinds of false
doctrines Nicheren claimed would be ruinous if peace did indeed have top priority. Some historians have argued Nicheren encouraged a Japanese sense of
special destiny and mission rather than a real commitment to peace – a debate
that influences Japanese Buddhism even today.

Overall, however, despite all the complexities, Buddhist commitment to
ahimsa never disappeared and might easily emerge in pure form, devoid of
compromise. Thus a Buddhist thinker during the Chinese Tang dynasty – the
regime that saw some Buddhist military activity early on – returned to basic
principles: "O, you, son of Buddha! You should not act on behalf of a country, nor join an army, nor organize an army to kill people ... No, a holy person should not even frequent an army, much less become the enemy of any
country."

Conclusion

Several points seem clear, in the relationship between Buddhism and peace.
First, obviously, the power of Buddhism as a missionary religion did not trans-
late into as consistent a commitment to peace – much less, as active an achievement of peace – as basic principles suggested. Interpretations of the faith varied
considerably, along with outright neglect or manipulation.

Second, however, Buddhist principles were in many ways both clear and
strong, creating the basis for recurrent and intense advocacy for peace. This
described long stretches of Buddhist history, in several parts of Asia – even
apart from the possibly special example of Ashoka. And it continues to define
an active Buddhist contribution in the present day, to which we will return.

This tension, between principle and frequent reality, was of course not unique
to Buddhism. We encounter similar dilemmas, for example in Christianity after
an early period, in the ensuing chapter. But it is legitimate to raise the issue of
partial distinctiveness even so. Was Buddhism a bit less burdened by compromise than other major religions? The relative lack of conflicts among Buddhist sects – particularly aside from the Japanese experience – may suggest an
unusual willingness to embrace toleration for the sake of peace. Did Buddhism
encourage slightly less regional violence, particularly in Southeast Asia, than
was true of many other regions? Tallying rates of warfare is difficult, and deciding whether religion played a leading role even where comparative differences
do seem to exist is even more challenging. The issues are worth pondering, at
least. The Buddhist approach was not a hollow invocation of peace, despite the
variations and limitations.

...ist tradition

: The Search for India's Lost Emperor. New York: The Overlook

ne Traditions of Nonviolence and Peace." *International Journal on*
3 (1993): 47–54.

...nd peace

Cook, ...ed. *Concise History of World Religions: An Illustrated Time Line*. Washington, D.C.: National Geographic Society, 2011.
Frost, J. William. *A History of Christian, Jewish, Hindu, Buddhist, and Muslim Perspectives on War and Peace*. Lewiston, NY: Edwin Mellen Press, 2004.
Palmer-Fernandez, Gabriel, ed. *Encyclopedia of Religion and War*. New York: Routledge, 2004.
Pennington, Brian K., ed. *Teaching Religion and Violence*. Oxford: Oxford University Press, 2012.

On Hinduism

Gandhi, Rajmohan. "Hinduism and Peacebuilding." In Coward, Harold and Gordon S. Smith, eds., *Religion and Peacebuilding*. Albany, NY: State University of New York Press, 2004, pp. 45–68.
Gupta, Krishna Govinda. "Some Phases of Hinduism." *Journal of the Royal Society of Arts* 57.2950 (1909): 582–96.

On Buddhism

Ives, Christopher. "Dharma and Destruction: Buddhist Institutions and Violence." *Contagion: Journal of Violence, Mimesis, and Culture* 9 (Spring 2002): 151–74.
Kraft, Kenneth, ed. *Inner Peace, World Peace: Essays on Buddhism and Nonviolence*. Albany, NY: State University of New York Press, 1992.
Strong, John S. *The Legend of King Asoka: A Study and Translation of the* Asokavadana. Princeton, NJ: Princeton University Press, 1983.
Victoria, Brian Daizen. "Teaching Buddhism and Violence." In Pennington, Brian K., ed., *Teaching Religion and Violence*. Oxford: Oxford University Press, 2102, pp. 74–93.

4 Religion and peace in the postclassical age

Two great religions – the largest in the world today – formed in the Middle East, during or shortly after the classical period. We deal here with a period that emerged well after the formative stages of Buddhism. Christianity arose when the Roman state was at its height, and began to spread through much of the Mediterranean region and a bit beyond over the next few centuries, even as the Empire declined. After Rome's collapse, and as the Mediterranean world fragmented, Islam emerged, from about 600 CE onward, and began to win converts quite rapidly, first mainly among the Arab peoples and then more widely. These two religions, often antagonistic, shared many features: the Prophet Muhammed viewed Christ as a holy prophet and deliberately built in part on Christian ideas, arguing that the messages he received from Allah perfected earlier religious teachings. Between them, Christianity and Islam divided not only the Mediterranean world, but other regions as well, though for quite a while Islam was particularly dynamic. For centuries after 600, and in important ways still today, the peace or lack of peace of many parts of the world depended heavily on the guidance of these two great faiths.

This chapter focuses on what Christianity, and then Islam, had to say about peace, and how their messages compared. While the emphasis rests particularly on beliefs, we must also look at practice, for the new religions launched important initiatives toward peace and war during the postclassical centuries from 600 onward. Again, these initiatives must be compared as well. Additional comparison, with Hinduism and particularly Buddhism, rounds out a consideration of the contributions of the great world religions toward peace, and the key complexities involved.

Before turning directly to the postclassical centuries, however, a brief look at yet another religion is essential. Long before the birth of Christ, the Jewish religion established important commitments toward peace and war that would affect both Christianity and Islam substantially. The three successive Middle Eastern religions are linked through their common founding beliefs – Muslim scholars, indeed, often refer to an "Abrahamic" religious tradition that identifies the links among all three. Both Christianity and Islam departed from Judaism in many ways, and peace was one of the differentiators: but the Jewish approach to peace remained influential (and some would argue, both troubling and promising) as the larger religions took shape and developed their missionary outreach.

Judaism and peace

The Jewish religion took shape in the centuries after 1100 BCE, though stories point to possibly even earlier origins. The initial Jewish experience, in other words, nestles at the intersection of the early civilization period in the Middle East, and the onset of classical empires such as the Persian and, later, the Roman regimes.

There is no question that the Judaism of the Old Testament – the initial religious documentation of the religion, gradually written down – was profoundly affected by the frequent conflicts in the region, which impinged on the Jewish people directly and which made war seem normal. Yet the religion itself was a new force, most obviously because of the emphasis on a single God rather than the usual polytheistic multiplicity, but also because of an unusually clear emphasis on the importance of ethics. Both features – the monotheism and the ethics – bore obviously relationship to the subjects of peace and war.

The Old Testament is notoriously filled with war, and not just casual conflict but frequent, bloody battles. Various books in the Bible testify to the importance of military leaders. Carnage is described in great detail. Exodus went beyond this, to claim "The LORD is a warrior; the LORD is his name." God often approved of wars directly, as in Deuteronomy: "and when the LORD your God has delivered them over to you and you have defeated them, then you must destroy them totally. Make no treaty with them, and show them no mercy."

Aside from sheer repetition of the military themes, the Jewish religion added two, related, components to support for war – in principle, major innovations, and in practice often a spur to battle from biblical days to the present. First and most important, war could now be conducted in God's name and for God's purposes. It might be essential, for example, to wage war on idolaters. A holy war could now be imagined, that could in turn license great cruelty in the name of divine command. This went well beyond the frequent support for military action by a "god of war" in a polytheistic pantheon. The new theme helps explain the recurrent justifications for efforts to destroy an enemy, to leave nothing standing. Furthermore, and this was the second point, war could now be seen as part of a divine punishment for a sinful people, again providing a legitimacy for war that could complicate any efforts to bring peace.

Part of the legacy of this first great Middle Eastern religion, then, was a partially novel, and unusually sweeping basis for military fervor and a boundless ness to military effort.

But the Jewish religion contained important seeds for peace, and here too there were innovations – even though, on the whole, the peace themes gained less visibility than the image of God militant. Peace scenes were described, and peace was sometimes presented as a desirable community goal. Accounts of peace following episodes of violence figured in, both for victors and for those defeated. In the book of Isaiah, peace is presented as preferable to the militarism of the Persian Empire.

A problem with the Jewish idea of peace, in these early centuries, involves its broad scope. The Hebrew word *shalom*, still used as the basic greeting in the language, is often translated as peace, but in fact it connoted a broader sense of wellbeing and justice. This does not mean there was no idea of peace, but it does complicate its interpretation: peace as we commonly understand it may not have been the main point. To the extent that God demanded justice, violence in its defense might be essential. Another Old Testament theme involved criticizing false prophets, who proclaimed peace but did not bring it – again, the idea of peace seemed somewhat elusive.

Despite these complexities, the religion did make a fundamental contribution to peace, beyond simply acknowledging it in the way most cultures did. Peace could become part of a prophetic vision of a better world to come, perhaps toward the end of existence of earthly activities as God prepared a final judgment. Thus the famous biblical passage:

> It shall come to pass in the latter days that the mountain of the house of the Lord shall be established as the highest of the mountains … and many nations shall come, and say, "Come, let us go up to the mountain of the Lord, to the house of the God of Jacob, that he may teach us his ways and we may walk in his paths." For out of Zion shall go forth the law and the word of the Lord from Jerusalem. He shall judge between many peoples, and shall decide for strong nations afar off; and they shall beat their swords into ploughshares, and their spears into pruning-hooks; nation shall not lift up sword against nation, neither shall they learn war anymore; but they shall sit every man under his vine and under his fig tree, and none shall make them afraid; for the mouth of the Lord of hosts has spoken.

The vision of turning instruments of war into agricultural tools is one of the most powerful ever written, and would be referred to in later situations well beyond the bounds of Judaism. And it intriguingly evoked, as well, the contradictions between agricultural prosperity and war, and the related importance of peace.

The contribution of peace in prophetic visions of a better future could go further still. Another Old Testament prophecy foresaw an age when "every boot of the tramping warrior … and every garment rolled in blood will be burned as fuel for the fire. For to us a child is born, to us a son is given … and his name will be called 'Wonderful Counselor, Mighty God, Everlasting Father, Prince of Peace.' Of the increase of his government and of peace there will be no end … from this time forth and for evermore." Humankind might, in other words, look for God to bring a reign of peace that would displace war entirely – but it would be God's agency that would turn the tide: "The zeal of the Lord of hosts will do this." This image of a future age of peace would powerfully affect

Christianity and particularly Islam. It could inspire efforts to reduce conflict, though it could distract by pointing so vividly toward the future and the need for divine intervention, rather than the present and what human effort could achieve.

Jewish society and culture, born in a time and place of frequent war, reflected its context. Yet, as in basic concepts about the nature of the divinity, the religion contributed important new ideas to the issue of peace. Elements of Judaism clouded the prospect of peace, as in the new injunction to fight under God's banner for divine laws and divine purity. But this was not the whole story: the new vision of a peace stretching out at some future time, again under God's leadership, could motivate as well. The hope for a Prince of Peace could extend beyond the Jewish tradition.

Christianity

Christianity was born as a religion of peace – the second such major religion, after Buddhism. Just as Buddhism transformed peaceful elements in Hinduism into a larger statement for peace, so Christianity built substantially on peaceful components of Judaism while reducing or ignoring the contradictory elements. The result was a major commitment to peace as a goal on earth as well as a condition in heaven – a source as well of recurrent, practical efforts by Christians and Christian leaders to establish peace from the early days of the religion to the present. The image of peace was carried in both the Eastern and the Western versions of Christianity, as they began to emerge during the religion's first centuries. Christian pacifism differed somewhat from the Buddhist commitment, in that condemnations of violence and killing were less specific; but a similar basic vision, of divine sponsorship of a goal for peace, clearly emerged.

The pacifism of early Christianity was not a final statement. As the religion gained acceptance in the later Roman Empire, from the fourth century onward, important qualifications were introduced: for if a Christian state required war, must peace be sought at all costs? The result was an ongoing debate among Catholic thinkers through the Middle Ages and beyond, about the terms and conditions of just wars. Strong impulses toward peace remained, but they did not uniformly predominate. But during the Middle Ages as well – in Western Europe from the sixth century to the fifteenth – frequent local wars and weak states also prompted a new series of measures, Church-sponsored for the most part, to limit violence and establish some elements of peace. Motives here mixed highly practical concerns with some of the spiritual preferences for peace born with the religion itself. The result was a series of interesting if limited experiments that enrich the history of peace, and that surfaced recurrently until the role of religion in European statecraft changed with the emergence of stronger monarchies and the advent of new religious divisions in the sixteenth century.

Here too, of course, there were important similarities to later developments in Buddhism, where practical politics and even a use of religion to justify violence arose as well. For Christians, however, the dilemma of the state on balance loomed even larger, from the later Roman Empire onward, because of political and theological patterns alike. The result was a clearer modification of initial pacifism than occurred in Buddhism, though not, even here, a total eclipse.

Early beliefs

Jesus Christ, the founder of the new religion and regarded by Christians as the Son of God, was explicit in his commitment to peace, and he and his followers were eager to have his message disseminated. In his Sermon on the Mount, Jesus spelled out the new doctrine:

> Blessed are the peacemakers, for they will be called sons of God ... You have heard that it was said, "Eye for eye, and tooth for tooth." But I tell you: resist no evil. If someone strikes you on the right cheek, urn to him the other also ... You have heard that it was said, "Love your neighbor and hate your enemy." But I tell you: Love your enemies and pray for those who persecute you, that you may be sons of your Father in heaven.

Not surprisingly, the word "peace" appeared in all of the books of the New Testament save one.

The point seemed clear: peace was now an overwhelming goal, far more important than the kinds of conflicts justified by older ideas. And in principle there might be no valid reason to go to war at all. The theme of peace was carried on in stories about the new savior: angels were said to have announced his birth with the words, "Peace on earth to men of good will." Christ himself might be celebrated as the heralded Prince of Peace, and as Christian religious holidays developed they often included elaborate references to peace. Christmas, most obviously, would ultimately fill with references to peace on earth.

For early Christians peace was a benefit in and of itself, but its pursuit – as the Sermon on the Mount suggested – highlighted qualities and virtues that would be rewarded in heaven, possibly after a final judgment in which the righteous were separated from the unsaved. And in the new Christian version of heaven, peace maintained a leading place. Eastern Orthodox Christians would soon be describing heaven as "a place of green pasture; a place of repose, wherein all sickness, sorrow and sighing are fled away." Or in the Roman Catholic catechism: heaven constituted a "blessed communion with God." "Scripture speaks of it in images: life, light, peace, wedding feast, wine of the kingdom, the Father's house."

Christ's message for this earth included a variety of specifics. Christian missionaries, beginning with the original disciples, were urged to greet others in the name of peace: "When you enter a house, first say 'Peace on this house.'" The New Testament offered direct attacks on war, in urging "put up again thy sword in its place: for they that take the sword shall perish with the sword."

Christ urged rulers to seek peace rather than contemplating going to war. At times, to be sure, the message was at least uncertain as to how much peace could be achieved in this life. "I have told you these things, so that in me you may have peace. In this world you will have trouble. But take heart! I have overcome the world." Among his final words to his disciples was the invocation, "Peace I leave with you; my peace I give you." Again, it could not be entirely clear whether he believed worldly peace was possible, as opposed to the confidence and serenity faith could provide to Christian believers here and now, and the sure hope that, for the virtuous, a heavenly peace awaited.

Christ's crucifixion, at the hands of agents of the state, added to the message of peace, for here was a martyr for humanity. Missionaries quickly spread the word that Jesus had been "making peace through his blood, shed on the cross." For a time, of course, many Christians believed that Christ would soon return, and that a reign of peace would greet this Second Coming, for those who were virtuous. This idea reduced actual, concrete efforts for peace, as believers waited for God's will to be done.

As the sense of immediacy faded, two new elements were added to the message of peace. First, the Christian missionary effort began to reach out to a variety of peoples, and not just Jews. This expanded the idea of peace, by creating a common sense of humanity now open to God's word. Christ was now portrayed as one who "came and preached peace to you that were far off and to them that were close"; cultural differences should not matter in God's mission of peace. Again, whether the peace Christians envisaged was a literal end to war, or a larger sense of peacefulness through religious faith was not always clear, but the potential universality of the message was an important step.

The second innovation, again particularly once expectations of an immediate Second Coming receded, was a growing realization of the incompatibility of this aspect of the Christian message, and the dominant policies of the Roman Empire. Here, Christianity could become a pacifist movement outright, in opposition to Roman militarism. Thus Lactantius, an early Christian thinker, stated flat out: "It is not lawful for a just man to engage in warfare." Many early Christian leaders argued that anyone who had engaged in war should be excluded from the church for at least three years. War was simply a manifestation of evil. This approach was enhanced, of course, through the periodic persecutions of Christians by the Roman state: it was relatively easy for this growing but still minority religion to see itself apart from the policies of emperors. Violent resistance was futile, but this could simply enhance the commitment to peace. One of the victims of Roman persecution, Irene, later gained sainthood in both the Catholic and the Orthodox traditions as the first patron saint of peace.

New complexities

With time, tensions between the Roman state and Christians lessened, and this opened the door to some different kinds of conversations. Some Christian leaders, for example, began to praise the *Pax Romana* as part of God's plan. This maintained a commitment to peace, but now as the result of some mixture of divine guidance and practical military policy. Christians had to work hard to explain that their pacifism was not responsible for the increasingly visible decline of the Empire – and this could modify peace goals as well, in favor of greater accommodations with the ruling powers.

Outright pacifism persisted. The great Latin Church writer Tertullian, writing in the decades about 200 CE, made it clear that imperial policy was often unacceptable. Tertullian insisted that the notion of a "Christian soldier" was nonsensical, because Christ had "dismissed all soldiers." Obedience to emperors must be limited, in the same interests of peace. It was fine to pray for one's ruler, but it was also important to impose constraints, including constraints over military ambition. Christianity should become a separate force in the Roman state, working for peace; and it also should promote peaceful relations outside the Empire, even with peoples regarded as barbarians. Another Christian writer stated more simply that warfare was nothing more than legitimized murder. Theologians in the Eastern part of the Empire echoed the same message: Christians must educate for peace; "peace and love, simple and plain blood sisters, do not needs arms or abundant supplies." Faith is the Christian weapon, and it inflicts no wounds. Christians should be "children of peace," using Jesus' example to avoid conflict. "Let us pray for the peace and settlement of the world and of the holy churches; that the God of the whole world may afford us His everlasting peace, and such as may not be taken from us." In these views, no accommodation with the Roman state should undermine the commitment to universal peace.

But further compromises did occur, and by the fourth century the dominant views of Christian writers began to shift accordingly. For, early in the fourth century, the Emperor Constantine converted to Christianity and ended imperial persecutions of Christians once and for all. He became a pious man, by all accounts, and indeed he dedicated a new church building to Irene, as patron saint of peace, soon after he made the city of Constantinople the new capital of the Eastern part of the Empire. But Constantine was clear that, under the new rules of engagement, Christians had to serve the Empire in turn; this was one of the prices for state approval. A law required that any Christian who refused to serve in the Roman army, or deserted, should be excommunicated. Church and State, newly united, recast the Christian relationship to pacifism.

From this point onward most leading Christian thinkers – headed by the formidable St. Augustine of Hippo – began modifying the systematic commitment to peace with a belief that certain kinds of wars could in fact be regarded as just. This does not mean that a preference for peace was abandoned. Augustine made it clear that war should be limited. He noted that it was far better to kill war with words than men by swords. But he explicitly recognized that war might be necessary. Thus while explicitly condemning any desire to harm, or take revenge, or try to dominate – all unacceptable motives for war – Augustine added: "certain wars that must be waged against the violence of those resisting are commanded by God or some other legitimate ruler and are undertaken for the good." It was the motives behind a war, not killing itself, that must be considered. Both religion and the state might legitimately prompt military action. By the same token it now became quite acceptable for Christians to serve as soldiers, though – as a gesture to earlier sentiments – priests of the church must not themselves bear arms.

So what was a "just" war? Christian thought tended to regard as just those wars designed to recover property or to repel enemies. But the category could include the administration of legitimate punishment or use as a weapon against unbelievers. Considerable thought, from this point onward, went into distinctions between wars with other Christians, and the wider latitude given to wars against infidels or heretics. Christians might legitimately war against other Christians if the latter had attacked or – more vaguely – when they were operating under legitimate authority. Wars against infidels did not need this kind of fine distinction. With time, furthermore, the latitude of the just war tended to widen. By the time of St. Thomas – eight centuries after St. Augustine – just wars involved service to rightful princes, or for a just cause, or where greater good would ensure – arguably, rather broad categories. Some hesitancy persisted. The Christian legalist Gratian, for example, noted that while wars might justly punish, peace was preferable to maximum possible punishment.

But the wider point is clear. The Christian religion retained the capacity to condemn certain kinds of war. It certainly continued to highlight the desirability of peace and, of course, the idea that peace would be part of heavenly reward. And a more fervent pacifist position might always resurface as part of Christian belief – a possibility that remains lively even to the present day. But majority Christianity now involved compromise and complexity. Wars might be essential for several legitimate purposes. Indeed – extending the same thought – war might even be necessary to carry out God's purposes, as in the defense of the one true faith. Gratian caught this point as well, writing that "[Military] valor is a gift of God, but must be used in accordance with His will." Mainstream Christian thinking had clearly changed since the early days, not beyond all recognizability, but substantially nevertheless.

Medieval Christianity

There was, however, a further chapter to be played out in the relationship between Christianity and peace, as the Roman Empire finally collapsed in the West and Europe entered its version of the postclassical period – usually, in the European context, called the Middle Ages. This chapter involved a dramatically new political and military context, in which both newer and older elements of Christian thinking came into play – creating important innovations in the history of peace in the process.

The fall of the Western Roman Empire, in the fifth century, and the migrations and invasions by Germanic peoples into wide stretches of Western Europe, led to a deterioration of state authority, and the basic capacity to keep order, that would last for many centuries. Christianity continued to gain ground during the period, and in most ways the Catholic Church was by far the most effective institution in the region. But conflict and disorder increased measurably, with regional wars and disputes exacerbated by periodic external invasions. This was a violent time, and religion was not the controlling factor. Gradually, a system of feudalism developed, based primarily on relationships between military leaders and their immediate followers; wars and preparations for war continued to be a dominant theme.

In this new framework Christian leaders tried to react, particularly by the tenth and eleventh centuries as considerable disorder persisted. Their motives might recall earlier pacifist strains, but they reflected more immediate concerns about protecting church people and church property and offering some solace to the weak and vulnerable. Debates about what constituted a just war, or the extent to which peace should be a primary goal, typically combined with more practical considerations.

In the first place, church leaders attempted to set up religious buildings as peaceful sanctuaries, safe from the ravages of war and disorder no matter what was going on in the larger society. In this effort they often mixed spiritual sanctions with very practical physical measures. Anyone who attacked church property was subject to excommunication – that is, banned from the church and denied access to the holy sacraments – and subjected to other spiritual warnings and punishments. At the same time, many church buildings – and particularly monasteries, as centers for prayer and peaceful work and contemplation – were fortified in ways that might protect them from attack. This was true in Russia as well as in Western Europe: some monasteries had the same kinds of walls and fortifications as some of the walled cities, and for essentially the same reasons.

Church officials – priests, monks, and nuns – were also supposed to be safe from involvement in war. This might not mean active commitments to peace, but the safeguards were meant not only for protection but to allow church leaders to play special roles in attempting to protect the most vulnerable groups from attacks in war or even to mediate in the interests of peace.

Concerns of this sort could easily broaden into outright efforts to promote peace. Again, various motives could intertwine. Recollections of commitments to peace in principle played a role. So, often, did a sincere desire to protect peasants and the poor from the damage military activities commonly caused. Medieval warfare featured a military elite of armed knights, often fighting from horseback, and ordinary people had little protection from their attacks. But in a Christian church now well established and often prosperous, worldlier concerns entered in as well, in a situation where states were too weak to offer protection. Bishops and monastic leaders wanted to protect their wealth and landed property, and they were quite willing to use spiritual measures toward this end. Excommunication – the equivalent of loss of citizenship not only in this life but also the next – was an effective countermeasure, reconnecting the church to the promotion of peace.

And the threat was not hollow: many accounts circulated about soldiers who had violated a peace agreement and were later banned from burial in consecrated ground. One eleventh-century story embellished the common pattern: an excommunicated soldier's friends buried him in the church cemetery despite the religious ruling, but the consecrated ground itself repeatedly tossed the body out. Ultimately the friends had to bury the body elsewhere and realized, so the story went, that heaven required that peace be observed. The larger point should be clear: the medieval church was trying to demonstrate that peace could be based on moral or spiritual grounds, and not government-based force.

Bishops, in particular, led the most sweeping efforts at peace. They rarely tried to attack military activities systematically, for the feudal lords depended on this outlet and bishops did not confront them directly. But they did try to craft a number of restraints.

Efforts crested from the later tenth century into the mid-eleventh, as Christian leaders sought to deal with a growing problem of violence and regional strife. For a brief period, earlier, an effective empire under Charlemagne had deliberately attempted to promote internal peace in a territory that stretched from present-day France and the Low Countries into parts of Germany and Italy. Church property was explicitly singled out for protection. But by the tenth century the Empire had collapsed, with an ensuing increase in disorder. This was the context in which churchmen sought new measures that would substitute spiritual promotion of peace for the efforts of the state. The arrival of a new millennium in 1000 CE – the passage of a thousand years since the birth of Christ – may have created additional anxieties about a possible end of the world and divine wrath that gave further impetus to the movement at its height.

Thus in various parts of France, during the last quarter of the tenth century, bishops convened a variety of local meetings with local feudal leaders, "to hear from them," as one notice suggested, "what advice they had to give about keeping the peace." Many councils attempted to impose an oath to respect church property and the goods of the poor – not peace in general, but protection from particular targets in war. Often, the lives of unarmed churchmen themselves were to be shielded.

Ultimately, this movement coalesced into an effort to promote the "Peace of God." Again, the actual goals were quite specific, not as sweeping as the term implied. But the movement did seek to constrain war in certain ways, and to make it clear that the power of God lay behind the constraints. Many meetings were held in rooms filled with holy symbols, including the bones of saints. Sermons emphasized the peace and harmony that the saints enjoyed, in contrast to the violence of everyday life on earth. The oaths required were meant to drive home the solemnity of the issues involved and the dire consequences of violations.

At times, additional enforcement might be implied. At a peace conference in one French city in 1038, the Archbishop had everyone over the age of 15 swear to a peace agreement and also to joint action against anyone who broke the agreement – even to the extent of taking up weapons. Peace, in other words, might require a war on war. The peace that was sought was fairly limited: church property and the persons of monks and nuns.

During the eleventh century the Peace of God movement – the attempt to protect certain categories from war – was supplemented by the Truce of God effort. Again, some millennial fears may have encouraged this expansion. Here, the target was a more general requirement that war cease on certain occasions, notably Sunday and other holy days, though on occasion the effort was extended to the end of the week as a whole. Again, oaths and holy relics were meant to provide incentive and enforcement. And while both the Peace and the Truce of God were quite limited – not at all attempting a general or widespread peace, but simply a set of restraints that would protect religious activities – the movement could lead to wider discussions of peace goals. Churchmen increasingly added peace themes to their sermons, with congregations sometimes shouting out "Pax, pax pax" or "God wishes it" in response. Those in attendance sometimes exchanged kisses of peace – so that, as one observer argued, "they may remain in the Peace of Christ and harmonious concord, and that peace may be upon them all and upon all people." And while the whole movement was sponsored by bishops, supported by monks who brought the holy relics to the meetings, the response of the laity – ordinary people and local lords alike – was often enthusiastic. Stories of the meetings carried the message even more widely, sometimes claiming that in the wake of a successful oath not only did greater peace ensue, but disease also ceased. Leaders claimed to be returning to the kind of peace Christ himself had exemplified, the same peace that he had urged on his disciples. Small wonder that some historians have referred to an effort at "peace propaganda" during the eleventh century. Thus another meeting began with the invocation, "how fair is the name of the peace and how beautiful is the repute of the unity which Christ left to his disciples when he ascended into heaven."

The Christian peace movement trailed off in the later eleventh century. Despite the various invocations, it had not always gained much effect in real life: local lords often continued to behave badly, and the idea that war was a logical purpose of feudal leadership had not really been dented. As in Japan, aristocratic militarism largely trumped religion. But by this point, regional governments began to become more effective, and one sign and purpose of their effectiveness was to reduce internal feuds and other kinds of military or paramilitary violence. The successful regional leaders – sometimes kings, sometimes powerful dukes – often claimed that they had taken over the enforcement of the Peace and Truce of God; the goals did not entirely die off. But – as with the later Roman Empire – increasing reliance on secular rulers might alter the Christian message. For now peace depended not on spiritual power, but the activities of an earthly ruler, who commonly considered war if not a goal, at least an acceptable means to an end. Thus one French bishop changed the message, in arguing that the keeping of the peace was up to the state:

The bishop's task is to pray; it is for the king to fight. Thus, kings should curb strife by force, end wars, and promote the concerns of peace. Bishops should exhort them to fight manfully for the public safety and should pray for them to be victorious.

Clearly, both the goals and the methods of the century-long peace movement were being revised.

Peace themes did not of course disappear, as part of the Christian repertoire, even though specific efforts at the Peace and Truce of God faded away. Sermons continued to discuss peace. Church leaders still attempted to intervene in local conflicts, to offer mediation and advice. At the theoretical level, discussions of what constituted a just war continued.

The Roman papacy attempted to promote peace on occasion. Efforts to protect Rome itself from war or invasion were a recurrent papal theme, the equivalent of the effort to protect religious property and institutions more generally. More broadly, Christian thinkers sporadically talked about a possible papal role in deciding whether a war was just or not, and in actually interceding to prevent or settle wars among Christians. One German notion urged the pope to forbid all wars, settling any differences among states and removing any ruler who rejected his decision. By the sixteenth century, popes claimed to be defining their role in terms of "protecting the Christian peoples against the infidels and barbarians ... judging the princes and arbitrating in their quarrels; maintain peace; restoring concord; insisting upon disarmament." There were even dreams of a papal militia of peace, "ever on the watch to punish the wanton disturber of peace."

These ideas were never realized, though they foreshadowed some modern, though less religious, notions of international organization for peace. The ideas did indicate the continued commitment of Christian leaders to a role for peace. And at least once, in a crucial decision at the end of the fifteenth century, the pope actually did orchestrate an agreement that helped reduce the possibility of great-power warfare in South America. In 1494 Pope Alexander V I brokered the Treaty of Tordesillas, in which Spain and Portugal accepted separate territories for exploitation in South America – both nations had appealed to the pope for help in limiting their growing, and increasingly belligerent, colonial competition. The agreement endured, and may have played a role not only in preventing Spanish–Portuguese warfare, but in creating the surprisingly peaceful framework within which Latin American states have normally operated since that time. The occasion was a unique one, but of real significance.

But there was a final side to papal policy that again suggests the complexities of the Christian approach to war and peace by the later Middle Ages. At the end of the eleventh-century Pope Urban II addressed a church council at Clermont, France. In one sense he urged a standard message of Christian peace. Christians should not fight with each other. He lamented "how the warfare and strife of the princes of the world endlessly brought about the destruction of peace," and he recalled the peace movement of the earlier time. He urged indeed a new Peace of God for the whole of Christendom. But he called for war against the Islamic control of the Holy Land, calling Muslims an "accursed race" who defiled the holy places and abused Christians. War, in other words, was quite legitimate in defense of the faith, and Urban actively promised the forgiveness of all sins for any Christian who died in the crusade, which meant presumably automatic access to heaven. And indeed, spurred by the call – which the pope believed would reduce war in Europe itself, by uniting Christians in the new cause – a series of crusades occurred that would lead ultimately to about a million deaths. This was a graphic testimony to the complexity of Christian beliefs as they had evolved over many centuries.

By the sixteenth century, the crusades were long past, and Western Christianity was about to enter a new time of trouble, in which novel religious divisions would provoke a bitter round of wars and in which, on the whole, the role of states in war and peace would increase still further. But the Christian connection to peace was not over, and many of the themes and divisions that had surfaced from the early church through the Middle Ages would show up again. And of course the complexity would persist as well. In more recent centuries Christians have been found leading ardent pacifism, working to settle or prevent war, condoning war, and actively promoting war in the name of the true faith. All these approaches, and more, could appeal to ample precedent.

Islam

The founder of Islam, the Prophet Muhammed, regarded himself as a messenger of peace. But Islam emerged in circumstances that were quite different from the context of early Christianity or Buddhism. The religion was tied to local states at the outset, and involved as well in wars between the city states of Mecca and Medina. The establishment of the new religion was directly wrapped up in local military campaigns, with Muhammed leading a force that ultimately defeated authorities in Mecca who had initially expelled the Prophet. Far sooner in its development than was the case for Christianity, this new religion had to deal with distinctions between just and unjust wars, and to consider goals that might qualify or outstrip the undoubted desire for peace. The idea the war might be useful in defending or advancing the faith, which did not initially surface in Christianity or Buddhism but only emerged as a result of later evolution, similarly cropped up much earlier in Islam. Sincere commitment to peace in early Islam, as a result, was more complicated at the outset than had been true of the two other great missionary religions.

This said, Islam did build in strong attachments to peace. Though deeply convinced of its religious truth, it was far more willing than the early Christian churches to tolerate other religions, less likely to feel that violent repression was necessary. It would be Christianity, after all, not Islam, that called religious crusades. Most important, over time, the evolution of Christianity took this religion closer to the same complexities that Islam had generated from the outset. By 1450, the two faiths were closer on peace issues than had initially been the case.

Example: in the twelfth century the Muslim political theorist al-Farobi, writing about the just war, made it clear that the use of force to repel an enemy or claim legitimate property, or more broadly to force people to accept what was best for them, was right and proper, assuming the guidance of a good ruler. But wars merely for conquest or to appease rage were unacceptable and immoral. Would most relevant Christian thinkers by this point have disagreed?

The key point is to be careful about over simple generalizations or comparisons, when dealing with Islam and peace. The issue has contemporary implications as well, given conflicts swirling within and around Islam, which requires even greater precision in building the historical record. Islam, like the other great religions, would have its own contributions to make in the development of ideas and policies for peace.

Three points stand out. First, there was less pure pacifism in Islam than in early Christianity or early Buddhism, and again more active discussion of various types of war including the famous (but complicated) idea of *jihad*. But some pacifist strains could emerge, nevertheless. Second, Muhammed and Islam had a deep appreciation of peace from the outset. Discussion of just wars must not obscure this element. And third, mainstream Islam evolved, during the postclassical period. Without renouncing initial beliefs, including the idea of necessary war, interest in war receded in what has been called the *Pax Islamica* – the third great reign of peace (though not of pacifism) in world history after Rome and Han China.

Early Islam and peace

abode –
a place of
residence
house or
home

Muhammed staked out a strong claim to peace, but in a context that highlighted conflict. A devotion to peace surfaced in many ways, in the Quran and other early work. In his last sermon, for example, the Prophet stated simply, "Hurt no one so that no one may hurt you." Allah invited believers to the abode of peace. Acts of peacemaking were seen as holy acts, worthy of praise and reward. "O people! Spread the greeting of peace, feed the poor and needy, behave kindly to your relatives … and thus enter Paradise in peace." The religion placed great emphasis on the peace that an individual gains through right relations with Allah, and the goal of a heavenly salvation that would be gained in peace. "Peace is on him who follows the [Quran's] guidance; and those who believe and do good are made to enter gardens, beneath which rivers flow, to abide in them by Allah's permission; the greeting therein is, Peace."

Muhammed highlighted the greeting of peace that became standard in Muslim interactions: *as-salamu alaykum*, or peace be with you." References to religious leaders, including the Prophet but also Jesus, frequently included the phrase "peace be unto him." The Quran held up an ideal society, the *Dar as-Salam*, or "house of peace." The Prophet promised that in the future an era of love and compassion would be brought back to humanity, and peace and well-begin would prevail throughout the world. History, in other words, was moving toward peace, with Paradise the final reward for believers. "See, the inhabitants of Paradise today are busy in their rejoicing, they and their spouses, reclining upon couches in the shade; therein they have fruits, and they have all they call for. Peace! – Such is the greeting, from a Lord All-Compassionate."

Tensions around peace and war

Three issues complicated the vision of peace that Muhammed advanced. First, the Quran clearly stated that obedience to the state was essential for good Muslims – even if the state was less than ideal. Like most of the major religions, then, but in this case quite clearly from the outset, Islam could legitimately offer support for a war that was framed in terms of the preservation or restoration of order.

Second, aspects of the vision of peace, including the basic greeting, may have involved more attention to personal peace, to the individual's relation with God, than to peace as a social condition. The emphases were not necessarily contradictory, but they could lead to some confusion. Elements of the Islamic promise of peace, in other words, might function for pious believers without requiring efforts to resolve conflicts in society at large.

Third – and most important – Islam talked of war in terms of religious duty: the famous concept of *jihad*. War in defense of the true faith, war to promote the true faith, might not only be justifiable but positively required of a good Muslim. And believers killed in such wars might be assured a place in heaven: "those who are killed in the path of Allah [are not dead]; they are alive with their Lord." The centrality of the *jihad* concept, and its various interpretations, looms large in any assessment of Islam and peace.

Jihad can and does mean many things. To most Muslims it has primarily come to identify the constant individual need to struggle against sin. In this sense it may have nothing to do with war at all, in the conventional sense, and might be entirely compatible with the larger interest in peace. But there is no question that the concept can be taken further, and was taken further in early Islam. Thus al-Shafi'i wrote, "The *jihad*, and rising up in arms in particular, is obligatory to all able-bodied believers, exempting no one, just as prayer, pilgrimage and payment of alms are performed, and no person is permitted to perform the duty for another." The need to defend Islam against attack by others forms the clearest definition for military *jihad*. Quite of bit of attention, during the postclassical period and beyond, went into discussions of protecting Islamic frontiers, under a concept called *ribat* that was sometimes linked to *jihad*. Some jurists ultimately argued that *ribat*, or defensive action, was actually more important than other forms of *jihad*, arguing that one night devoted to protection was worth a thousand nights of prayer.

However, the legitimation of *jihad* could go further still, to include military offensives, even unprovoked attacks, against a number of other categories. Bandits were one target: the Quran specifically urged "punishment of those who combat Allah ... and go about to commit disorders on the earth; they should be executed or crucified or have their hands and their feet cut off or be banished from the land." Apostates were another group, Muslims who renounced the faith or who dissented from Islamic leadership. And finally, there were nonbelievers in other societies, who could and should be attacked. The Quran particularly identified polytheists, urging the faithful to "fight those of the polytheists who are near you, and let them feel your severity." But the category of nonbelievers might be more general still. As one jurist put it, "It is our obligation to commence a war on nonbelievers, [even] though they may not intend to commence a war on us. Because Allah has made it an obligation on us to kill the unbelievers, so nobody ... would be in a position to suspend this rule, so that all the people would say that there is no god but Allah." War, in principle, might become almost perpetual – though one rule of thumb in early Islam suggested participation about once a decade – until the whole world had been converted to Islam.

Carried to extremes, or taken out of fuller context, the most aggressive definitions of *jihad* might seem to overwhelm the interest in peace which Muhammed had expressed. And indeed at least one small Islamic sect, in the postclassical period, did take the *jihad* injunction so literally as to engage in virtually non-stop campaigns. The Kharijite group emerged early, devoting great military energy in attacking other Muslims for what they felt was a lack of adequate religious zeal. But this was not the typical stance, which returns us to the more complex problem of combining an understanding of *jihad* with what was, beginning again with Muhammed himself, a real interest in peace.

As a first step, it is important to remember that while *jihad* was a distinctive concept, unusually sweeping and explicit, it resembled ideas about war that developed in other religions. We have seen Buddhist leaders praise war against non-Buddhists, reconciling with peaceful principles by contending that nonbelievers were subhuman. Christians recurrently developed ideas about holy war, both in defense of the faith but in offensive efforts against other religions, that resembled though in less systematic fashion the thinking behind *jihad*. Judaism had harbored similar elements. So Islam was not unique in the need to reconcile some militant beliefs and initiatives.

In practice, and again beginning with the Prophet himself, a number of religious groups were normally excluded from injunctions of *jihad*. Jews and Christians, and in some cases Zoroastrians, were identified as "people of the book," far different from polytheists. They were certainly encouraged to convert to Islam, and were taxed more heavily if they failed to do so, but they were not normally the subjects of outright violence. Formal treaties codified these arrangements in many parts of the Middle East and North Africa. Most versions of Islam, indeed, proved quite tolerant, which contributed to peace in fact – for instance, in religiously diverse societies such as Spain under Muslim rule – and which in theory helped blend *jihad* with a quest for peace. The Quran stated directly: "There is no compulsion in religion."

A number of other limits were placed on *jihad*. For quite a while – in a pattern similar to that of medieval Europe – fighting was supposed to be suspended during holy periods, most notably the fasting month of Ramadan. This provision was not maintained systematically, for another passage of the Quran had argued: "they will ask you about war in the sacred month. Say: to war at that time is bad, but to turn aside from the cause of Allah, and to have no faith in him ... and not to drive out [enemies] is worse in the sight of Allah." *Jihad*, in other words, might trump religious restraint.

A more consistent effort applied to the authorization of *jihad*. Most Muslim leaders were at pains to insist that the ordinary faithful must not strike out on their own, that *jihad* had to be balanced with concerns for order. Only a legitimate religious leader could call *jihad*. A Shiite jurist thus stated, "One of the conditions of *Jihad* is the presence of a just Imam, since he is the one and only to issue such a command ... Therefore, *Jihad* is not a religious obligation when an infallible Imam is not present. If someone goes to *Jihad* upon the instruction of an unjust imam or an ordinary ruler, then he deserves punishment since he has committed a sin." This restriction did not apply to wars of defense, when "the religion or lives of Muslims are in danger," but significantly restrained the commitment of acts of offense.

Without contradicting the obligation of *jihad*, much discussion was devoted to other limitations. Jurists generally argued that noncombatants, for example women and children, should not be subject to attacks under *jihad*, unless they were indirectly helping the enemy cause. Great attention, and disagreement, focused on other constraints: some authorities argued that all enemy property could be destroyed, others that livestock at least should be spared. It was clear that, normally, only able-bodied men were subjected to any requirement of participation in *jihad* offensives.

Even beyond this, and more fundamental to a genuine interest in peace, additional thinking increasingly went into sorting out wars, under the umbrella of *jihad*, into just and unjust, or good and bad, categories – a set of distinctions that involved concerns very similar to those conducted in other societies. Muhammed himself had urged caution about *jihad*, making sure that religious distinctions were carefully thought through: "When you go to war in Allah's way, make investigation, and do not say to anyone who offers you peace: You are not a believer." While major wars during early Islam were actually fairly infrequent – Arab armies swept over large parts of the Middle East and North Africa without consistent opposition – there was enough strife to encourage an effort to define limits more clearly; and the potential open-endedness of *jihad* had a similar effort for many groups. Good wars, for the purposes of defense or for conquests that would lead to gain for Islam, became known as *futuh*; but there was also *fitan*, or bad war, where believers had been wrongly tempted into defying God's ordinances by, for example, fighting with other Muslims.

Finally, from Muhammed onward a great deal of attention went into preventing or resolving conflicts not only within Islam but also beyond. Here was one way that a genuine commitment to peace proved compatible with other aspects of Islamic thought. Muhammed and many followers highlighted their role in reducing traditional tribal battles and feuds, which definitely constituted a wrong type of war. The Quran itself urged the importance of arbitrating disputes:

> O you who believe! Obey Allah and obey the Apostle, and those among you invested with authority; and if you differ upon any matter, refer it to Allah and the Apostle ... This is the best and fairest way of settlement.

Muhammed himself submitted to arbitration a dispute with a Jewish tribe, thus establishing that this principle applied to dealings with non-Muslim groups, and not just to Islam itself. Later Islamic rulers frequently appealed to arbitration to settle problems with subordinates, helping to keep peace within various parts of the Middle East.

Like Christianity and Buddhism, Islam became a widespread and complex religion, with many potentially conflicting components. The need to focus on defining war and its limits was unusually explicit, because of the context in which the religion first emerged and the idea of *jihad*. But there was unquestionably a real interest in peace, as part of the religious vision and as a matter of practical politics. The resulting conversations and disagreements linked this dynamic faith to patterns in other major religions in many ways. And while outright pacifism was rare, even it could emerge from Islamic principles. One sect, the Maziyariyya, ultimately dropped the concept of *jihad* entirely, while much later, in the twentieth century, a Muslim group in northern India would be persuaded to convert to an entirely nonviolent approach as they joined in the effort to protest British rule.

The Pax Arabica

Muslim interest in peace and the successful development and evolution of the Arab Caliphate between the eighth and the thirteenth centuries, a state that at its height controlled the bulk of the Middle East, North Africa and even Spain, combined to yield a prolonged period of peace in the whole region. While the idea of *jihad* did not disappear, it commanded less active interest in a state eager to preserve stability and avoid unnecessary conflict. More and more Muslims began to see long interruptions of *jihad* as normal. Tensions in mainstream Islam, over the issue of peace, receded as a result.

Leaders during the Abbasid caliphate, such as Harun al-Rashid (c.786–809), thus actively sought to negotiate peace settlements with neighboring Christian states, even sending a delegation to Western Europe proposing a strategic peace. Peaceful delegations were also sent to the Chinese court. Envoys to African countries might refer to the inhabitants as "our kinsmen," again as a gesture of solidarity. Growing scholarly attention focused on the importance of good relations among states and on concepts of international law. Considerable discussion applied to the safe treatment of foreign envoys even from hostile states.

Internally, commitment to the use of arbitration increased. Toleration of Christian and Jewish communities gained even greater emphasis: Harun al-

Rashid made it clear these groups were to be treated "with leniency." Leaders provided growing attention to the idea of security or protection under the Islamic state, again even to non-Muslims, citing precedents from the policies of Muhammed. Under this policy former enemies might be forgiven: as the Prophet had said, "anyone who puts down his arms will be safe." An increasing number of rulers began to emphasize clemency to opponents. One caliph described his preference for persuasion over war as follows: "I apply not my lash where my tongue suffices, nor my sword where my whip is enough, and if there be one hair binding me to my fellowmen, I let it not break. If they pull, I loosen, and if they loosen, I pull."

Arab scholars were often aware of the evolution that had occurred, and the increasing emphasis on peaceful relations. The great North African historian Ibn Khaldun, while confirming the idea of *jihad* in principle and accepting war as natural, devoted considerable effort to defining those types of wars that were simply wrong. And he saw the mature caliphate as an example of passage from militarism to a higher form of civilization.

Even more interesting was the revisionism of the eleventh-century philosopher Ibn Rushd (known in the West as Averroes). Ibn Rushd believed that ideas of *jihad* had been misinterpreted and overgeneralized. War, including war against unbelievers, might be useful. But "there are times in which peace is preferable to war." Muslims have wasted too many lives trying to fight unbelievers, and Islam should pull back from the systematic injunction which, he argued, had not been the Prophet's original goal.

Growing attention to spirituality within Islam, particularly from the Sufi movement, also heightened the commitment to peace. A Sufi leader in the eleventh century thus defined the basis for *jihad* as self-discipline, weaning one's appetites from lower desires and purifying the internal state of the individual. A century later the Sufi scholar al-Jilani talked of transforming the whole idea of *jihad*: "we have returned from the lesser *jihad* to the greater *jihad*," which meant that the conquest of the self was a greater struggle than the conquests of external enemies. Other reform movements sought to focus *jihad* on protecting the weak and oppressed, whether Muslim or not, rather than condoning warfare.

Conditions and attitudes during the *Pax Arabica* help explain why the Christian crusades, targeting the Holy Land from the late eleventh century onward, appeared so shocking to Arab opinion. War in the name of religion seemed increasingly strange, particularly in an environment in which considerable religious toleration had been established. The brutality of the Crusaders against Muslims was particularly noteworthy, and again hard to understand in the context of the Abbasid caliphate.

Of course the *Pax Arabica* did not last forever, and other strands of Islam remained available. A renewed sense of *jihad*, indeed, was stimulated by the crusades directly, and ultimately it was a military response that ended the Christian threat. Still, the precedents established in postclassical Islam tended to bring initial Muslim commitments to peace into greater relief while adding elements, like Sufism, that further diverted attention from war. Even as the Arab caliphate began to collapse, ending definitively in 1258, important precedents had been established that would be taken up by later Islamic regimes, in terms of priorities and policies that would emphasize peace.

Conclusion

Extending tensions first developed in Judaism, Islam and Christianity generated legacies that, depending on interpretation and circumstance, could either promote war or sponsor peace. Both religions – Islam from the outset, Christianity over time – produced claims on the state and a desire to defend particular definitions of religious truth which often complicated peace goals. These complexities resembled the patterns that developed in some of the later Buddhist kingdoms but, on balance, they qualified pacifism more consistently. But Christianity and Islam added to the repertoire of arguments and precedents about peace, and about God's ultimate preference for peace over war. The implications of their debates over peace and war, and their mutual relationships, are still being worked out in world history today.

More broadly still, the importance of the rise of major religions, including Hinduism and Buddhism as well as the Abrahamic faiths, pose obvious challenges to historical analysis, from their origins onward. All the religions, if not initially then over time, included elements that could actively support or even initiate war – even Buddhism was involved here, though perhaps with less ferocity; but they all embraced elements that could support peace and condemn those who violated it. The idea of divine guidance and spiritual support for the cause of peace was an important addition to the human repertoire. On the whole, the major religions encouraged aspirations for personal peace more clearly than commitments in social policy, but they could all provide both guidance and restraint in the conduct of actual states.

During the postclassical centuries after 600, as religions spread and religious motivations intensified, various leaders and thinkers across Afro-Eurasia picked and chose within each faith, at times using faith itself as a reason for war, more commonly contending that religion did not systematically preclude war. These internal ambiguities constituted one reason that the incidence of war did not clearly decline, along with the fact that religious impulses nowhere fully triumphed over other, more secular factors. Religious leaders and intellectuals did develop new options and alternatives, as in medieval Europe or the Abassid caliphate, but they did not systematically prevail. Warfare remained frequent. Yet the new religious support for peace, and distinctive features within each religion like the image of Christ as Prince of Peace or the Hindu attack on violence or the Islamic approach to tolerance for the sake of reducing religious conflict, were not merely historical curiosities. They helped shape new beliefs and new activities, and they expanded the bases for peace efforts, at the time and as part of an ongoing legacy for subsequent periods. The age that saw the spread of major religions was not an age of peace, overall, but new policies as well as new ideas were established that nourished efforts at the time and contributed to precedents available for later use.

Further reading

Frost, J. *A History of Christian, Jewish, Muslim, Hindu, and Buddhist Perspectives on War and Peace*. Toronto: Edwin Mellen Press, 2004.

On Judaism

Chester, Andrew. "The Concept of Peace in the Old Testament." *Theology* 92.750 (1989): 466–81.
Gichon, Mordechai. Foreword to *The Military History of Ancient Israel*, by Richard A. Gabriel. Westport, CT: Praeger, 2003, xi–xix.
Leiter, David. *Neglected Voices: Peace in the Old Testament*. Scottdale, PA: Herald Press, 2007.
Trimm, Charles. "Recent Research on Warfare in the Old Testament." *Currents in Biblical Research* 10.2 (2012): 171–216.

On Christianity

Cadoux, C. John. *The Early Christian Attitude to War*. London: Headley Bros. Publishers, 1919.
Callahan, Daniel F. "The Peace of God and the Cult of the Saints in Aquitaine in the Tenth and Eleventh Centuries." *Historical Reflections* 14.3 (1987): 445–66.
Cowdrey, H. E. "The Peace and the Truce of God in the Eleventh Century." *Past & Present* 46.1 (1970): 42–67.
Holmes, Arthur. *War and Christian Ethics: Classic and Contemporary Readings on the Morality of War*, 2/e. Grand Rapids, MI: Baker Academic, 2005.
Lowe, B. *Imagining Peace: A History of Early English Pacifist Ideas, 1340–1560*. Philadelphia, PA: Pennsylvania State University Press, 1997.
McGrath, Alister E. *The Blackwell Encyclopedia of Modern Christian Thought*. Oxford: Blackwell, 1999.
Moses, Paul. *The Saint and the Sultan: The Crusades, Islam, and Francis of Assisi's Mission of Peace*. New York: Doubleday Religion, 2009.
Teschke, Benno. "Geopolitical Relations in the European middle Ages: History and Theory." *International Organization* 52.2 (1998): 325–58.

On Islam

Black, Antony. *The History of Islamic Political Thought*, 2/e. Edinburgh: Edinburgh University Press, 2011.
Ehlstain, Jeane Bethke, ed. *Just War Theory*. New York: New York University Press, 1991.
Ferguson, John. *War and Peace in the World's Religions*. New York: Oxford University Press, 1978.
Hashmi, Sohail. *Just Wars, Holy Wars, and Jihads: Christian, Jewish and Muslim Encounters and Exchanges*. New York: Oxford University Press, 2012.

Istanbuli, Yasin. *Diplomacy and Diplomatic Practice in the Early Islamic Era*. New York: Oxford University Press, 2001.

Johnson, James Turner. *Ideology, Reason and the Limitation of War: Religious and Secular Concepts, 1200–1740*. Princeton, NJ: Princeton University Press, 1975.

Kadri, Sadakat. *Heaven on Earth: A Journey through Shari'a Law from the Deserts of Ancient Arabia to the Streets of the Modern Muslim World*. New York: Farrar, Straus and Giroux, 2012.

Kelsay, John. *Arguing the Just War in Islam*. Cambridge, MA: Harvard University Press, 2007.

Kelsay, John and J. Johnson, eds. *Just War and Jihad: Historical and Theoretical Perspectives on War and Peace in Western and Islamic Traditions*. New York: Greenwood, 1991.

Khadduri, M. *War and Peace in the Law of Islam*. New York: AMS, 1979.

Popovski, Vesselin, Gregory Reichberg and Nicholas Turner. *World Religions and Norms of War*. New York: United Nations University Press, 2009.

5 Peace in a new age of empires

The three centuries between 1450 and 1750 – often called the early modern period – were dominated by wars of various sorts. New technologies were involved, notably the growing use of cannon and other guns and the advances in navigation that permitted growing global contacts – military contacts included. New motives were involved: more and more states defined key goals in terms of territorial expansion and success in battle. Peace, for many of these states, was little more than a respite while energies recovered, with the next war merely a matter of time. New ideological rifts contributed to conflict, notably the battles between Protestant and Catholics in Europe and elsewhere, but also some new confrontations between Sunni and Shiite states in the Islamic world. One of the common characterizations of this period in world history – the age of gunpowder empires – correctly places emphasis on the widespread eclipse of peace.

Two specifics embellish the standard focus and its distance from interests in peace. As unprecedented European colonial empires emerged – first Spain and Portugal, then France, Britain and the Netherlands – they did not, like earlier empires in China, Rome and the Middle East – settle into a mature emphasis on their capacity to maintain peace. Mutual competition, including military competition, and the desire for steady expansion precluded this evolution; European colonialists remained heavily armed. Some of the new Asian empires more clearly reverted to the older pattern; the Ottoman Empire, for example, moved away from its own origins in war to a considerable interest in peace. But the European newcomers marched to a different drummer. Correspondingly another key theme of the early modern period, the rise of greater Western power in the world, did not bring claims about contributions to peace. European leaders thought they had a number of things to brag about, including commercial zeal and an interest in technological innovation, but peace was not among them. Not only their new empires, but their growing role in world trade, depended heavily on force of arms – which is one reason several of the regions that could do so sought to limit Western access in hopes of greater peace.

There were, nevertheless, some important developments on the peace side in the early modern centuries, even if they took a back seat to the strutting of empires. It should be obvious by now – as peace history to this point abundantly suggests – that few periods are monopolized either by war or by peace – human beings and states usually seek some alternation, if nothing else. Indeed, the rise of new types of wars directly generated some of the new initiatives and groups dedicated to peace: here was a key source of innovation. Europeans thus experimented with new types of peace treaties, in hopes of limiting subsequent war, particularly around the now-bitter internal religious divisions in their society. Many of them came, however grudgingly, to the realization the new levels of tolerance were essential if not only warfare, but particularly bitter warfare, was to be curbed. Innovative efforts at peace occurred elsewhere as well.

The early modern period also requires exploration in terms of how earlier approaches to peace – developed for example in Confucianism or in Islam – played out in this new age. New Islamic empires were forged from military conquest, for example, but once installed several of them played up some of the commitments toward peace that the Islamic religion and Arab peace precedents had already established. China hardly demilitarized during these centuries, but it did not emerge as a major warring state; here, but also now in Japan, the role of Confucian thinking in encouraging alternatives to militarism took on renewed importance.

Again, the early modern centuries are not really fundamental in the history of peace, though some of the new ideas and precedents had important implications. The most striking new commitments were often relatively modest – like emergence of Quakerism in Britain, or the alliance system developed by several North American Indian tribes, or the dramatic ideas of one emperor in India. But peace interest remained lively, in various settings, and the result would feed into the more sweeping ideas about peace that would emerge after 1750. Three centuries deeply involved in war would ultimately generate reactions in turn.

* * * * *

No overall pattern helps organize discussions of peace initiatives during the early modern period – there is nothing comparable to the commonalities and differences in the spread of world religions. It was true that several otherwise different societies tried to modify the role of religion in spurring conflict and war, with new approaches to tolerance. But specifics varied, and in some cases the adjustments did not last. Beyond this, three largely separate regional patterns do provide a manageable framework for the analysis of peace in the early modern world. In many parts of Asia older cultural supports for peace, such as Confucianism or Islam, gained additional traction, in combination with some interesting innovations. Several of the new Asian regimes spoke and acted with peace goals in mind. Developments in Europe, though overshadowed by military expansion and rivalry, included new expressions of Christian interest in peace but also some innovations in treaty settlements and new proposals for international organization. Finally, American initiatives, linked in some cases to European ideas, produced some interesting developments.

New regimes in Asia

After some initial adjustments in the fifteenth and early sixteenth centuries, the early modern centuries formed an unusually peaceful time for many societies in Asia. The Ming dynasty opened one of the really peaceful periods in Chinese history. Developments in Japan were even more striking, as the society enjoyed greater peace than at any point before or since, at least since organized states began to emerge in the islands – though there were some costs involved. The Islamic world is less easy to categorize, but new empires produced greater stability for some regions, and a few regimes generated some new ideas about peace.

The contrast with developments in Europe – discussed in the next section – was striking. There was far less explicit discussion of peace, as East Asia, particularly, relied on traditional prescriptions for the most part. But there was more peace in fact. It is not easy to figure out, in the absence of many sweeping proclamations, whether peace was a high priority goal or a byproduct of the consolidation of government power. Correspondingly, it is difficult to pinpoint the legacy of this interesting period. Asian peace would be shattered in the nineteenth century, as a result of external interventions – by the West, and in the Middle East also by Russia – and new internal tensions. It would become difficult if not impossible to recapture the guiding principles of the previous centuries.

Confucian societies

Late in the fourteenth century a new dynasty, the Ming, began to replace the period of Mongol rule. The Mongols had maintained a successful regime in many ways, but they were deeply resented by Chinese elites, who welcomed the opportunity to drive them back to central Asia. The new dynasty quickly claimed allegiance to basic Chinese traditions, including Confucianism, though they proved tolerant of various religions including Buddhism. The first Ming emperor also proclaimed his interest in peace. He sent emissaries to other states, including even the Byzantine Empire, with a greeting that included the statement: "We cannot but let the world know Our interest to maintain peace within the four seas."

In fact, initial Ming policy was a bit more complicated. In addition to expelling the Mongols, the Ming emperors organized a series of naval expeditions through the Indian Ocean. The intent, apparently, was to establish a wider tribute network, of the sort China had often tried to organize in central Asia. The goal was not conquest, but recognition of Chinese superiority and a regular exchange of visits and gifts. The expeditions, organized in great ships, included military forces, and several skirmishes occurred, for example in Southeast Asia. Again, peaceful relations may have been a goal, but only if special Chinese interests were recognized.

A new Ming emperor called the expeditions to a halt in 1433. Thereafter, Ming policy focused on stability, economic growth particularly in manufacturing, and careful control of relations with the outside world. Military activity did not stop. The Empire extended Chinese control over Tibet, for example, initially as part of the process of driving the Mongols away; messages to Chinese representatives in Tibet referred to the restoration of peace, but in fact military involvement was essential. And some expeditions continued in central Asia, against remnant Mongol forces, though not always with much success.

The signature policies were largely defensive, however. The government organized contacts with European traders mainly through the Portuguese port of Macao, which minimized the need for wider confrontations with the West. Great energy and expenditure were devoted to building a more formidable Great Wall – the Wall that still today attracts the fascination of tourists and astronauts alike, against possible recurrence of nomadic invasions. Here, arguably, was an investment in peace, as opposed to the larger military presence that would otherwise have been necessary. All of this was consistent with Confucian interests in political stability and social order. The challenge, of course, is trying to figure out how explicitly peace factored into to the priorities of the emperors and their bureaucrats.

Japan, in the same period, presents a different case, where the achievement of peace was far more novel. Through the sixteenth century the country continued to experience frequent regional wars, orchestrated by the feudal lords and their samurai soldiers. Indeed, the man who ultimately introduced greater central control was himself held prisoner by one of the great lords when he was a boy – though we have no way of knowing whether this experience helped shape later goals. By the middle of the sixteenth century Japan was increasingly visited by European traders, and an active interest in European guns and other European trappings including Christianity emerged.

This was the context in which a new general, Hideyoshi, the former boy prisoner, gradually emerged victorious. A combination of military victories and careful negotiations subdued the great lords, and the authority of the central state expanded. A "great peace" – sometimes called the Tokugawa peace, after the name of the new regime – descended on Japan. Feudalism was not abolished, and military exercises continued, but many samurai were turned into state bureaucrats in fact.

The Tokugawa regime took several measures that simultaneously confirmed its power and promoted greater internal peace. Peasants were forbidden to carry swords: strict social hierarchy was essential. Contacts with the outside world were largely curtailed. Most European merchants were now forbidden access to Japan; only Dutch traders, viewed as relatively nonthreatening, were exempted, and they were strictly regulated, their dealings confined to the single port of Nagasaki. Large, seagoing ships were banned in Japan itself, as ultimately was foreign travel. The fleeting fascination with European guns was another target, because of the danger they posed if used in internal warfare. Gun production was strictly regulated, and few were now manufactured in any given year. In essence, to use a modern term, Japanese society was effectively demilitarized, under government control. Religious and other freedoms were limited in the process; the government brutally eliminated the new Christian minority.

Two other developments supplemented the new policies. First, from the later sixteenth century onward, growing internal trade created a more extensive urban culture, including enjoyment of a variety of consumer amenities. Here was a clear alternative to the kinds of military emphases that had previously loomed so large. More important was the rapid spread of Confucian ideas, promoted as well by the new government. Buddhism persisted, but was increasingly confined to the religious sphere. Education and policy alike were increasingly shaped by Confucian interests in social stability.

As with China, the new Japanese regime did not produce sweeping statements about peace. As a goal, peace itself was part of a policy package that included the emphasis on authority and even intolerance, and a strong dose of isolationism.

Yet the fact was that, by the seventeenth century, the "Confucian world" of East Asia was a remarkably peaceful one. None of the governments involved undertook significant military adventures or aggressive foreign policies. A brief Japanese invasion of Korea, at the end of the sixteenth century, was an exception not to be repeated for three centuries. Chinese foreign adventures had also been halted, in favor of peaceful trade and careful defense. Even the decline of the Ming dynasty and its replacement by the Qing did not produce lasting disruption in China, and the Qing proceeded, in the eighteenth century, to negotiate a border agreement with the expanding Russian Empire that long helped preserve peace in that quarter. The relationship between Confucianism and peace, however implicit, took on new importance.

The Islamic empires

Three new Muslim empires were created by force of arms shortly before or during the early modern period. All relied to some extent on successful use of guns, and all demonstrated recurrent interest in military expansion. The Ottoman Empire gained control over much of the Middle East, southeastern Europe and parts of North Africa; the Safavids controlled Persia; and an invading Mughal dynasty took over much of the Indian subcontinent. Obviously, the military origins of the new regimes, and ongoing interests in conquest, long complicated any pursuit of peace. But at least two of the new regimes recalibrated their mission after a while – as more mature regimes often do – and began to foster more nuanced discussions and policies.

The Mughal state in India was the first to innovate, in the sixteenth century. The founder of the state, Babur, quickly realized the need for religious tolerance, as a Muslim force increasingly ruling over a Hindu majority. He advised his son: "It is but proper that thou, with heart cleansed of all religious bigotry, should dispense justice according to the tenets of each (religious) Community … The progress of Islam is better with the sword of kindness, not with the sword of oppression. And bring together subjects with different beliefs … so that the body politic may be immune from various ailments."

But it was Babur's grandson, Akbar, and his adviser Abu'l-Fadl who developed the most systematic approach to peace at the end of the sixteenth century. Akbar was a remarkably successful general, skilled in the use of cannon, and he expanded the territory under Mughal control by force. But he sought to preserve this territory by other means.

Tolerance toward the Hindu majority remained crucial. Abu'l-Fadl wrote explicitly of the need to avoid religious violence so that "dissensions within and without be turned to peace and the thorn bush of strife and enmity bloom into a garden of concord." But Akbar pressed further, contending that he had direct spiritual inspiration to redo some Islamic tenets that, in his view, were contrary to the interests of peace. He claimed to be ashamed that he had ever used force to promote religious conversion, and he attacked any insistence that Muslim law be followed to the letter, for peace was more important. He granted full equality to Hindus, and tried to reduce conflicts among different Islamic sects including often contentious Sunnis and Shiites. Religious strife was, in this view, "a basic cause of human misfortune." The all-powerful emperor must have the right to alter religious practices in light of a higher morality, a morality focused on "universal peace," "universal concord," and "love for all men." Universal peace, in turn, should be, as Abu'l-Fadl put it, "the foundation of the arrangement of mankind. "Foreign policy should follow the same principles (though Akbar worried about the expansionist claims of the Ottoman Empire, and tried to cement an alliance with Portugal to block it). In 1582 Abu'l-Fadl urged kings "to establish among themselves the bonds of friendship and cooperation so that the peoples, for God's glory, may enter into good and worthy relations among themselves."

These ideas and policies can be interpreted in several ways. Claims of direct religious inspiration may have been quite sincere. It is obvious that the results supported not only the effort at peace but the clear supremacy Akbar claimed not only within the state, but within religious life as well. The doctrines also reflected the kinds of interests the Mongols had earlier developed in maintaining power amid tolerance, and spiritual beliefs within Hinduism and Islam as well. The ideas, in other words, were not entirely new, nor entirely isolated from the diverse religious and political context of India and central Asia. At the same time, the fact that Akbar ruled near the end of Islam's first millennium may have promoted a particular interest in religious innovation. The end result was an extraordinary moment, when a reigning monarch chose to associate himself so clearly with the active promotion of peace.

It was, however, a moment. Mughal successors in the seventeenth century did not maintain Akbar's policies and interests, ultimately pulling back from the equal treatment of Hindus and sponsoring excessive efforts at military expansion as well. As with Ashoka earlier, history suggests how challenging it is to maintain commitment to peace as part of the apparatus of monarchy.

The Ottoman Empire produced no equivalent of Akbar, but it too ultimately fostered some new peace discussions. The Empire was founded on conquest and maintained efforts at expansion, off and on, until the later seventeenth century. The conquest of Constantinople in 1453 was crucial, and the Empire quickly seized other Byzantine territories. Victory over an Egyptian force followed, with new territories in that direction. More consistent struggles pitted the Ottomans against various states in the Balkans and ultimately the Habsburg monarchy, and also against the Safavid Empire in Persia.

But the expansion period did draw to a close, in the seventeenth century, and the Ottomans indeed began to struggle to hold on to some of the territory acquired. This in turn opened more extensive discussions of policy – how to organize better militarily, how to follow Islamic law, but possibly how to pay more attention to the benefits of peace. Thus Katib Çelebi published a book called *Code of Action for the Rectification of Defects*, around 1651, in which he argued among other things that the military was costing too much, at the expense of prosperous agriculture – not a clarion call for peace, obviously, but at least an indication that some commitments might be revisited. By the early eighteenth century innovations might go further still, even implicitly questioning the validity of expansionist jihad. An advice book for rulers, by Na'ima, urged a policy of "making peace with the Christians of the whole earth, so that [the Ottoman state] may be put into order and [the Ottomans] may have respite."

Ottoman sultans never committed to a sweeping policy of peace. They did become increasingly pragmatic, among other things willing to sit down with enemies and hammer out peace settlements, when strictly military initiatives had failed. Thus despite a sweeping rivalry with the Safavid Empire, including bitter disputes between the Ottomans as Sunni Muslims and the Safavids who committed to Shi-ism, an agreement was reached in the early seventeenth century (Treaty of Zuhab, 1639) that set a boundary between Persia (Iran) and the Ottoman domains (today, Turkey and Iraq) that has lasted to the present day. Recurrent settlements with the Habsburgs and Russia tended to be more transient, but there was increasing willingness to negotiate.

Developments in Islam hovered somewhat in between the quiet but successful commitments of many East Asian countries to give considerable priority to peace, and the combination that developed in Europe, of ongoing military ambition plus a steady stream of intellectual discussions of peace. The example of Akbar suggested that quite dramatic peace initiatives were possible within at least a partially Islamic framework, while Ottoman adjustments opened some opportunities as well.

Stirrings in Europe

Three forces increased the interest in, and incidence of, war in early modern Europe. First, Europe's quick appropriation of explosive powder, and the development of guns, combined with advances in shipping, allowed European armies and navies to exercise new military might in many parts of the world. Force was used in the conquest of the Americas, on the seas where Europeans tried to intimidate other traders, and in parts of Asia and Africa. Second, more and more European states – beginning with city states in Renaissance Italy, then extending to national monarchies such as France and Spain – defined one of their key purposes in terms of military aggrandizement. Wars and military alliances within Europe increased accordingly, even as the old regional conflicts associated with feudalism declined. Finally, the rise of Protestantism in the sixteenth century caused new religious battles, within and among states, for two centuries. The belief that particular definitions of the Christian faith must be defended or attacked with the weapons of war long overwhelmed the Christian tradition of peace-seeking. Religious motives plus the interest of kings in military expansion led particularly to the Thirty Years War in the early seventeenth century, which devastated Germany, but there were other major conflicts as well.

Obviously, Europe did not present the kind of examples present in several of the key Asian regimes, in which the establishment and preservation of substantial peace became a commitment of major governments. No major ruler undertook the kind of rethinking that developed among the early Mughal emperors.

Beneath the surface, however, and partly because of increasing warfare, some new thinking emerged on the subject of peace. Obviously, the new ideas did not immediately prevail, but they formed an additional repertoire for some gestures at the time and later on. And, at the more official level, the very frequency of war generated some innovative efforts at peace making that offered some interesting precedents for the future.

The result raises some important challenges for analysis. Most obviously, from the early modern period onward – and indeed, the first stirrings occurred a bit before – European intellectuals and religious leaders generated a surprisingly steady stream of peace ideas; or, if stream is a bit too strong, at least a steady trickle. The pattern outlasted the early modern period itself, and to some extent, in various forms, it has continued to the present. Some of the ideas reflected older thinking, including original Christian ideals; but there were recurrent new elements as well, and these constitute another reason for inclusion in a wider history of peace. It is true that most conventional histories unduly neglect this strand of Western history, one of the many illustrations of the extent to which peace history has been buried. At the same time, it is also true that many of the peace discussions had little intersection with actual policy. The intellectuals certainly knew that Europe was a war-torn place – this helped spur their arguments. But with some exceptions they had little visible impact on actual political leaders; peace discussions and diplomatic and military decisions emanated from different people and different camps. Few actual rulers displayed the kind of peace interest that was now occurring occasionally in Asia. The resulting European gap created obviously challenges for the peace advocates, including what they should actually do about decisions concerning military service. It creates challenges for our own historical analysis, in terms of how much weight to give this new, but largely unsuccessful, strand in the Western experience.

The Renaissance

As early as the fourteenth century, as the Renaissance developed in Italy, some innovative commentary applied to peace. The Italian Renaissance highlighted growing interest in philosophies somewhat separate from Christianity, and in reviving works of the Greek and Roman past. In this context, and amid major power struggles in Italy, a philosopher named Marsiglio of Padua wrote a book called *Defender of the Peace*, in 1324, one of the more important statements of political philosophy during the whole century. Marsiglio was genuinely interested in peace, but his real purpose was promotion of the role of the secular states as against religious interference from the papacy and other authorities. Kings and emperors, not religious leaders, could apply their human reason to developing and maintaining peaceful relationships. The idea that rationality, rather than faith, could devise goals and tactics necessary to promote peace was new, though it made little headway initially.

Other commentary emerged in the fourteenth century, spurred by the increasing conflicts between Catholic popes and secular rulers. A French lawyer, Pierre Dubois, worried about wars among Christians and urged a union of Christian empires, to be headed by the pope. Dante, the great Italian poet, wanted a unified monarchy but under secular control, with the emperor responsible for earthly happiness and peace. And there were other suggestions about how to organize a Christian peace, some of them, however, predicated on defeating the new Ottoman Empire as a predominantly Muslim power.

More sweeping efforts to promote peace, at the intellectual level, occurred as Renaissance spread to northern Europe, where it combined with important components of Christian tradition. Several north European humanists, as the Renaissance intellectuals were called, wrote extensively about peace. In the Netherlands, Erasmus (1456–1536) urged the significance of peace. One key essay was explicitly entitled "Antipolemus, or, the Plea of Reason, Religion and Humanity against War." Erasmus argued, "If there is in the affairs of mortal men any one thing which it is proper uniformly to explode, and incumbent on every man by every lawful means to avoid, to deprecate, to oppose, that one thing is doubtless war." Wars produce more misery and destruction than any other cause, yet, Erasmus noted, wars were conducted not only by pagans but also by Christians; the easy assumption that war was a natural condition must be opposed. Man was created "not for war, but for love and friendship; not for mutual destruction, but for mutual service and safety; not to commit injuries, but for acts of reciprocal benevolence." All of this should counter the tendency for actual men to commit acts of violence, to destroy farms, to ravage women:

Peace is at once the mother and the nurse of all that is good for man; war, on a sudden and at one stroke, overwhelms, extinguishes, abolishes, whatever is cheerful, whatever is happy and beautiful, and pours a foul torrent of disasters on the life of mortals. Peace shines upon human affairs like the vernal sun. The fields are cultivated, the gardens bloom, the cattle are fed upon a thousand hills, new buildings arise, riches flow, pleasures smile, humanity and charity increase, arts and manufactures feel the gentle warmth of encouragement, and the gains of the poor are more plentiful.

Attacking the frequent invocation of religion as a cause of war, Erasmus urged a return to the doctrines of Christ and his embrace of peace. Like other Northern humanists, he sought to combine a revival of basic Christian doctrines with the new interest in rationality, and both conduced to his deep interest in peace. "If we acknowledge Christ to be our Lord and Master, who is love itself and who taught northing but love and peace, let us exhibit his model in our lives and conversation. Let us adopt the love of peace, that Christ may recognize his own, even as we recognize him to be the Teacher of Peace." And his ideas were not mere abstractions. Erasmus wrote specifically against a possible European war on the Ottoman Empire, after a 1529 attack on the city of Vienna: "no matter how serious or how just the cause, war must not be undertaken unless all possible remedies have been exhausted and it has become inevitable." And again, lest Christians portray the Ottomans simply as warmongers, he urged that Christians' own warlike tendencies must be examined.

Early strife between Protestants and Catholics spurred Erasmus further, along with other Renaissance thinkers, for here was war among Christians – war clearly against Christian principles – brought really close to home. A pamphlet called *The Complaint of Peace*, in 1521, again condemned the ravages of war – "every blossom of happiness is instantly blasted ... and every thing that was formed for long duration comes to a speedy end, and every thing that was sweet by nature is turned to bitterness." War, quite simply, was contrary to religion, a true sign of human madness. For animals showed a devotion to peace that humans might well emulate. And when the example of Christ is added in, with the clear messages of peace throughout the New Testament, how could Christians, particularly, continue to engage in violent conflict? No truly Christian person can legitimately kill others in war. Reason and religion alike called for peace. Rulers and ordinary people alike should come to their senses. Kings must gain control of their passions, and make a fundamental commitment to end bloodshed and thoughts of conquest. "Let the greatest share of honor always be paid ... to kings that entirely reject the war system, and by their understanding and guidance, not by force and arms, restore to bleeding human nature the blessings of harmony and repose." And Erasmus urged the ministers of religion to unite toward the same goals, and use their influence to change the thinking of Europe's rulers.

Erasmus was not alone. Another key northern humanist, the English Thomas More, wrote actively on behalf of peace. His 1516 book *Utopia*, sketching an ideal society, did not focus primarily on peace, but rather on tolerance, abolition of private property, and devotion to human wellbeing. But peace was a key component of the society he sketched and on this subject as on other he used the idea of utopia to criticize common policies. "Most princes apply themselves to the arts of war ... instead of to the good arts of peace. They are generally more set on acquiring new kingdoms by hook or crook than on governing well those they already have." In this vision, Utopians prayed for peace, and did not directly participate in war even when it became essential as a matter of defense against unjust aggression, employing mercenaries as troops instead and seeking to avoid extensive bloodshed. Here, the reluctant definition of the only kind of war that might be justifiable recalled Cicero's thinking on the same subject – another source of the precedents that helped spur the Renaissance interest in peace. More's utopian ideas, linked to earlier efforts such as Plato's Republic, would inspire periodic ventures that sought to define an ideal society, in Russia and North America as well as Western Europe, on into the twentieth century, with peace generally a key aspect of the vision.

Additional voices included a German intellectual, Sebastian Franck, who argued that all wars were contrary to God's wishes and urged that humanity was a single basic community. Shortly after 1600 French author Emery Crucé went further still, in urging peace among Christians, Jews, and Muslims – for even the "ungodly ones," as he put it, are humans like the rest of us. Crucé even sketched the need for a permanent international organization, which would include Persia, China, Ethiopia, and the Caribbean, each with equal voting rights, to help assure peace on a global scale.

The new intellectual approach to peace clearly combined a recollection of earlier Christian commitments, plus disgust at how far many actual Christian states had drifted from those standards, with an interesting claim that human reason could devise a better approach to peace. And while for the most part the new advocacy depended on hopes that rulers could be reformed, the expansion of the vision to embrace humanity and to suggest an unprecedented level of international organization in the interests of peace shows how recollections of past precedent were combining with some striking innovations. The ideas had little impact at the time, but they could be used, after another century or so of bitter war, to generate a clear sense of alternatives. And some of them, obviously, even suggested approaches that would not be taken up until the twentieth century.

The Reformation

A second new current soon added to the European interest in peace – though still as a minority phenomenon: some unexpected side effects of the Protestant Reformation. Protestant pacifism was far removed from the polished rhetoric of the Renaissance, though it shared an interest in getting back to the early principles of Christianity. Even before the Reformation some religious reformers in Bohemia (now the Czech Republic) had preached a revival of Christian ideals of peace, in some cases arguing that no act of violence could be morally justified, and of course the Northern humanists recalled early Christianity as well. Again, the dominant contemporary claim that war could be conducted for Christian purposes came under specific attack.

But it was the new, usually small radical sects that sprang up in the wake of the Protestant movement that had more lasting results. Once Christian unity was broken by Martin Luther's successful challenge to Catholic control, a number of groups emerged with their own versions of Christian truth. Germany was the initial seedbed of innovation, but groups ultimately sprang up in other areas as well. Several of them focused strongly on restoring the original Christian message of peace. They varied in what they sought to do with this message: whether the goal was preservation of the group's own spiritual purity, or an effort to influence the larger society.

As early as 1525, in Germany and adjacent Switzerland, the Protestant attack on the Catholic Church began to generate more radical sects that tried to push the new ideas toward greater extremes. Luther, for example, the key instigator of the Reformation, was no pacifist: he accepted the need for war in the name of religious truth and indeed wrote one of the great militant anthems of Christianity, "A Mighty Fortress is Our God." This was not the approach of most of the smaller radical sects, however. Disagreements with mainstream Protestant groups centered on other doctrinal issues – for example, whether baptism should be for adults only – but differences over peace emerged early on.

The first breakaway group was known generically as the Anabaptists, who quickly adopted a platform of complete separation between church and state and, for believers, a stance of non-resistance. They argued that Christ had provided the example of "enduring suffering without retaliation." On the strength of this, Swiss Anabaptists refused to join town militias on grounds that it was against divine command. Individual pacifists urged their leaders to "use neither the worldly sword nor engage in war," comparing war with devastating plagues. Other commentary promoted resistance to state taxes that might support military action – as one critic suggested, there was no difference between "slaying with our own hands" and giving someone else the money to "slay in our stead."

From Anabaptist roots a group of Brethren formed in the Netherlands and ultimately became known as Mennonites. In the seventeenth century another group established the Amish sect. Both groups pledged firmly to peace. Mennonites, indeed, were particularly vocal in their peace advocacy, arguing that neither reasons of state nor religion could ever justify war. "Our weapons are not weapons with which cities and countries may be destroyed … But they are weapons with which the spiritual kingdom of the devil is destroyed." Mennonites became early supporters of religious toleration, again largely on grounds of the primacy of peace. One Mennonite tolerance tract, by Pieter Twisck in 1609, specifically noted that "the Steel Sword of the Worldly Government Does Not Extend over Conscience to the Compulsion of Belief" and that "Heretics and Disbelievers Must Not Be Converted with the Violence of Worldly Government but with God's Word." "The Gospel Does Not Have to be Defended with the Sword."

Another strand of minority Protestantism opened up in Britain, in the wake of bitter civil and religious wars in the mid-seventeenth century. The wars pitted Catholic sympathizers and some Anglicans against many Protestant groups; though there were internal political issues involved as well, particularly a struggle between the monarchy and Parliament. In this context, George Fox began around 1650 to form a new religious group to protest what he saw a failure of religious ideals. The group, ultimately called the Society of Friends, also became known as the Quakers for the physical manifestations of religious passion that would sometimes occur in meetings. Quakers turned quickly to a variety of social reforms, and though pacifism was not an initial emphasis individual Quakers began refusing military service. Then in 1661 a new statement of Quaker doctrine, by Fox and others, introduced pacifism more explicitly. "We certainly known and do testify to the world, that the Spirit of Christ … will never move us to fight and war against any man with outward weapons, neither for the Kingdom of Christ nor the kingdoms of this world." The Declaration went on to promise to "seek the good and peace of all men." Quaker defense of peace, and refusal of military service, became a standard principle from this point forward.

The radical defense of peace had three consequences, even as European wars continued to rage despite the sects' ideas. First, the pacifist doctrines brought attack and persecution from many authorities, including mainstream Protestant leaders, which in turn caused widespread migration, to many different parts of Europe and ultimately to the New World. It was North America that would ultimately become the principal home to the heirs of Anabaptism. Quakerism began to gain converts in North America, as early as 1656, while sending emigrants from the British Isles as well.

Second, while the urgent revival of Christian pacifism had little direct effect on the world of policy, the existence of these groups did revive a complication that had not been systematically addressed since Constantine: what was the state to do with people whose consciences simply did not permit them to fight? As early as the sixteenth century a few states were willing to grapple with the phenomenon that, in more modern times, would become known as conscientious objection to military service. In 1575 Prince William of the Netherlands gave Mennonites the option of substituting other duties for direct induction into the army – constructing ramparts, for example. This may have been the first instance in which a government acknowledged an individual right to object to military service on grounds of conscience, and represented something of a compromise with Mennonite principles. Mennonites proved willing to support the Dutch war effort with voluntary financial contributions, again in lieu of bearing arms directly. Issues of conscientious objection would spread to the New World in the eighteenth century. Colonial governments in places like Pennsylvania did not press Mennonite or Amish immigrants to serve in the French and Indian War in 1750, though Mennonite leaders did formally remind the colonial legislature of their principled objections to military service. These were only halting first steps in which would become a complicated modern history of conscientious objection, but it did set the issue in motion. Overall, the radical sects would have far more success in defending their own clean consciences than in influencing wider policies – another illustration of the tensions between personal purity and larger military developments that had surfaced earlier in several of the world religions.

Third, while the radical sects were not widely influential (though Quakers, who often became quite successful economically, did occasionally form more direct connections with political leaders), they unquestionably helped keep the peace discussion going while placing additional emphasis on key issues like religious tolerance. They connected, as a result, with the types of peace advocacy that resumed in wider intellectual circles, in Western Europe, by the later seventeenth century. But before resuming this strand, an actual policy development must be noted, as European rulers, and not just peace dissidents, finally realized they had to deal with the relationship between religious division and a need for greater peace.

The Treaty of Westphalia

Frequent wars were no novelty in Europe, but they became more vicious during the sixteenth century under the spur of battles over religious truths. Religious clashes between Catholic and Protestant states also combined with all sorts of political motives, such as the desire by German princes for more power against the emperor of the loosely organized Holy Roman Empire or rivalries for dominance between Spain and the rising French monarchy. Many rulers saw military expansion as part of their mandate, and these appetites crisscrossed the new religious map.

In 1555 the German states agreed in the Peace of Augsburg, to respect religious diversity within their ranks (though not within individual states). Lutheran states thus could be Lutheran, in recognition that Christian unity could not be restored. The arrangement quickly collapsed because it did not include other key Protestant groups, notably the Calvinists, and because Holy Roman Emperors could not give up the goal of restoring Catholicism throughout their domains. Europe was not ready to surrender insistence on a single Christian truth for the sake of peace. Religious strife in France, between Spain and the Netherlands, and later in the English civil wars further highlighted the elusiveness of peace.

By 1648 it was time to try again. The Thirty Years War, launched in 1618 and concentrated mainly in Germany, resulted from the now-familiar religious strife, but also the battles between princes and emperor and, now, foreign intervention as well. Sweden, a growing military power, intervened directly on behalf of Protestants, as did France because of opposition to the power of the Habsburg emperor; Spain, joined to the Holy Roman Empire by a common dynasty, sent troops on the other side. An ongoing war between Spain and the Netherlands factored in as well. The war truly devastated Germany, in terms of lives lost and property destruction, and at the same time it became clear, by the 1640s, that it was impossible to win outright.

The result was the convening of the first real international peace conference in European history, centered mainly in the city of Muenster, in the region of western Germany called Westphalia. The ensuing treaty did end the Thirty Years War (though conflict between France and Spain continued for more than a decade). More important in terms of the larger history of peace, the settlement advanced or completed a number of new principles.

First, the so-called Peace of Westphalia celebrated considerable religious tolerance. The papacy was not represented at the conference, and the pope disowned the results. But the settlement clearly established that each European state could have its own religion and that partial toleration might be granted to minorities within each state. One of the clauses of a key Westphalian Treaty identified the "grievances of the one or the other religion" as "for the most part the cause and occasion of the present war," and the settlement vowed to remove this justification for conflict. The irrevocable end of European religious unity was recognized, and within Germany imperial courts were charged with resolving any subsequent disputes. Christian religious conflict did not end in Europe – recent battles in Northern Ireland attest to that – and full tolerance was not yet recognized – but large wars on behalf of one Christian group or another really did draw to a close. The Peace implicitly stated what many European philosophers had come to believe: tolerance was preferable to ongoing warfare. Soon thereafter the establishment of partial toleration within the Netherlands and also in Britain pressed this point further. At Westphalia itself, France and Sweden sought to guarantee this aspect of the peace in Germany.

Second, the Peace was organized in meetings among representatives of virtually all the states of Europe, with a smattering of philosophers thrown in; only Britain and Russia, and of course the Ottoman Empire as well as the papacy, were not present among the major states of the continent. Here was a precedent for some notion that the states of Europe had some responsibility for putting the pieces of their region back together when war dismembered it. Peace conferences would dot the European experience from this point until the gathering in Versailles after World War I, by which point other regions, outside Europe, might be represented as well.

And third, the settlement affirmed the sovereignty of individual states and a principle of noninterference – a huge blow to the idea that the papacy had some wider authority or, within Germany, that the Holy Roman Emperor could meddle with the affairs of individual princes. This principle arguably reduced the motives for certain kinds of conflicts, though it did nothing at all to inhibit conflicts among theoretically sovereign states.

Historians generally agree that the key features of Westphalia constituted an important departure in European history – particularly the removal of religion as a legitimate reason for major states to go to war within the continent. It is less clear how the settlement should be viewed in a larger history of peace.

For European war quickly resumed, based more exclusively on the ambitions of individual kings, such as the rising absolute monarchs in France. The idea that international conferences would be available to help settle wars might be helpful, but it hardly represented a new priority for peace itself.

Back to the philosophers

The resumption of warfare, the new principles of diplomacy including the reduction of violent religious dispute, plus momentum from the earlier philosophical and religious discussions of peace set the stage for additional commentary in the later seventeenth century. The commentary rehearsed many earlier arguments, and it was no more effective in stopping actual wars than its predecessors had been. There were, however, two new elements worth noting. First, arguments about peace increasingly included at least a vague sense that wars were bad for business and that the middle classes had motivations for peace that might differ, for example, from those of the more military-minded aristocracy. And second, again based partly on intellectual precedent but partly on real events like Westphalia, philosophers increasingly turned their attention not just to arguments in favor of peace, but to discussions of possible mechanisms on its behalf. The older notions, of relying just on religion or, even more, of hoping for better motivations on the part of rulers, gave way to at least vague interests in new structures.

As political philosophy became a growing passion during the seventeenth century, most commentary now contained some thoughts on war and peace. Even before Westphalia, Hugo Grotius had thus written an extensive analysis of the reasons for just wars, but also the types of wars that were not warranted; yet he assumed that certain rules should apply even in a case of war, that were applicable to all international parties, and he explicitly contended that peace was part of the laws of nature. Writing under the impact of the English Civil Wars, Thomas Hobbes urged highlighted this brutal, warlike disposition of man that could (and should) be restrained only by the strong authority of a state; but he despaired of any real peace among states. In contrast the most important political theorist of the age, John Locke, writing as greater stability returned to Britain, highlighted the importance and possibility of peace. War was an act of destruction, and not a normal human expression. People formed societies in the interests of the preservation of freedom and property – and peace. And peace both is and should be the norm in social experience. Locke was obviously not a pacifist – societies could have legitimate reasons to resort to violence; nor was peace his main topic. His work illustrates the extent to which some discussion of peace was becoming a standard part of progressive philosophy.

More explicit discussions of peace persisted as well, and this is where some of the innovations showed more clearly. Thus William Penn, a Quaker convert and businessman in England (and, later, the colony of Pennsylvania) argued that war was bad for property, and that peace was actually far more profitable than war. Of course, speaking as a Quaker, peace was beneficial to everyone, but the most important reasons tended now to shift toward helping sustain production and an increasingly commercial economy. Penn went on to urge the formation of an all-European parliament, based on the wealth of each nation, aimed at safeguarding the peace among states. He urged full religious tolerance, even (a novelty for Protestants still) for Catholics.

Writing early in the eighteenth century, a political philosopher in France, Charles Castel de Saint-Pierre, carried some of the new thinking about peace unusually far – in some ways anticipating enthusiasms about the possibility of earthly progress that would be more characteristic of the Enlightenment a few decades later. Saint-Pierre brought to his work an experience as a working diplomat, for he almost certainly served as a negotiator at one of the conferences that produced a settlement to the last round of Louis XIV's wars. Saint-Pierre had reform ideas on virtually every topic, from girls' education to diseases, but his main work was a huge, three-volume study of a *Plan for Perpetuating Peace in Europe*. Saint-Pierre despaired that kings, by themselves, could ever abandon war. So what was needed was a union or federation of sovereign states that could hold individual aggression in check. The League would be authorized to intervene to protect the peace (and also to put down revolts within states; Saint-Pierre was no flaming radical). It would additionally maintain an international court to help adjudicate disputes.

Saint-Pierre – widely known at the time, though not since – has predictably been credited with some of the ideas that would ultimately lead to the World Court and the League of Nations. More directly, his work influenced a number of Enlightenment intellectuals, notably Jean-Jacques Rousseau and Immanuel Kant. He thus bridges the extensive philosophical interest in peace in Europe's early modern period, with the more sweeping speculations of the later eighteenth and nineteenth centuries.

Finally, peace discussions expanded geographically within Europe, as well as in European colonies in North America. Active debate about peace surfaced in Poland in the seventeenth and eighteenth centuries, reflecting older Christian tradition, some of the newer ideas, and also Poland's own, increasingly difficult military situation caught among the rising powers of Prussia, Sweden, and Russia. A statement in the seventeenth century – "who indeed would dare to kill a being for whom Christ has died" – picked up directly on Christian pacifism. Later discussions also tried to reconcile military service with a Christian conscience and opened the possibility, for Catholics, of conscientious objection. Clearly, ideas about peace were gaining a wider reach.

For the work of the later seventeenth and early eighteenth centuries confirms the importance of a tradition now well established: that some consideration of peace, and not simply the more conventional topic of just versus unjust wars, had become standard fare for at least a few European thinkers in every generation. Practical effects remained limited. The frequency of peace commentary in Europe clearly reflected the recurrent wars, in contrast to patterns in Asia. Yet there were definite connections between the commentary and some of the larger changes in European society. Most notably, the need to comment on religious conflict receded, and at the same time attention turned on the whole to more secular arguments for peace and – as Saint-Pierre so abundantly illustrated – some effort to sketch mechanisms, beyond royal good will or divine guidance – and could generate real change. This trajectory would continue, and amplify, in the next phase of European history.

The Americas

Peace issues inevitably arose as Europeans began to penetrate the Americas after 1492. In the main, the story was one of conquest, with tremendous military advantages on the side of the colonizers and the spread of new diseases adding to the imbalance. However, encounters with Native Americans, in some cases with their own concepts of peace, did produce some interesting ideas and proposals toward different approaches. And the fact that the principal encounters took shape beginning in the sixteenth century, when humanistic discussions of peace were expanding in Europe itself, added a further dimension.

A number of Spanish theologians and jurists, during the sixteenth century particularly, expressed deep concern about treatment of Native Americans. They urged that Indians had rights, that every human being deserved freedom. While advocating continued Christianization of the natives, they also hoped for peace. Thus Francisco de Vitoria, one of the leaders of what became known as the Salamanca School, contended that it was unjust to use war to impose control or even religious conversion on a free people; defense alone legitimized warfare.

Even more important were the views of Bartolomé de Las Cases, who visited the New World several times and frequently commented on Spanish policy. Las Cases was dismayed at the treatment of natives as a result of Spanish conquest of Cuba and defended native peoples in many publications. He too believed that a violent imposition of Christianity was appalling, that only persuasion was justified. Las Casas abandoned his own plans to run an estate in Latin America, and worked on an elaborate peace plan which he presented to other humanists, including Erasmus, while also winning support from the Catholic Church in Spain: the plan suggested mixing European peasants with the natives in agricultural estates supervised by the clergy. The Spanish king rather liked the plan, but opposition of colonial landowners killed it. In 1537 Las Cases returned to the charge, writing a book called *The Only Method of Attracting Men to the True Faith*. He challenged authorities to let him try his peaceful approach in Guatemala, and indeed his missionary work, including preaching in local languages, was so successful that the region was briefly called the "Land of True Peace." In a later memoir Las Cases wrote of his commitment to acting against the "unspeakable violence and evil and harm" the natives suffered from the European conquest. Work of this sort, plus wider advocacy by Jesuit missionaries, did impede efforts actually to enslave native laborers and encouraged colonial powers to claim some interest in peaceful methods.

Other writers, many of them Catholic missionaries, continued to hammer home the point that Spain was prevailing in the Americas by force rather than virtue. Álvar Nuñez Cabeza de Vaca, after an expedition to Florida in which he was captured by natives for a time, thus presented the Spanish government with a new account of the need to treat Indians more humanely, and later led an abortive expedition intended to illustrate his ideas. This kind of work bore some fruit, at least rhetorically, when a new Spanish monarch, Charles V, began to claim the mantle of the Roman leader Augustus, as an emperor of peace. Charles' successor, Philip II (1554–1598) replaced the word "conquest" with "pacification," when defining the new Spanish policy toward the Americas. In 1573 the Council of the Indies declared the "Discoveries are not to be called conquests ... Since we wish them to be carried out peacefully and charitably, we do not want the use of that term to offer any excuse for the employment of force or the causing of injury to the Indians ... [Spanish officials] are to seek friendship [with the Indians] through trade and barter, showing them great love and tenderness and giving them objects to which they will take a liking."

Similar arguments emerged in French colonial policy. French leaders were well aware that colonists were vastly outnumbered, and initially urged a relatively peaceful approach. There was some belief that French culture and Christianity would be so obviously attractive that force would not be necessary. And indeed a number of peaceful negotiations did occur with tribal groups, though by the eighteenth century French policy tended to stiffen, with a greater sense that the natives were "naturally" inferior.

British encounters in North America produced their own policy discussions, from the seventeenth century onward. Theorists like John Locke urged that the British should "keep ourselves within the rules of peace" and treat Indians with respect and (a special Lockean emphasis) tolerance. But Indian attacks convinced many leaders on the spot that "gentle" methods had failed as a result of the "treacherous violence of the Savages." Edward Waterhouse, in the Virginia colony, claimed that war was fully justified in this circumstance, and that it was perfectly legitimate to "destroy them who sought to destroy us." Of course actual policy varied, and short-term peace negotiations often paid off; but a larger rhetoric of peace tended to fade.

The British and French did interact with one native group, the Iroquois, who had their own proud tradition of peace. A confederacy of five Iroquois tribes, in what is now northern New York and the Great Lakes region of the United States and Canada, may have formed a peaceful union as early as the thirteenth or fourteenth centuries, and possibly even before. Legend enshrined the confederacy as the work of a great peacemaker, and a vast array of rituals and symbols reinforced the system. The rules of the confederacy, or the "Great Peace" were preserved through arrangements of wampum shells. The confederacy in practice involved periodic meetings of leaders from the five Iroquois tribes, which was responsible for resolving any disputes. The confederacy was hardly pacifist: the rules of engagement required that hostile tribes outside the union be brought into compliance or attacked. But within the group endemic fighting did cease. In 1720 a sixth tribe, the Tuscarora, formally joined the League.

The Iroquois peace was one of the more interesting and successful ventures of a largely hunting and gathering people, over an impressive span of time. The approach was tested by the arrival of Europeans, with whom the Iroquois quickly came into conflict. Periodic negotiations did occur, however, for example with the French in 1644 and 1645. Familiarity with the possibility of peace arrangements may have influenced Iroquois behavior, which included treating colonial representatives with great care and courtesy. Some of the same symbols, such as wampum belts, that were current in the confederacy were presented to European agents.

Some historians have contended that Iroquois principles had a wider influence on some British colonial leaders. Several colonists, including Benjamin Franklin, did participate in a treaty discussion in 1745 that led most directly to an agreement by which Iroquois gave up claims to vast stretches of land in return for payment. Franklin and his colleagues may have learned from these discussions how impressive the Iroquois precedents were, which, the argument goes, spurred them in their later quest for greater self-government within the colonies and for peaceful relations among them: in other words, an Iroquois link to the ideas that would ultimate shape the new United States. On balance, historical opinion inclines against much influence, but it is clear that interactions could take various shapes.

One final exchange shows the range of possibilities when particular European ideas combined with the American setting. When William Penn, the English Quaker, established the colony of Pennsylvania around 1681, he saw an opportunity to put into practice his ideas of peace and tolerance. Much of this was aimed at European settlers, for Penn encouraged various religious groups to migrate; and an act of 1673 specifically established that no citizen of the colony was required to bear arms if he had a religious objection. But Penn's views had implications for the treatment of native peoples as well. Pennsylvania on balance featured less frontier warfare with Indians than was normally the case. Penn himself established good relations with the Delawares, learning their language, and made a point never to break treaty arrangements.

Over time, in Pennsylvania as in most of the European holdings in the Americas, any effort at a special approach faded, the victim of quarrels over land and the steady push to expand European territory. The Americas in the early modern period contributed nothing very durable in the history of peace, if anything serving as a dramatic example of the importance of warfare during the period as a whole. But the countercurrents were interesting. European ideas and native precedents could generate some sense of alternatives, clearly affecting the rhetoric and self-image of some colonial leaders and, once in a while, influencing policy as well.

Conclusion

Connections among different parts of the world intensified during the early modern period. This began to be reflected in some discussions of peace, particularly on the European side, with references to international bodies, but also in some of the ideas about international harmony generated in the Mughal and Ottoman Empires. On the whole approaches to peace (or lack thereof) continued to reflect regional distinctions. Confucian commitments thus differed from the approaches taken in the Islamic empires, while the European context was different still. Only in the Americas did some mingling of the new European ideas and more local initiatives have some modest impact.

The period as a whole was marked by military aggression from many quarters. Some regions stood apart, however, through a combination of tradition and policy innovation – this was the case particularly in East Asia. And the military emphasis did help generate an interesting and partially novel set of intellectual discussions of peace and tolerance. These in turn had some limited results at the time. The question was, obviously, whether they might set a basis for a clearer set of peace ideas and peace priorities in the future.

Further reading

Bangs, Jeremy Dupertuis. "Dutch Contributions to Religious Toleration." *Church History* 79.3 (2010): 585–613.

Bauer, Ralph. *The Cultural Geography of Colonial American Literatures: Empire, Travel, Modernity*. New York: Cambridge University Press, 2003.

Belmessous, Saliha. "Assimilation and Racialism in Seventeenth and Eighteenth-Century French Colonial Policy." *American Historical Review* 110.2 (2005): 322–49.

Black, Antony. *The History of Islamic Political Thought, from the Prophet to the Present*, 2/e. Edinburgh: Edinburgh University Press, 2011.

Brock, Peter. *Studies in Peace History*. Syracuse, NY: Syracuse University Press, 1991.

Brock, Peter. *Varieties of Pacifism: A Survey from Antiquity to the Outset of the Twentieth Century*. Syracuse, NY: Syracuse University Press, 1998. eBook Collection (EBSCOhost).

Kende, Istvan. "The History of Peace: Concept and Organizations from the Late Middle Ages to the 1870s." *Journal of Peace Research* 26.3 (1989): 233–47.

Koskenniemi, Martti. "Empire and International Law: The Real Spanish Contribution." *University of Toronto Law Journal* 61.1 (2011): 1–36.

Russell, W. M. S. "William Penn and the Peace of Europe." *Medicine, Conflict and Survival* 20.1 (2010): 19–34.

On Native Americans

Crawford, Neta C. "A Security Regime among Democracies: Cooperation among Iroquois Nations." *International Organization* 48.3 (1994): 345–85.

Lee, Wayne E. "Peace Chiefs and Blood Revenge: Patterns of Restraint in Native American Warfare, 1500–1800." *The Journal of Military History* 71.3 (2007): 701–41.

On Protestant minorities

Crowley, William K. "Old Order Amish Settlement: Diffusion and Growth." *Annals of the Association of American Geographers* 68.2 (1978): 249–64.

Schlabach, Theron F. "Mennonites, Revivalism, Modernity: 1683–1850." *Church History* 48.4 (1979): 398–415.

On Westphalia

Christenson, Gordon. "'Liberty of the Exercise of Religion' in the Peace of Westphalia." *Transnational Law & Contemporary Problems* 21.3 (2013): 721–61.
Straumann, Benjamin. "The Peace of Westphalia as a Secular Constitution." *Constellations* 15.2 (2008): 173–88.

6   Peace in an industrial age

As the nineteenth century ended, and the new twentieth century was about to get underway, a host of European and American commentators looked back on the previous hundred years and tried to figure out what the next hundred would be like. On the whole, the mood was decidedly optimistic. Newspaper columnists trumpeted the many signs of progress that the nineteenth century had bequeathed: there was more education, more freedom (so they said), more democracy, far better technology, more wealth, better science, and better health. Granted, progress had been most noteworthy in the Western world, but thanks to Western guidance other regions were posting gains as well. The *New York Times* new century article noted explicitly that "the other races" were making some commendable progress in catching up to the blessings of modern civilization.

Achievements in peace figured strongly in this optimistic commentary, regarding what one American article simply called a "Wonderful Century." Editorialists noted the huge wars that launched the nineteenth century, around the French Revolution and Napoleon, but then the absence of anything like that scale of conflict since. Specific gains added to the sense of progress. Agreements like the Geneva Convention, plus advances in medicine, reduced suffering in war, while new international arbitration conferences and the establishment of an International Court offered alternatives to war of any sort. Larger humanitarian advances confirmed the trajectory: "The principle that man is his brother's keeper has gained new recognition." Yet all this was nothing compared to what would happen in the coming century. War, already declining, would disappear completely, argued the most committed visionaries. For war was becoming both too dangerous, thanks for more destructive technologies, and too offensive to the contemporary human conscience. The twentieth century would see the "complete vindication of arbitration, the abolition of standing armies, and the peaceful co-operation of all the nations of the globe." Or more bombastically still: "On the threshold of [the new century] are the footprints of Divine Love. Its banner is the Golden Rule. Its leader is the Prince of Peace ... Altruism is displacing selfishness as a social force. A century of honor lies behind us."

The place of peace in a definition of modern progress is an important fact, legitimately included as one of the contributions of the long nineteenth century to the history of peace. Yet, obviously, the folly of the anticipations is an even more important fact: just 14 years later, World War I would shatter any visions that humanity had moved beyond violent conflict.

And the war was no accident. The history of the long nineteenth century was more troubled than the optimistic editorialists acknowledged on the eve of a new era. To be sure, some turn-of-the-century commentators, though particularly in Europe, already recognized a darker side, referring particularly to the possibility of new rivals to Western supremacy, particularly from East Asia: in their view, the civilized advances based on the leadership of Western standards might soon be jeopardized. As one British editorialist put it: "The day will come, and perhaps is not far distant, when the European observer will look around to see the globe girdled with the continuous zone of the black and yellow races."

But even aside from this complexity, the actual history of war and peace in the nineteenth century was far more complicated than the optimists realized – even aside from the massive struggles of the Napoleonic era. Two points are essential. First of all, while Europe after 1815 was relatively peaceful, there were several smaller wars, particularly around Italian and then German unification, that showed the destructive potential of modern industrial weaponry and, as well, set in motion new rivalries with other European powers – rivalries that would lead directly, though not immediately, to World War I. Also within the Western orbit, the American Civil War, essentially the world's first fully industrial war, showed how much more dreadful war was becoming, in terms of death and destruction. Second, the nineteenth century was, famously, a century of Western imperialist expansion. The United States and Canada pushed steadily westward, crushing native opposition. The European great powers swallowed up the whole of Africa and much of North Africa, Southeast Asia and Pacific Oceania as well. China was tamed, though not fully conquered, through force, beginning with the Opium War of 1839, and then river boat gunnery. All of this involved war and military intimidation. The wars were not large, because new weaponry allowed small Western forces to win without much difficulty (though often with huge losses of life on the part of local combatants, through artillery and machine gun fire). Westerners did not even necessarily recognize the conflicts as wars, because they involved so little effort. But a century of imperialism placed most of the world directly under Western military threat or control. Outright battles might end with European victory, though flare-ups of resistance would persist; but this was not peace, by any definition save that of Western conquerors. Mark Twain himself reflected this vision in his own turn-of-the-century remarks in 1900: "I bring you the stately maiden named Christendom returning bedraggled and besmirched, dishonoured from pirate raids in China, Manchuria, South Africa, and Philippines, with her soul full of meanness, her pocket full of boodle, and her mouth full of pious hypocrises. Give her soap and towel, but hide the looking glass."

The long nineteenth century in world history, from 1750 to 1914, was marked above all by Western industrialization, which created vast new economic and military power, and by the fact that, for the moment, the West essentially monopolized this dramatic new economy. Other parts of the world, with rare exceptions, fell behind the West economically, prodded to accept Western industrial goods in return for cheap raw materials and food exports. The new military edge was crucial. Where in the early modern period Western navies had gained decisive global advantage, now naval power was further enhanced – thanks to steam ships and bigger guns – and at the same time Western land armies were now decisively superior as well. Western victories in Egypt, in 1798; in China, 1839; in Russia's Crimean backyard, in 1854–55, and of course in Africa demonstrated the new, if temporary, power balance. Only in Ethiopia and Afghanistan were Western forces defeated. Everywhere else they either won or, as in Japan and Korea, successfully intimidated.

This was also a new age of nationalism. This new form of loyalty, developed first in the West in the later eighteenth century and then gradually spread around the world by 1900, was not always militaristic. Nationalists could focus on cultural identity, and they might in principle embrace the rights of other nations as well as those of their own. But the spread of nationalism often had military and competitive overtones, initially in Europe itself and soon in a number of other societies. Given Western example, it was not surprising that nationalist attention frequently involved aspirations for military strength. One of the first Japanese moves, in response to the need to reform after 1853, was to reorganize and rearm the nation's military forces, and soon to adopt a very new policy of aggression in East Asia.

This does not mean that there is no history of peace in this period – for the end-of-century optimism, however exaggerated, already suggests the contrary. A peace vision was not ultimately triumphant – as the advent of World War I clearly demonstrated – but this does not mean that it was absent, or incapable of significant innovation. Several themes predominated.

First, there were new ideas. The European Enlightenment of the later eighteenth century contributed additional thinking and enthusiasm to the notion that peace was both desirable and possible, though it built on the Western peace discussions that had run through the early modern period. The early nineteenth century would add further arguments to considerations of peace, including a new socialist vision.

Second, the fact that war was becoming, or potentially becoming, more dreadful, thanks to modern weaponry, spurred new efforts as well. This was indeed the dawning of modern peace organizations, reflecting the ongoing power of the new ideas but also an increasing sense of need given the destructive potential of modern weaponry and modern nationalism. By the century's end, actual new policies came into place as well. Some, like the Geneva Conventions, were bent on moderating the worst effects of war, by fostering international agreements on the treatment of war prisoners and wounded. But some aimed at reducing or eliminating war altogether.

These two factors – new ideas and new needs plus organizational responses – combined to produce real peace movements, by the nineteenth century itself.

Obviously some religions, at some points, had constituted peace movements of a sort, but along with other goals; now, organized activity focused on peace as the priority goal, and without commitment to a single religious doctrine. And peace movements, combined with the growing imperialist competition, further generated some unprecedented institutional changes designed to limit war by the final decades of the nineteenth century. New kinds of international courts, peace conferences, even the revived Olympic Games were designed to provide alternatives that would replace violent conflict with other forms of settlement and other, nondestructive forms of competition. It turned out of course that these were halting, inadequate first steps, but they were genuine innovations in the history of peace that would set the stage for further changes later on.

The most obvious deliberations and changes in the history of peace during the long nineteenth century emanated from the West, though a Russian role was also noteworthy toward the end and American participation became increasingly extensive. It will be important, as a final challenge toward identifying the strands of peace in an age of imperialism, to be open to other voices as well, as various peoples struggled to find out how resistance to Western domination might best be shaped. And one society – Latin America – deserves attention for its relatively low level of nation-to-nation conflict.

Enlightenment and revolution: The first phase of the long century

The torrent of ideas

The Enlightenment encouraged an explosion of thinking and planning about peace. Not all the ideas were new, but the volume was, as peace became part of a vision of earthly progress that was fundamental to this intellectual current. The variety of specific proposals was novel as well, and there were some clear departures from precedent in a number of comments. Finally, Enlightenment thinking about peace became so pervasive that the French revolution of 1789, conceived amid the new ideologies, had to offer its own commitments as well, though they soon fell short of effective policy.

Virtually all the Enlightenment philosophers had something to say about peace. Voltaire, for example, frequently referred to the earlier work of Saint-Pierre, but he particularly urged the centrality of religious tolerance for peace:

> The only way to bring peace to people is to destroy all dogmas which divide them, and restore verity, which would unit them; that would be a permanent peace. And such a peace is by far not a dream ... Every man should be actively working ... on the destruction of fanaticism, and restore peace, what this monster has chased away from the empires, from the families, from the hearts of miserable mortals.

The other great French *philosophe*, Rousseau, wrote even more widely on peace, though with more diffuse focus. Rousseau sought peace, but not at all cost: liberty was more important. He also loudly doubted that kings could ever establish peace, which must come from political systems that reflected popular will. He did see peace as a possibility in a well-constituted society, with a clear social contract; but somewhat anachronistically he argued that peace was only possible if all citizens were good Christians: "It is impossible to live at peace with those we regard as damned; to love them would be to hate God who punishes them."

Another line of argument emanated from eighteenth-century economists, who increasingly advocated free trade. Greater trade and prosperity, and peace, should be part of the same policy package. Adam Smith, effectively the father of modern economics, saw competition and profit as the great motives for individuals, from which war would merely distract. The Utilitarian philosopher Jeremy Bentham made the connections to peace more explicit: Trade should be a great goal, whereas "all war is in essence ruinous." Governments too often limit commerce and seek war; the priorities must be reversed. Armies and weaponry should be reduced to a very low level, freeing a tremendous amount of revenue for economic growth; and all conquered territories must be freed, for a country with no colonies would have no reason to be attacked. Utilitarians argued that only defensive wars could be justified, and even these would end when nations became more fully immersed in trade networks. Competitive trade and profit-seeking increases wealth, and "binds together by one common tie of interest and intercourse, the universal society of nations throughout the civilized world." John Stuart Mill, the great nineteenth-century liberal, carried this line still further:

> It is commerce which is rapidly rendering war obsolete, by strengthening and multiplying the personal interests which are in natural opposition to it. And it may be said without exaggerations that the great extent and rapid increase of international trade, in being the principal guarantee of the peace of the world, is the great permanent security for the interrupted progress of the ideas, the institutions, and the character of the human race.

Continuing the work of Grotius and others, scholars also highlighted opportunities in international law. In 1789 a German law professor, George de Martens, urged a study of the various treaties European nations had crafted with each other; this would produce a sense of positive international law, which in turn would resolve disputes and maintain peace. The obvious point is that arguments in favor of peace were drawing on a growing array of arguments, now largely secular, while also linking to the larger Enlightenment conviction that through reason and political reform the nature of human society could be dramatically improved. It was also significant that peace arguments were making their way into various national intellectual traditions, with very different specifics but quite common goals.

Enlightenment-based discussions of peace also spread widely geographically. A number of Russian intellectuals, including A. Radishchev, thus endorsed the importance of peace in international relations, seeing this as part of a larger package of social and political reforms that would respond to popular wishes. Along with Christian thinking about peace, this new current encouraged unprecedented Russian involvement in larger peace efforts, that dotted the nineteenth century after 1815.

It was the sense that peace could and should be achieved as part of human progress that was the most important point. Thus at the end of the eighteenth century the Marquis de Condorcet, who believed fervently in the possibility of steady human advance, included strict limits on war (though not full pacifism) as part of his vision. No war is just unless it is purely defensive, and strong states should not need such wars, while weaker states should develop alliances toward the same end. Professional militaries should be replaced by citizen armies.

The most systematic peace statement emanating from the Enlightenment period was the product of the German philosopher Immanuel Kant, in his 1795 work on *Perpetual Peace*. Kant urged that people devote themselves to an ethical imperative aimed at social peace: "The morally practical reason utters within us its irrevocable veto: *There shall be no war.*" To this end, several diplomatic principles were essential. No independent states should be conquered; standing armies should be completely abolished; no peace treaty should be regarded as valid if it tacitly allowed for some future war; no state should interfere with another by force; and if war did occur, no state should act so badly that a subsequent peace would become impossible. Kant also picked up the economists' argument that the quest for profits – the "trading spirit" – would help prevent wars.

Like Rousseau, Kant had no confidence in monarchs; world peace depended republics with parliaments. He envisaged some federation of states – "a league of peace" – that would be charged with maintaining peace and providing a higher authority to which people in any part of the world could appeal, without the need for violent conflict. Kant criticized earlier peace treaties, like Westphalia, because they had no enforcement mechanism over individual states, though he was somewhat vague about how his federation would be consistent with the principle of noninterference. Still, the work was without much question the most elaborate discussion of peace, and mechanisms to attain peace, ever produced to that point.

Contacts with policy

It was a testimony to the volume of the new thinking that it began to pass from the intellectual to the political domain. The loudest connections occurred during the French revolution. Thus an early act of the Revolution was grandiosely entitled the "World Peace Declaration" of May 1790, declaring that the revolutionary French nation would "never wage war for conquest, and would never use its forces against the freedom of any people." A law in 1792 offered French assistance to other countries seeking peace as well as freedom. In point of fact, the revolution was quickly embroiled in war. It was attacked by conservative states, but quickly became aggressive in its own right, conquering adjacent territory in Europe. And the revolution introduced the fateful idea of mass recruitment to the military: since all French men were now free citizens, they owed military service to the nation. In this context, the idea of conscientious objection to military service was disallowed (as was the case as well in the American Revolution, when many members of Protestant sects who objected to war were jailed for up to two years, and heavily fined). Along with new weaponry, the advent of widespread military conscription constituted a clear challenge to peace efforts, substantially undermining the revolutionary rhetoric.

Less vividly, however, some other European developments by the later eighteenth century pointed in the direction of peace, and they had some relationship to the new peace arguments particularly in the economic sphere. Arbitration of disputes was one key focus. Growing oceanic trade produced increasing opportunities for clashes among merchants and navies, and while a few blossomed into outright wars – an odd conflict between Britain and Spain in the eighteenth century, the "War of Jenkins' Ear" was one instance – the governments involved realized that many could be settled more constructively. Thus, with growing utilization from the sixteenth century onward, a number of cases were submitted to a national court for dispute resolution. So-called "prize courts" determined whether one nation's ships had legally seized ships or goods from another nation. A British judge, dealing with a dispute with Sweden in 1799, discussed the principles involved: though his court was British, "it is the duty of the person who sits here to determine the question exactly as he would determine the same question if sitting at Stockholm; to assert no pretensions on the part of Great Britain which he would not allow to Sweden in the same circumstances." A number of controversies between Britain and the new United States were also settled in this fashion. The Jay Treaty of 1794, setting up arbitration procedures for maritime disputes between Britain and its erstwhile colony, is sometimes hailed as a landmark in this field. A later dispute, in 1862, when a British ship joined Confederate forces in attacking American shipping during the Civil War, was also ultimately referred to arbitration, but this time with neutral or uninvolved nations (Switzerland, Italy, Brazil) involved as well. Revealingly, in 1907 an international negotiation in Hague, Netherlands, would create an international prize court, so that dispute resolution would not depend on trusting another country; but this was part of a massive expansion of peace efforts discussed below. For the moment, it's vital to note that some mechanisms were created early on.

Another, and far more sweeping, test of new interests in peace occurred at the close of the Napoleonic Wars, at the Congress of Vienna in 1815. From the 1790s onward, and then under the brilliant generalship of the Emperor Napoleon, France had been engaged in wars that involved most other European powers. It invaded many territories, setting up dependent regimes from Poland to Spain. By 1815, however, a coalition of European countries finally gained the upper hand. An unprecedented number of kings and diplomats gathered to pick up the pieces.

The resulting Treaty of Vienna was not necessarily heavily influenced by the new thinking about peace. Indeed, these were conservative statesmen, bent among other things on restoring monarchies, so the wilder Enlightenment ideas were not popular. Nor were there any grand declarations about peace or a progressive future. Indeed the Treaty itself, establishing what nation controlled what territory in Europe or the colonies, reads like a massive real estate transaction. But there is no question that a durable peace was the intent of the negotiations, no question either that of all the great peace conferences in Europe from Westphalia onward, this was in many ways the most practical and successful.

For the Vienna settlement was guided by a desire to set up a balance of power that would prevent a new round of French ambition and, more generally, create a potentially harmonious framework among the great powers more generally. Most countries – Russia and Prussia, for example – got some new territories that were designed to make them stronger players in the European system, and more content as well. At the same time – and this showed the practical hope for peace – France was not dismembered nor hideously punished; huge French resentments did not result, and the nation quickly resumed a prominent place among European nations.

The settlement was imperfect. Nationalist ambitions were scorned, to the dismay, for example, of Poles placed under Russian rule, or Belgians under the Dutch (the Belgians would quickly undo this aspect of the settlement, with a revolution in 1830 that established independence). It soon became clear that issues in Italy and Germany had not been resolved, with resultant unification wars in the 1850s and 1860s. But huge, multi-nation wars in Europe did end for a century, and key players, like France, really did curb their appetites for an even longer period.

Finally, Vienna unquestionably involved a new sense of a practical need for peace. The Russian tsar talked vaguely of the importance of "brotherhood" among kings. Soon after Vienna a loose alliance was formed among Britain, Prussia, Russia and Austria in the interests of promoting harmony along with a conservative order: the British negotiator referred to a "system of general government as may secure and enforce upon all kings and nations a system of peace and justice." Durable international institutions to protect peace did not result, but ideas in that direction were clearly in the air. Here was another innovation, picking up on the intellectuals' discussion of a possible international system that would be developed further later on – though mainly after another, and even more devastating, round of European war.

National approaches: The idea of neutrality

Finally, and again by the early nineteenth century, a few individual nations began to carve out a distinctive path toward peace, partly in response to the fury of the Napoleonic Wars, but partly in relationship to the innovative ideas by now widely disseminated. Two nations – Switzerland and Sweden – launched on a path of neutrality, of nonparticipation in war – that both have maintained in the main to the present day. And the new United States, though decidedly not neutral, began to discuss its desire to avoid contamination from the old European order and establish an American approach to peace.

Switzerland had participated extensively in the kind of feudal wars that marked much of Europe before the early modern period, and it provided troops for other countries as well (including guards for the papacy, a tradition that still continues). But in the Treaty of Westphalia the nation was separated from the Holy Roman Empire, and began a tradition of reduced involvement in European disputes. French revolutionary invasion in the 1790s interrupted this stance, but the Congress of Vienna not only restored Swiss independence but assured its neutrality for the future. This status reflected the deep Swiss resentment of the French incursion and a desire to avoid this kind of attack in future. It also, implicitly, reflected a Swiss willingness to renounce any aggressive military ambitions of its own, in favor of a commitment to peace.

Neutrality was a new principle, and Switzerland was its first illustration. It involves mutual pledges: first, other powers pledge not to invade; but second, the neutral nation itself promises not to take sides in surrounding wars. And indeed Switzerland has not been directly involved in any war since 1815. Neutrality does not require demilitarization: indeed, Switzerland has always maintained a well-trained citizen army, capable of defensive action. Swiss neutrality has frequently been tested. In both the world wars of the twentieth century, both sides tried to manipulate Switzerland, and the nation was frequently accused of cowardice in staying out of the action. Questions about involvement with international organizations also arose. If the League of Nations or United Nations wanted member states to contribute to a military force to restore order in some part of the world, could a neutral nation participate? Switzerland ultimately bowed out of the League because of these complications, and joined the United Nations only in 2002. But neutral Switzerland, in addition to maintaining its own peace, amid growing economic prosperity, has also provided service in other conflicts, representing countries for example (like the United States in Iran) that are involved in disputes too bitter for normal diplomatic relations.

More broadly, the neutrality principle, first established clearly in 1815, was respected as a matter of convention for almost a century. Then, at The Hague conference in 1907, it received formal international support and definition.

The case of Sweden was slightly different, but here too 1815 was an important date. Sweden had of course been one of the European great powers in the seventeenth century, actively involved in the Thirty Years War and possessed of substantial territory in Northeast-Central Europe. It lost ground to Russia and Prussia during the eighteenth century. It continued to play a role during the Napoleonic Wars. A new king – a former French Napoleonic general – began to chart a new course, however. Sweden participated in the alliance that brought Napoleon down, but it was last to enter – and many allies thought the new king was trying to spare Sweden any losses. In the ensuing treaty arrangements Russia gained Finland from the Swedes, which automatically reduced potential conflicts with the Russians in future. Sweden voluntarily retreated to regional status, withdrawing from broader European affairs. And, like Switzerland, the Swedes have not directly participated in a major war since 1815.

Sweden's new policy reflected an understanding, from the king on down, that the kingdom was no longer a major military player and that the role of small but satisfied power was most appropriate. Temptations toward wider involvements arose, but they were largely rejected. As with Switzerland, this was a policy of peace backed by moderate but solid defensive military strength. The nation remained essentially neutral in a number of conflicts between France and Britain, on the one hand, and Russia during the nineteenth century. It also firmly supported freedom of trade in the Baltic, against periodic Russian efforts to assert control. Sweden provided some very limited defensive help to Denmark in a struggle with Prussia around midcentury, but without much result. New Swedish kings sometimes searched for a more active role; one wrote in 1873 that he "longed for the day" "when Sweden with advantage and honor could draw the sword against the ... enemy." Again, this was not yet the systematic commitment to neutrality that had developed in Switzerland. Over time, however, the Swedish people developed their own deep preference for neutrality, to a desire to be left alone to live in peace. There was simply no appetite for a more activist policy, and by the time of World War I Sweden's non-involvement was, domestically, widely popular. Further tests awaited, particularly in World War II when Sweden reluctantly provided passage for Nazi troops to attack Norway. Later in the twentieth century, however, Swedish neutrality gave Swedish leaders opportunities to help lead in peace efforts in various global areas. Here too, the neutrality option proved very interesting, a national commitment to peace independent of the rest of the world.

The case of the United States was quite different, but again reflected some of the peace sentiments that were flourishing among intellectuals and policymakers around the turn of the nineteenth century. As the new nation took shape after the 1776 revolution, leaders from George Washington onward expressed a fairly consistent desire to avoid getting bogged down in European disputes and wars. Again, there was no question of a fully distinctive policy like neutrality – though George Washington signed a Neutrality Act in 1794 designed to keep the nation distant from the conflict between Britain and France. Periodically at least, the United States would take sides in disputes with Britain and others, and of course its westward expansion would involve periodic wars with Indian tribes and also with Mexico. But the national self-image, gradually taking shape, did include a sense that the nation's motives should be purer than those of the old European powers, less prone to war.

Thus Washington talked of being "disengaged from the labyrinth of European politics and wars." In his 1796 Farewell Address, the first President went on to advise firmly against any set allegiances with European powers, taking advantage of American distance from old world controversies. There was no reason for war to reach American shores, and the idea of neutrality was explicitly evoked: Americans should make sure that national neutrality is "scrupulously respected." The nation's military stance should be defensive, its approach to other nations peaceful and even-handed. And the retiring President added a related warning about military excess: "Overgrown military establishments are under any form of government inauspicious to liberty." Other leaders in the early republic picked up key elements of this message, particularly as it suggested American freedom from war-prone precedents. Alexander Hamilton brashly wrote of a "great American system" that could control relationships with the old world, while Thomas Jefferson, as President, talked about "peace, commerce and honest friendship with all nations, entangling alliances with none." Jefferson also opposed a standing army. An even more striking idea came from Benjamin Rush, a medical doctor and signatory to the constitution who in 1793 suggested the establishment of a Peace Office for the new nation – the first proposal ever for a peace-based government unit, and an idea that would begin to gain reality only in the twenty-first century (though not in the United States). Rush wanted the new office to promote not only the nation but also Christianity and Christian education. But peace was part of the charge as well: the new unit should "inspire a veneration for human life, and a horror at the shedding of human blood" and should "subdue that passion for war ... militia laws should everywhere be repeated, and military dresses and military titles should be laid aside."

In practice, the United States tried consistently to limit European interventions in the Americas. In 1823 President James Monroe, worried about European interference in the new republics of Latin America, castigated imperialism as "dangerous to our peace and safety." Since Britain, also, worked to limit European capacity to interfere with free trade to Latin America, in fact relatively few substantive issues arose. But an orientation toward some special New World arrangements that would depart from European precedents, presumably in the interests of relative peace though also United States hemispheric leadership, moved out early in the national experience.

New expressions of interest in peace from various governments and leaders, the turn to neutrality in special circumstances, plus the considerable success of the Vienna settlement constituted an important set of developments that bore some relationship to growing considerations of peace among intellectuals. The result was not, ultimately, revolutionary, save in specific cases like Switzerland. Enough movement occurred to keep peace interests alive more generally; not enough, however, to satisfy them. The next stage in peace history during the long nineteenth century returned attention to discussions and advocacy, but with some new arguments joining in and, above all, some new organizational zeal.

Peace organizations: A new element in world history

Eager discussion of peace continued on many fronts after 1815, with United States and Russian intellectuals increasingly involved along with West Europeans. The commentary in one sense maintained the trajectory already established in the Enlightenment, and some of the same arguments were involved. But interest also increased because of the fact of the recent Napoleonic Wars, which heightened a desire to develop alternatives, and because of some newer political philosophies as well. Many organizations received strong support from the rising professional and middle classes, for whom peace was part of a new sense of progress and a commitment to economic prosperity. This was the atmosphere in which what can be called the modern peace movement first emerged, though in a confusing welter of specific and mainly national organizations.

Key ideas

Economists in many countries maintained the argument that war was bad for business, many adding that the advent of industrialization and the resultant opportunities for economic growth should divert attention from war in any event. In France Benjamin Constant contended that an age of trading had replaced the more savage age of war, a clear sign of advance in civilization. Many actual industrialists made the same pitch, truly believing that what they were doing constituted a milestone in human progress that again would simply displace war. Jean-Baptiste Say, another economist, claimed that his discipline itself would promote peace, by explaining to the public the changing nature of relations among states; a "science of peace" could become an economics subfield and educate about the rationale for eliminating military expenditures in favor of commercial investments. In Germany Gustav von Schmoller similarly contended that the "progress of civilization" favored economic growth and a sense of shared interests among trading partners, rather than reliance on the "coarsest and most brutal weapons." Still other theorists purported to show how competition and free trade would advance prosperity and create a sense of brotherhood and "ensure universal peace."

Other voices now contributed. Geography again expanded: an important new voice was V. F. Malinovski, from Russia, who argued that peace was the only path to human development. Nationalism was a principle of hatred. Malinovski, also an active diplomat and a conservative, pushed as well for the principle of balance of power as the basis for "peace in Europe."

But it was the advent of socialism and the incorporation of peace platforms in socialist ideology that constituted the most important innovation. In the 1820s the French theorist Henri de Saint-Simon, who sought social progress through an emphasis on science and technology, featured substantial emphasis on a new "world government," overseeing the activities of individual states and backed by the force of public opinion. The government – and he really ended up talking about a European-wide body, not a global entity – would sponsor educational advance, a common moral code, and big public works projects, all of which would serve the perpetuation of peace. Power would be taken from the military and given to scientists and industrialists. Whether Saint-Simon is best viewed as a socialist or a technocrat is open to debate, but he did feel that only a full reorganization of society would lead to peace, and also that this was eminently achievable as well as desirable. This he shared with the more influential socialist thinkers who emerged in the 1840s.

And this contingent, of course, was headed by Karl Marx. Marx's version of socialism, laid out from 1848 onward, focused on the decisive role of ownership of the means of production in all other aspects of a society. In modern, industrial society, the capitalist class owned these means, and through this controlled the state, culture – and of course diplomacy. Warfare was a central part of the capitalist order. But the wave of the future lay with the working class, who would ultimately revolt and overturn the capitalist order, and through this set the basis for a totally new society. Marxism, obviously, was not pacifist: violent struggle would be central to the revolution. But once the revolution produced a classless society, peace would be one of its results: "the exploitation of one individual by another will be ended, the exploitation of one nation by another will also be ended ... as the antagonism between classes within the nation vanishes, the hostility of one nation to another will come to an end." In the meantime, while wars would continue, the working class and the socialist movement had no reason to support them – and this meant that, in a somewhat convoluted way, this new and growing political current provided important new support for opposition to militarism of every sort. And other socialists, without accepting the entire Marxist theory, agreed that in the coming order, not only social justice, but also peace, would be the result.

The persistence of peace discussions, on new and old bases, helps explain the more important innovation of the second quarter of the nineteenth century: the proliferation of organizations explicitly devoted to the cause of peace.

Pacifist groups

The decades after 1814–15 truly constituted the birthplace for an amazing variety of pacifist or peace-seeking organizations: nothing like this had ever occurred before. The focus was almost entirely Western (though including Russia), which was a clear limitation. But many participants were convinced that their enthusiasm, and the justice of their cause, would carry the day in any event.

Peace organizations formed part of a larger flowering of reform groups of various types – ultimately embracing temperance movements, prison and asylum reform, anti-slavery, women's rights, and the protection of labor. Various efforts interconnected, which could both strengthen the peace movement by associating it with other causes, and distract by multiplying goals. Lots of people now believed that the world could and should be made better, and fast; the peace organizations were a key part of this process.

Probably the first such group emerged in the United States in 1814, in the Massachusetts Peace Society, which in 1828 expanded to become the American Peace Society. The group issued a regular periodical, called the *Advocate of Peace*, beginning in 1834, and sent speakers around the country in an age when the lecture was an extraordinarily popular medium. Quaker involvement was strong. The movement sponsored national meetings and participated in international gatherings, ultimately moving its headquarters from Boston to

Washington in obvious hopes of influence national policy. Under the leadership of William Ladd, from 1828 onward, a strong focus on new mechanisms for dispute mediation emerged: Ladd urged that "unless some means of terminating disputes by amicable and rational methods are devised," retaliation, revenge and war would be the inevitable consequence. A "spirit of peace" was important, but more specific mediation procedures were essential, and Ladd sketched the need for an international organization to agree on laws to preserve peace, though he envisaged only Christian and "civilized" nations. More broadly, American organizations, and individual pacifists like Henry Thoreau, were active in criticizing particular national war efforts, such as the Mexican American War, though most ended up supporting the Union cause in the Civil War as a policy action justified against slavery.

In Britain the Peace Society emerged in 1816, again with Quaker involvement, for the self-proclaimed purpose of promoting permanent and universal peace; it urged arbitration in disputes and a process of gradual and simultaneous disarmament of all nations. Here too there was a regular publication, the *Herald of Peace*, and a host of conferences and lectures.

The same pattern occurred in most European countries. France, Belgium, Switzerland and Germany all had early groups, complete with publications. By 1843 the networks among these organizations was sufficient to permit a first international congress, which enhanced the sense of global collaboration while discussing disarmament, international arbitration, and some kind of international federation of states. Soon, an International League for Peace and Liberty formed, the first of many loosely organized international coordinating bodies. The efforts, by midcentury, involved a true Who's Who of European intellectuals, including novelists like Victor Hugo in France. Hugo, for example, in a comment to the British Workingmen's Peace Association, urged that military leaders, far from being praised, should be "cursed" for their role in "these horrible executions of men," another indication of how peace discussions were beginning to transcend purely national lines. Actual attendance at meetings was usually fairly small, but the hope was that influential patrons plus the purity of the ideas would progressively influence rulers and governments to change their ways. And in fact, petitions were usually received amid all sorts of kind words about the importance of peace – even if actual policies changed not at all. The organizations also sponsored resolutions on peace to various parliaments – in Spain, Sweden, and elsewhere – though these were routinely turned away. Occasionally, additional mechanisms were discussed: one British proposal suggested pressing banks to refuse to lend money to war efforts.

The spate of organizations also promoted both peace research and peace education. In France Frédéric Passy organized the International and Permanent League for Peace, urging a pacifist philosophy that decried the ineffectiveness of military action. He advocated a permanent international congress to serve the interests of humanity, with police power, or what he called a "war on war." Passy's sponsorship of a variety of studies under the heading The Library of Peace effectively launched the notion of regular, scholarly peace studies.

Patrons

Organizations and individuals also sponsored serious efforts at peace education, trying to reach out to ordinary people through literature, lectures, even personal visits, while seeking to raise money for further efforts. Elihu Burritt, in the United States, was a pioneer. Self-taught, committed to moral improvement as a reform-minded Protestant, Burritt wanted to persuade people of the uselessness of military responses and the importance of alternatives such as arbitration. He urged peace as a precondition for prosperity, citing the dire economic consequences of war. He urged people to support peace through their votes and petitions. Copying the temperance movement, he suggested a commitment to total abstinence from war. He reached out actively to women, and their involvement in peace work became increasingly critical. Obviously Burritt additionally sought to have his pacifist materials available in the schools. He also collaborated with colleagues in Britain, and by 1850 he had raised close to 70,000 signatures in the two countries for a complete disavowal of war. Some of his most interesting efforts sought to combat the easy popularity of military songs and parades, seeking alternatives that would sustain the higher calling of peace.

Peace organizations gained new support, and new complexities, after 1850. As women's rights groups formed in a number of places – largely overlapping the countries in which the organized peace movement was strong – they often added a peace platform. Moreover, peace issues played a particularly interesting role in the kinds of discussions that were taking shape as feminism was first defined in the Western world. The question was: did women deserve equal rights as human beings or also because they brought some special qualities to civilization as a whole? And, if the latter, was one of those qualities not peace? If women gained the vote, more specifically, would peace become more likely than if men remained in charge? Here was an important, if debatable, linkage between two important movements for reform.

Workers' organizations, including those inspired by Marxism, also entered the lists. Marx insisted that his groups stay apart from the peace movements, which he regarded as capitalist-inspired. He argued that the new International Working Men's Association was in itself a peace movement, and that the global association of workers from various countries would ultimately "make international wars impossible." But other socialist leaders participated in peace organizations directly, and many socialist parties, as in Germany, firmly opposed imperialist ventures and military expenditures. Worker groups also sponsored major rallies in favor of peace. Of course – as with the religions that insisted that world peace depended on conversion – worker support for peace often assumed the need for a socialist revolution before the goal could be reached. But significant collaborations, amid otherwise separate organizations, were possible even so.

Certainly, the activities and impetus of the peace movements continued through the nineteenth century and beyond, though after 1914 they had to encounter the hard reality of one of history's most dreadful wars. Even before 1900, however, some participants began to raise questions about overall strategy – particularly, participants who were central to pacifism itself, and not also engaged in feminist or socialist causes. The issue was simple: the reformist peace movements hoped to mobilize opinion and create a sense of options, but their fundamental platform assumed an ability to change the goals and habits of rulers and governments. It was not clear – even before the outbreak of World War I – that this strategy would work.

And some leaders grew discouraged. Victor Hugo, for example, who eagerly supported the idea that peace conference resolutions should go to all rulers, became increasingly pessimistic after one experience after another where a government responded with good intentions but then did nothing to stem militarism. Hugo wondered loudly, late in his life, whether a more literally revolutionary approach might not be needed. Or Leo Tolstoy, in Russia, whose monumental *War and Peace* detailed the horrors of the Napoleonic Wars, similarly combined continued Christian pacifism with growing cynicism. Tolstoy opposed war policies and even risked government attack by supporting a small group of Russian Orthodox believers who turned against war and even sponsored a weapons burning demonstration. "How can so-called enlightened men preach war … (given) all that has been written, is being written, has and is being said, about the cruelty, futility and senselessness of war." He praised Russians who refused to enter military service and even corresponded with the rising Indian leader Mohandas Gandhi about the importance of non-resistance. But always there was the problem of reforming governments that showed no willingness to reform:

> In all history, there is no war which was not hatched by the governments, the governments alone, independent of the interests of the people, to whom war is always pernicious even when successful. The government assures the people that they are in danger from the invasion of another nation, or from foes in their own midst … and after assuring the people of its dangers the government subordinates it to control, and [claims that] this condition compels it to attack some other nation.

Peace movements persisted, and we will pick up their interactions later. Further, by the end of the century they were joined by several new government initiatives, some of which they directly sponsored, in the final chapter of peace history during the long nineteenth century as a whole. To some observers this further set of innovations promised to turn the corner between ardent profession of peace, and actual progress. It was this same set that helped support the optimistic projects of turn-of-the-century journalists. But first, one additional component deserves attention.

The world outside the West

Like so much of world history, peace history in the long nineteenth century is disproportionately Western. This is where the new ideas and the new organizations sprouted. The rest of the world, of course, did not simply melt away or become entirely subordinate to Western trends. The force of Western imperialism and Western industrialization did reduce margins for independent action. And the same forces inevitably tended to encourage responses in kind. Japan, as it successfully struggled to remain independent, early on decided to copy Western models of military organization and armament, and soon was engaged in a virtually unprecedented set of aggressive wars. China and the Ottoman Empire struggled, less successfully, to adapt their military structures. Nationalism, as we have seen, spread widely, and on the whole it tended to encourage rather than minimize conflict. In this whole process, earlier traditions of peace were easily overridden or ignored.

An interest in peace did not, however, evaporate, and there were even some interesting innovations outside the strictly Western orbit. Three cases deserve particular attention, though efforts to formulate peaceful responses to Western imperialism were also significant in India, in the National Congress movement that emerged in the 1880s, and in several African centers. The cases were very different, with varied implications for the future as well, but they suggested how new issues could intersect with older cultural traditions to produce vigorous peace ideas that were not simply dependent on the latest discussions in Europe and the United States.

In Iran, a new religious movement stemmed from the Shiite version of Islam, beginning in 1844. Sayyid Ali Muhammad Shirazi led a minority group in what was called the Babi movement, which (after some vigorous persecution by the government) turned into the Baha'i movement in 1866. Because of government attacks, Baha'i followers migrated widely in the later nineteenth century, to the Ottoman Empire, to Europe and ultimately to the United States. Baha'i beliefs varied, but a significant number of followers adopted a deep belief in non-violence. The Baha'is advocated wide religious tolerance, but also aspired to become a universal religion by incorporating elements of various religious traditions. During the 1860s Baha'i leaders began urging European governments to halt military expenditures, which created needless financial burdens on the poor, and to establish peace as an alternative. Promotion of peace and lobbying against military budgets became a consistent Baha'i message from the 1870s onward. In 1882 a new Baha'i leader wrote a book in Persian, *The Secret of Divine Civilization*, which went even further, advocating peace through a union of nations, along with universal disarmament.

The impact of the Baha'i movement on actual policy was not great, but the movement persisted, with some 2 million followers worldwide by the early twenty-first century. The movement certainly reflected the connection between earlier religious traditions – in this case, the pacifist strains in Islam – and a sense that, in contemporary conditions, further innovation and more explicit commitments were essential.

New thinking on peace also emerged in China, which was beset by internal violence and Western military pressure throughout the second half of the nineteenth century. Here, a number of new leaders, including Kan Youwei and Sun

Yatsen, focused on adapting Confucian values to contemporary conditions. The goal – not a new one – was a society that would provide social justice and harmony, and internal and external peace. These leaders opposed imperialism and nationalism, urging Chinese independence but also a universal world order that would abolish nation states. Kang, for example, believed that the current "Age of Disorder" would yield to a final system which he called the Age of Great Peace, drawing on many earlier Confucian texts for his inspiration. Ou Jujia, similarly, claimed that increasing wisdom would lead to universal peace. He saw a widening embrace of the whole of humanity in a social vision: "trust and harmony will prevail and fighting and murder will cease." Confucian teaching would spread widely, and would provide a foundation for all governments to embrace a common international law.

Developments in Central America saw significant advances in peace arrangements, but of quite a different order from the cultural innovations and continuities in Persia and China. Latin American independence movements, early in the nineteenth century, had been violent risings, and much of the remainder of the century saw civil wars or border conflicts – though huge conflagrations did not occur and Latin American nations were not part of larger international tensions. Early in the twentieth century, the small nations of Central America took several novel steps to assure greater harmony. In 1902 the Treaty of Corinto, among four nations, set up compulsory arbitration for disputes, and established a permanent treaty of arbitration. This arrangement obviously reflected larger international discussions of arbitration, but went further in making the process obligatory. Then in 1907 a larger peace conference, sponsored in part by the United States and Mexico, reflected renewed regional bickering. Five states signed a peace treaty and established a new Central American Court of Justice. Further international conferences followed, mainly seeking to iron out some economic disputes.

The significance of these moves should not be exaggerated. The arbitration panel in fact did little and was moribund within five years. The Central American Court lasted only a decade, and decided only nine cases. The regional innovation was nevertheless interesting, in applying some vaguer international models to a more specific setting. And the developments did begin to establish a situation in which the states involved, hard-pressed economically in any event, were able to keep military expenditures unusually low, with small armies focused more on internal politics than on external disputes or ambitions. As a society, Latin America in general would prove to be surprisingly free from significant warfare during the twentieth century – though not from often violent internal unrest. While the threat of United States interference played some role in this process, particularly in Central America itself, as the giant northern neighbor sought a favorable context for business ventures and a peaceful southern frontier, a willingness to negotiate directly and an absence of widespread territorial ambition promoted peace as well. No Latin American nation as yet committed to the kind of peaceful policy characteristic of places like Sweden. But the new pattern of negotiation in Central America suggested a distinctive if implicit regional spirit that would pay off – in contrast to so many twentieth-century patterns elsewhere – in promoting peace in the decades to come.

The international scene: The new institutions of the later nineteenth century

Continued discussion of peace opportunities but also some additional innovations, Western-sponsored but now on a more international scale, capped the long nineteenth century and helped create the optimism about the future that was displayed so strikingly in turn-of-the century commentary. The ongoing pace of peace thinking and the expansion of private organizations helped explain new initiatives. Though the spate of international peace congresses had ended in 1859, advocacy groups continued to gain ground: by 1914 there were 190 peace societies in Europe alone, publishing 23 journals in ten languages. While devoted followers were obviously in a minority, some products of the peace movement became surprisingly popular, like a German novel *Lay Down Your Arms!* (1899), which radiated the common optimism that true peace was right around the corner.

Yet developments in these final pre-World War I decades also had ominous undercurrents. Growth of military expenditure, particularly in the European nations, became extremely rapid, as heavy artillery and new types of shipping, ultimately including the battleship, expanded arsenals. More and more industrial nations also adopted extensive military drafts, as the size of peacetime armies exploded. New alliance systems, completely with pledges of support in case of attack, soon pitted France, Britain, and Russia, on the one hand, against Germany and Austria-Hungary, with Italy, Japan, and several other nations ultimately joining in. Imperialist expansion helped distract the major powers, but this merely whetted appetites and, as we can see in retrospect, made direct conflict more likely, and more palatable, down the line. The spread of excited, often militaristic nationalism easily outstripped peace rhetoric. The outcome of these developments was not fully realized until 1914, but many observers sensed the potential, and this, too, helped explain efforts at innovation.

Major initiatives

An early sign of the desire for change occurred in the 1860s. As a result of witnessing the dire results of a war between Italy and Austria, a Swiss observer, Henri Dunant, began agitating for international agreement on the treatment of those wounded or taken prisoner in war. Various governments supported his humanitarian efforts, and the result, in 1864, was the first Geneva Convention. A number of governments signed on, first mainly in Europe but then more widely; Japan, for example, observed the standards in its 1890s war with China. And the Convention would be revised and expanded many times, to cover new problems – such as the use of deadly gas in World War I. The Geneva Conventions suggested new opportunities for international agreement and the obvious distaste for the human damage caused by modern weaponry. They did not, of course, support peace explicitly, and indeed by making war more palatable might work in the opposite direction. The same applied to the creation of the international Red Cross, in the same period.

A more tangible step toward peace occurred in 1889, with the formation of a new Inter-Parliamentary Union (IPU), sponsored jointly by a Frenchman and a Briton. Both men – William Cremer in Britain, Frédéric Passy in France – had attempted to persuade several nations to accept arbitration in case of mutual conflict. Rebuffed, they decided to join together to promote international encouragement for the principle of arbitration. The IPU, soon headquartered in Switzerland, was the result. The group sponsored annual conferences, with promotion of peace a fairly standard topic, and urged mediation in a number of conflicts. The IPU also organized discussions aimed at revising history textbooks, which by this point were typically aggressively nationalistic, toward promoting a cultural context more favorable to peace.

The IPU helped encourage a key next step in international arrangements, the first peace conference, in The Hague, Netherlands, in 1899. The conference was also sponsored by the Tsar of Russia, who was eager to promote a reduction of armaments in part from a real concern about growing international rivalries, in part because of a specific realization that Russia was falling behind, technologically, in the current arms race. Mixed motives should not conceal the fact that the Russian government was identifying a real problem, which negotiations between individual states – Britain and Germany were the chief rivals – were unable to solve. Tsar Nicholas urged his fellow rulers:

> The maintenance of general peace and a possible reduction of the excessive armaments which weigh upon all nations present themselves, in the existing condition of the whole world, as the ideal toward which the endeavors of all Governments should be directed … The Imperial Government believes that the present moment would be very favorable for seeking, by means of international discussion, the most effective means of ensuring to all peoples the benefits of a real and lasting peace and, above all, of limiting the progressive development of existing armaments.

The result was the first official conference ever called not after a war, but in order, in principle, to prevent one.

The conference in fact passed a number of regulations about the conduct of war on land and sea. Participants also agreed to a Convention for the Pacific Settlement of International Disputes, which in turn established the Permanent Court of International Arbitration, sitting in The Hague. If countries agreed to send a dispute to the Court, each would select arbitrators to participate. In fact, 16 cases would be brought to the Court by 1914, involving often fairly minor but intractable disputes between or among countries like the United States and Mexico, several European countries and Venezuela, France and Britain and so on. Many disputes involved property claims, including payment of government debts or fishing rights in certain waters. But France and Britain settled a controversy over territory in the Middle East, and France and Germany used the Court to resolve a skirmish between their forces in Morocco. France and Italy clashed over Italian seizure of French boats during a minor war with Turkey, and the Court ordered the Italians to pay damages in most of the cases. Few of these incidents would likely have led to outright war, but the new mechanism certainly reduced tensions. And even though the Court hardly met the Russian tsar's high hopes for peace and disarmament, its utility for the international community has assured its operation to the present day.

A second Hague conference met in 1907, but few significant results accrued. An effort to require arbitration simply failed, so a voluntary system, with each state having to consent to the procedure, persisted instead. As international tensions visibly escalated, in the decade before outright world war, there was no new mechanism available to respond.

There were, in the same period, a series of more opportunistic efforts to end small wars. Several times one or more European powers intervened, either diplomatically or through expeditionary forces, to settle disputes, for example between Greece and the Ottoman Empire. These moves, however, were really part of the more general phenomenon of imperialism, and brought no systematic innovations concerning peace. A more important intervention occurred during a war between Russia and Japan in 1904–5. Japan, winning the war but unable to gain a settlement directly, appealed to the American President, Theodore Roosevelt, who convened a conference in New Hampshire and brokered a peace. Again, however, no new structures or principles emerged, though Roosevelt won a Nobel Peace Prize for his efforts.

Games and prizes

Several other initiatives, though nongovernmental, showed the growing interest in peace. In 1896 a French aristocrat and conservative, Baron de Coubertin, revived the Olympic Games, which historically had joined the city states of Greece in competition. Coubertin's idea was that athletics could release passions that might otherwise fuel actual conflict, though he was also interested in promoting physical fitness and celebrating amateurism amid growing professionalization in sports. He believed that national pride could be expressed constructively, and international understanding would gain from the mingling of athletes and even spectators. The games, Coubertin argued:

> may be a potent, if indirect, factor in securing universal peace. Wars break out because nations misunderstand each other. We shall not have peace until the prejudices which now separate the different races shall have been outlived. To attain this end, what better means than to bring the youth of all countries periodically together for amicable trials of muscular strength and agility? The Olympic Games, with the ancients, controlled athletics

and promoted peace. It is not visionary to look to them for similar benefactions in the future.

Initially, the games were largely European affairs, with countries like the United States joining in, but gradually of course they would expand, and they would indeed serve, particularly during the Cold War, to channel nationalist competitions. The Baron's hopes were unrealistic, but his reinvention may have contributed to some peace goals.

A second private innovation, this one beginning in 1901, involved the introduction of the Nobel Peace Prize, founded by a Swedish entrepreneur who sought to reward achievements in several sciences but also in peace work. Alfred Nobel had invented dynamite, and may have been concerned about his legacy given its destructive potential, so the peace focus was more than a general sign of the times. Early peace prizes went to many of the people who were leading groups like the Inter-Parliamentary Union; the first woman to receive the prize was the German author of *Lay Down Your Arms!*, a tireless advocate for the abolition of war. From its inception, and certainly over time, choices for the Nobel Peace Prize – made by a committee chosen by the Norwegian parliament – have often designated important if sometimes unexpected figures in the struggle to advance peace.

A final innovation was more regional. In 1910 Andrew Carnegie, the Scottish immigrant who made a fortune in the American steel industry, established the Carnegie Endowment for International Peace, with the now-familiar goal of "advancing the cause of peace among nations." The Endowment meant to study the causes of war and the means of preventing same, while promoting international law and the peaceful resolution of disputes. Funds were also available for organizations working on these goals. Here too, and also in several movements in Europe, new calls emerged for a revision of history textbooks. Coincidentally, Carnegie also funded the Peace Palace in The Hague, where the new arbitration court operated. Obviously, lots of people, from various backgrounds and with various political affiliations, from socialist to conservative, were working hard on peace by the dawn of the twentieth century.

These developments capped what in many ways was an extraordinary century and a half of new ideas, new associations, even new policies aimed at converting hope and optimism into reality. Progressive claims about the possibility of peace, around the turn of the century, were not just idle talk; they linked to some very real, arguably impressive developments. But the key test: whether relevant governments had changed their own goals and priorities, had not yet been met, and the hesitations around The Hague conferences were already a sign of disjuncture. There was worse to come.

* * * * *

The long nineteenth century indisputably played a major role in the history of peace. New ideas, organizations, and policies took root, forming precedents that continue to influence the world today. Clearly, however, peace did not win out. Several wars in the Balkans, a clearly troubled region at this point, led fairly directly to the larger bonfire of World War I. This war, in turn, shattered many hopes and tragically demonstrated that many new institutions fell short of their goals. Reason of state, armament levels and industrial dependence on weapons sales, plus rabid popular nationalism combined to overwhelm peace aspirations and apparatus. The lesson was bitter, as it revealed the fragility of many of the ideas that had flourished from the Enlightenment onward.

Yet it would be a mistake to dismiss the peace innovations of the long nineteenth century. Key ideas and organizations would survive or revive: many developments in the century after World War I have been extensions of nineteenth-century thinking and experimentation. World War I was a terrible blow, but as we will see many ensuing reactions sought to pick up the pieces, adding a bit more international organization, a bit more attention to disarmament, a bit more passion. Even today, after many additional disappointments, world leaders continue to work on ideas and precedents born before 1914. And, as we will see, some gradual progress may finally have resulted. Some of the limitations of nineteenth-century approaches still apply as well, however. There was a complex history still to come, even as much of the world was engulfed in battle after the summer of 1914.

Further reading

Bohman, J. and M. Lutz-Bachmann. *Perpetual Peace: Essays on Kant's Cosmopolitan Ideal*. Cambridge: Cambridge University Press, 1997.

Brock, P. *Pacifism in Europe to 1914*. Princeton, NJ: Princeton University Press, 1972.

Caedel, Martin. *The Origins of War Prevention: The British Peace Movement and International Relations, 1730–1854*. Oxford: Clarendon, 1996.

Heffermehl, Fredrik S. *The Nobel Peace Prize: What Nobel Really Wanted*. Santa Barbara, CA: Praeger, 2010.

Hudson, Manley O. "The Central American Court of Justice." *The American Journal of International Law* 26.4 (1932): 759–86.

Mazower, M. *Governing the World: The History of an Idea, 1815 to the Present*. New York: Penguin Group, 2013.

Miller, Paul B. *From Revolutionaries to Citizens: Antimilitarism in France, 1870–1914*. Durham, NC: Duke University Press, 2002.

Nicholls, David. "Richard Cobden and the International Peace Congress Movement, 1848–1853." *Journal of British Studies* 30.4 (1991): 351–76.

Ralston, Jackson H. *International Arbitration, from Athens to Locarno*. Stanford, CA: Stanford University Press, 1929.

Šabič, Zlatko. "Building Democratic and Responsible Global Governance: The Role of International Parliamentary Institutions." *Parliamentary Affairs* 61.2 (2008): 255–71.

Scott, Shirley V., Anthony Billingsley, and Christopher Michaelsen. *International Law and the Use of Force: A Documentary and Reference Guide*. Santa Barbara, CA: Praeger, 2010.

Svarverid, Rune. *International Law as World Order in Later Imperial China: Transla-
tion, Reception and Discourse, 1847–1911*. Leiden: Brill, 2007.
Wank, Ke-wen. *Modern China: An Encyclopedia of History, Culture, and Nationalism*.
New York: Garland Publishers, 1998.

On the U.S. peace movements

Chatfield, Charles. *The American Peace Movement: Ideals and Activism*. New York:
Twayne, 1992.
Davis, Calvin DeArmond. *The United States and the First Hague Peace Conference*.
Ithaca, NY: Cornell University Press, 1962.
Hawkley, Louise, and James C. Juhnke, eds. *Nonviolent America: History through the
Eyes of Peace*. Newton, KS: Bethel College, 1993.
Janis, Mark Weston. *The American Tradition of International Law: Great Expectations,
1789–1914*. Oxford: Clarendon Press, 2004.
Juhnke, James C., and Carol M. Hunter, eds. *The Missing Peace: The Search for Non-
violent Alternatives in United States History*. Kitchener, ON: Pandora Press, 2001.

On The Hague Peace Conference

Caron, David D. "War and International Adjudication: Reflections on the 1899 Peace
Conference." *American Journal of International Law* 94 (2000): 4–30.
Choate, J. *The Two Hague Conferences*. Princeton, NJ: Princeton University Press,
1913.
Eyffinger, Arthur. *The 1899 Hague Peace Conference: "The Parliament of Man, the
Federation of the World."* The Hague: Kluwer Law International, 1999.
Rosenne, Shabtai, and Terry D. Gill. *The World Court: What It Is and How It Works*.
Leiden: Martinus Nijhoff Publishers, 2003.
Van Krieken, Peter J., and David McKay, eds. *The Hague – Legal Capital of the World*.
Cambridge: Cambridge University Press, 2005.

7   Peace in the decades of war

World War I was both a devastating blow to the peace movements, and a stimulus to renewed effort. During the war itself, between 1914 and 1918, peace activists found themselves marginalized if not jailed outright, as popular support for a peace stance initially melted away. The war clearly revealed how shallow many peace efforts had been, at least beneath a thin leadership level. But the war was so devastating, so contrary to well-established ideals and expectations, that it generated a resurgence of peace efforts in its wake. The war killed at least 10 million people, and injured 20 million more – maimed veterans would be a vivid reminder of the war's destruction long after it ended. The war devastated economies. On many battle fronts it featured prolonged stalemates, in which little change occurred for months, even years – where every modest effort might produce a hundred thousand casualties. By any measure, modern or traditional, this was simply a horrible war, in which the power of modern military technology was unleashed on a wide scale for the first time. Small wonder that, once the conflict finally ground to a halt, many people sought assurances that this kind of thing would never happen again – including some former soldiers who vowed that no matter what the future issue, nothing would ever justify violence of this sort, that war settled nothing. Small wonder that an audience for peace initiatives expanded once more. The contrast between the war and earlier idealism might be forgotten in the first excitement of conflict, but it reemerged starkly after four years of bad news with the bitter experience of actual modern warfare now added in.

The years between 1914 and 1945 – the decades so dominated by war or threat of war – saw three major developments in the history of peace, plus another setback that would have its own lasting consequences.

First – again, after World War I itself – governments and political leaders tried a number of additional strategies to promote peace, going well beyond what had been attempted during the long nineteenth century. Some of the new steps built on peace ideas generated during the war itself, as it dragged on so brutally. A new League of Nations was meant to provide a format in which conflicts could be resolved. Explicit disarmament conferences tried to control this aspect of the environment. Official rhetoric about the importance of peace reached new heights. Most of these developments clustered in the 1920s, and did not extend into the increasingly militaristic atmosphere of the 1930s with the rise of Hitler and a new military regime in Japan, but the precedents, and the accompanying limitations, would obviously create additional guideposts for the future.

Second, outside of officialdom, outright pacifism, along with prolonged war-weariness, gained new ground. Many labor and feminist movements made their commitments more explicit, embarrassed by the breakdown of World War I. In the United States, isolationism was a somewhat related response, though not explicitly pacifist.

Third, outside the increasingly shaky Western orbit, a new philosophy of nonviolence emerged in India, under the leadership of Mohandas Gandhi. Nonviolent resistance applied primarily to the struggle against British imperialism in India at this point, but it had major implications for pacifism more generally, at the time and subsequently. Western leadership in peace was so obviously unreliable that it was hardly surprising that initiatives would open up elsewhere, combining innovation with the deployment of older peace traditions.

Peace initiatives were consistently disputed during these decades, creating more agonizing complications than nineteenth-century advocates had encountered. Some groups thought they learned from World War I that violence was essential. Fascist and Nazi movements praised action and war, and by the 1930s, spurred additionally by the devastating economic depression, they increasingly translated thought into action. The rise of militarist regimes, combined with divided response by other states, made another major war increasingly inevitable during the 1930s. Peace efforts failed once again. Right before conflict resumed in Europe, an attempt to appease Nazi Germany, in a 1938 meeting in Munich, seemed to dramatize the powerlessness of anything but military response. This too would leave its mark when the decades of world war finally ended.

Peace efforts amid total war

When war actually broke out in August, it became clear that most segments of the relevant populations either actively embraced the effort or at least offered no resistance. Governments had been worried that the working class, for example, so widely exposed to socialist ideas and leadership, would be recalcitrant: but workers, and most of their labor leaders, in fact opted for nationalism and obedience over ideological purity. Indeed, national unity became a watchword everywhere. The same reactions applied to women, as a group: as troops paraded off to the fronts, many women and girls were active cheerleaders. No large groups or population segments opposed the war. In fact, response to the war declarations clearly combined high excitement and great ignorance: excitement, because after decades of peace at home many people were clearly pining for new adventures; ignorance, because virtually no one imagined what a dreadful and bloody deadlock would soon develop. Governments actively encouraged the supportive mood by issuing inaccurate and dramatic propaganda about the evils of the enemy – German forces were portrayed, for example, as killers and maimers of Belgian babies as they violated this nation's neutrality in order to move quickly into northern France. Official measures were also taken to identify and constrain individuals who might effectively resist the war effort.

Peace activity

In this context, the few people still devoted to the priority of peace faced an obvious challenge in figuring out what constructive steps might be taken. Many leaders were arrested or accused of treason or other crimes. With time, however, peace efforts revived, though amid great difficulty. The horrors of the war itself, and the reluctance of governments to consider any kind of peace compromise, created opportunities for renewed interest in peace.

In Britain, key political leaders, including those from the Liberal and Labour parties that had often opposed war in the past, largely acquiesced to the war effort and even joined a unity cabinet. The few who dissented simply resigned. But some Labour party members quickly formed a group opposed to obligatory military service, and this group grew rapidly when conscription was enacted in 1916. Individual intellectuals, like Bertrand Russell (who was not, however, a systematic pacifist) spoke out strongly against the war, urging international unity and advocating nonviolent, passive resistance against the war effort. (Russell was arrested for encouraging citizens to refuse any work that supported the war effort.) Then in 1915 a League of Nations Society was created, hoping to promote a new international association that would arbitrate future disputes and prevent war. This group carefully avoided opposition to the current war effort or even calls for a negotiated peace, but pressed for a role for its key ideas whenever the war finally ended. By 1917 other voices, including British officer and poet Siegfried Sassoon, began to emerge, when it became clear that the government was resisting any kind of compromise settlement; Sassoon stated, bluntly and publicly, that soldiers were dying in a conflict that had no valid cause.

Russian socialists quickly branded the war an imperialist conflict, condemning labor leaders who supported the war as traitors to the international proletariat. They had little initial impact, however, as their movement was already illegal. Exiled leaders like Vladimir Lenin joined with other anti-war socialists, mostly in Switzerland, in opposing the war effort. In 1917, as revolution broke out in Russia, the German government facilitated Lenin's return to Russia, where he ultimately seized control of the revolution and pulled Russia out of the war.

A few German socialists, including Rosa Luxemburg, similarly opposed the war, drawing police attention. And the papacy spoke out, by 1917: a papal "Peace Note" provided one of the first attempts to define a compromise settlement to end the prolonged conflict. The pope further urged disarmament and "instead of armies, the institution of arbitration, with its lofty peacemaking function," with sanctions against any government that would refused to submit disputes to this process. Actual papal negotiating efforts fell on deaf ears.

Finally, support for the idea of the League of Nations came from many other European countries, including France but also Europe's nervous neutral states – Sweden, Norway, Switzerland, and the Netherlands.

Because the United States did not initially enter the war, peace ideas initially had greater leeway. A number of leading politicians, including the Secretary of State, William Jennings Bryan, quickly spoke out against the war, urging international arbitration of all disputes. As it became clear that a number of Americans, possibly including President Woodrow Wilson, favored the Allied cause against the Germans, more formal pacifist groups formed. The American Union against Militarism organized in 1915 and included many prominent intellectuals and political leaders. The group urged the United States to remain neutral, contending that war harmed liberty and humanity alike. Once the country actually joined the war, AUAM offices were frequently raided by police; in protest, another group was formed, which urged free speech and the right to conscientious objection, and this ultimately (in 1920) became the American Civil Liberties Union. In 1915 yet another group, again backed by key figures including former President William Howard Taft, began urging the formation of a new League of Nations; the group's title, indeed, was League to Enforce Peace. As in Britain, the idea here was a new entity that would have the power to arbitrate international disputes and use economic or military sanctions to enforce its decisions. In 1916 Woodrow Wilson himself addressed the group, and promised United States support for an appropriate effort after the war.

In 1915 the industrialist Henry Ford organized an American expedition to Europe to join with likeminded European pacifists. The resultant meeting occurred in Stockholm, Sweden, since only the neutral Scandinavian countries allowed representatives; Allied and Central governments alike banned participation by their citizens. But the effort quickly took on the air of a stunt, rather than a serious initiative.

And after the United States actually entered the war, the terms of debate narrowed. People like Theodore Roosevelt condemned American pacifists as "evil enemies of their country." They were "traitors to the great cause of justice and humanity" – the mantle the war effort now adopted. Roosevelt claimed that it would be an act of "baseness," "of unworthy cowardice and a betrayal of this country" to accept any peace "except the peace of overwhelming victory" which would include expelling the German emperor. Quickly, in fact, the United States passed a new Sedition Act (1917) and then an Espionage Act criminalizing speeches or publications that questioned the war. A number of newspapers were closed.

Apart from national settings, a variety of individuals and organizations sought a broader response in the interests of peace. Labor leaders from several countries attempted to form an international conference in 1917, but they were blocked by police actions of the relevant governments. Women proved to have somewhat greater leeway. A number of individual women, including the German Rosa Luxemburg but also American social worker Jane Addams, spoke out strongly; Addams actually organized a Women's Peace Party. A Hungarian feminist, Rosika Schwimmer, toured the United States in 1914, urging peace and international feminist unity on behalf of peace; she presented a petition signed by thousands of European women to Woodrow Wilson. In 1915 women from both neutral and warring nations were invited to a meeting in The Hague, and a number of delegates were actually able to get to the gathering – the International Congress of Women. (American delegates sailed in a neutral Dutch ship, bearing a homemade flag with Peace spelled in blue letters, though the ship was held up for several days by the British navy.) Resolutions spoke out against "the madness and horror of war, involving as it does a reckless sacrifice of human life and the destruction of so much that humanity has labored through centuries to build up." They urged people that, since all nations thought they were fighting for national self-defense, there should be no barrier to an agreement based on common interests – there was no reason to keep fighting. An "honourable peace" could be established. "The Congress therefore urges the Governments of the world to put an end to this bloodshed, and to begin peace negotiations" toward a permanent settlement. Principles of peace would include: no transfer of territory without the consent of people living in it – "the right of conquest should not be recognized"; future international disputes to be referred to arbitration, with "social, moral and economic pressure" brought to bear on any country that resorts to war; and women gaining equal political rights and foreign policies in future subject to "democratic control."

Even resolute women, of course, had their limits. Women's leaders from several warring nations, including Canada as well as France and Belgium, refused to join in on grounds that the cause their nations were fighting for was entirely just. Only three British representatives were able to bypass government opposition to the movement, and only then because they snuck in early. The Congress sent delegates to every government, where they were usually courteously received but then ignored. Most of the government ministers argued instead that negotiations were impossible, because they would be taken as a sign of weakness; only complete victory made any sense. And many delegates themselves were accused, back home, of treason. One female American professor was simply fired (from Wellesley College).

Closely related to the efforts of peace leaders and movements amid harsh new constraints, the war also raised huge challenges for ordinary individuals who objected to war as a matter of personal conscience. Not surprisingly, many peace leaders, in countries like Britain, explicitly urged conscientious objection as a way to protest the war effort. A group called the Anti-Enlistment League opened in the United States in 1915, before the entry into the war, to dissuade young men from joining the military. Overall, the number of conscientious objectors had clearly risen by this point, reflecting many religious traditions as well as new peace concerns. It was also true that compulsory military service made it far more difficult simply to avoid war through informal arrangements.

But the wartime atmosphere made conscientious objection an arduous, sometimes dangerous process.

Ben Salmon was a Catholic conscientious objector in the United States, and an open critic of the claim that this was a "just war." Yet both the Catholic Church and the *New York Times* described him as a "spy suspect," while the American military charged him with desertion and spreading propaganda, first sentencing him to death and them commuting this to 25 years hard labor. Salmon appealed directly to President Wilson, arguing that Jesus died for the principle of "thou shalt not kill," which Salmon saw as "unconditional and inexorable." "When human law conflicts with Divine law, my duty is clear … prison, death, or both, are infinitely preferable to joining any branch of the Army."

Other objecting groups encountered difficulties, including Mennonites and Jehovah's Witnesses. In the United States about 2,000 objectors refused any cooperation with the military (among about 25,000 objectors overall), and were imprisoned in military facilities, where in many cases they were actively tortured. Two Hutterite draftees died as a result. Eventually, most American conscientious objectors were allowed to do agricultural work or relief service in Europe, while some became firefighters or hospital attendants.

The Russian government, a bit more responsive, allowed Mennonites to take on hospital or forestry jobs instead of fulfilling the military obligation. In fact, a wide movement against war took shape in this country, with Tolstoyans as well as pacifist Christian sects participating in proclaiming conscientious objection. Britain, establishing full military service in 1916, explicitly exempted objectors, allowing them to do civilian service, so long as they could convince a Military Service Tribunal of the quality of their objection. Over 10,000 gained options, but another 6,000 were forced into the army and then imprisoned when they refused orders. Several Quakers were involved. The Tribunals were notoriously hard on objectors, reflecting widespread public opinion that they were lazy or cowardly, seeking to benefit from the sacrifices of others. As in the United States, prison conditions were harsh, and a number died as a result of their treatment. Many military leaders wanted objectors shot outright, and they did seize some directly without the knowledge of civilian authorities. Objectors were also banned from voting for five years after the War. Clearly, in many countries, the clash between personal commitment and the demands of modern war grew more intense, though nowhere were huge numbers involved.

Overall, peace movements and conscientious objection revealed a determined commitment to peace on the part of crucial, though often small, minorities, all the more impressive given the opposition by governments and orchestrated, inflamed public opinion. The efforts would pay off in larger pacifist movements after the war – and this would prove important. Impact on the war itself was negligible, and ironically, perhaps tragically, the same applied to the war settlement. Only the movement on behalf of a new international association bore fruit, in peace discussions that focused otherwise mainly on nationalist goals rather than constructive compromise.

The Versailles Conference

Indeed, the attacks on peace advocates during the war, and the resultant distraction from continued careful thinking about peace, help explain another crucial feature of the war itself: it ended really badly. As we have seen, the major governments involved in the war were bent on total victory, not compromise, which meant in practice that war could only end when Germany essentially collapsed. And the ensuing peace conference at Versailles was a disaster, in marked contrast to the Vienna gathering that had worked to settle the Napoleonic Wars. Vienna, for all its flaws, demonstrated a real interest in an ensuing peace. Versailles was much more fully dominated by revenge and fear. The result was a series of treaties that provided abundant motives for subsequent conflict. It would be an exaggeration to say that Versailles guaranteed World War II, but it unquestionably provided much of the motivation.

The Congress of Vienna had not necessarily explicitly embraced some of the newer Enlightenment thinking about peace, though the Russian tsar was at least aware of some of the rhetoric, but it may have included some elements along with more conventional balance of power considerations in Europe. The conference at Versailles explicitly embraced peace ideas in one area – the creation of the new League of Nations – but ignored them in favor of other goals in every other respect – and balance of power was also jettisoned in the process. The substantial rejection of peace movements during the War itself clearly formed part of the context in which bad decisions were made.

The key problems at Versailles involved the attempt to punish and weaken Germany, as if it bore some special responsibility for the war, while at the same time simply dismantling the Austro-Hungarian Empire in favor of a welter of weak but highly nationalistic states in East-Central Europe. Germany was asked to accept limitations on armaments and to pay war reparations, while losing substantial territories particularly to France and to newly independent Poland. Reversing the provisions of Versailles became a major goal of German nationalists, including the new Nazi movement, but even many other Germans were offended: this aspect of the Versailles settlement could work only insofar as other powers were able to keep Germany in line. French leaders certainly hoped for peace, but they were more focused on punishment and on short-term protection from renewed German attack. Leaders of several other countries, like Italy, saw the Versailles conference as a chance to grab additional territory, as a reward for the war effort, and emerged actively dissatisfied with what they were able to get. The dismantling not only of the Austro-Hungarian but also the Ottoman Empires removed two multinational governments that had kept some semblance of peace in their regions, and opened both territories up for new conflicts. Most of the Versailles negotiators assumed that small-nation nationalism must be given a chance in East-Central Europe, and while this view was not explicitly anti-peace, it did not place long-term peace considerations at the forefront. Versailles was also hampered by continued assumptions of Western superiority, that precluded adequate attention to demands from countries like

Japan, or to nationalist aspirations in places like Africa or India (or for that matter with to new revolutionary regime in Russia).

The only sign of systematic thinking about peace – and it was an important one in principle – was the agreement at Versailles to establish the new League of Nations. The League built directly on peace thinking that had developed over several centuries in Europe, and it explicitly sought to go beyond the institutional experiments of the later nineteenth century. Woodrow Wilson, the idealistic American President, particularly pushed the League idea, which in his mind would partly counterbalance his embrace of small-nation nationalism, but there were many other supporters as well. The establishment of the League was hampered, however, by unwillingness to include key players like Germany or revolutionary Russia, and it was badly damaged by the ironic refusal of the United States ultimately to participate at all. Most obviously, the League's operations would be severely hampered by the tensions that immediately emerged from the other aspects of the Versailles settlement: the League would prove incapable of handling the issues that arose from German resentment, the weak structure in East-Central Europe, or Italian or Japanese imperialist frustration. Still, the League not only as a new symbol, but as a focus for some genuine achievements in managing conflict, deserves further exploration as part of the larger effort to adjust policies toward preventing the renewal of the kinds of hostilities that had produced the world war.

At the end of World War I, with full realization of the devastation that had occurred, a number of leaders began to talk in terms of "the war to end all wars." Woodrow Wilson, among others, used the phrase at least once, and so did postwar British officials. In fact, the term had been introduced as early as 1914 itself, as British author H. G. Wells argued that German militarism had to be defeated but that the same process would allow an "end" to war. Wells and others helped popularize the phrase by 1918. The one sense, the rhetoric was hollow: as we have seen, the actual peace settlement did not set up favorable conditions for peace. But the aspiration was interesting, for it reflected the obvious conflict between the beliefs about peace that had developed prior to the war, at least vaguely, and what had just happened in fact. Somehow, many people now hoped, the discrepancy must be repaired. So much suffering should lead to a transformation that would restore humanity to a path of progress. Later on, when it became clear that war had not ended, the phrase generated not hope but ridicule, casting peace idealism more generally into some disrepute. It was hard to strike the right balance.

Postwar strategies

At Versailles but even more so in the years immediately following, a number of steps reflected serious efforts to address key problems that had led to world war. The League of Nations was the most ambitious venture, but significant disarmament conferences occurred recurrently into the 1930s – when the process broke down entirely. And there were more specific initiatives as well, at least partially related to the quest for a new assurance of peace: these included key aspects of American isolationism and some important new treaty arrangements in Central America. Never before had so much energy been expended, at the official state level, to promote a framework more favorable to peace.

The League of Nations

Innovation toward peace was the primary motive behind the creation of the new League. The idea received wide support, not only from the idealistic Wilson but also from the governments of France, Germany and Italy, a leading socialist group in Britain, and the League to Enforce Peace.

Early discussion centered on the radical possibility of giving the League a military capacity, in order directly to enforce peace in any part of the world. A French plan argued that a military force, contributed from member states, would be able to implement League decisions and end localized conflict – and the idea was literally a global force. President Wilson, however, vetoed this ambitious proposal on grounds that the American Congress would never ratify an arrangement that put American troops under any international command. Wilson pinned his hopes, instead, "in our having confidence in the good faith of the nations who belong to the League."

Despite this revealing setback, the League document did talk about possible action in case of war. The League Covenant sought to protect the political independence of all members "against external aggression," though the actual response to such aggression would have to be discussed. Another article highlighted concern about war or threat of war; "the League shall take any action that may be deemed wise and effectual to safeguard the peace of nations." All of this was rather vague, and references to possible economic sanctions against aggressors were arguably a pale substitute for military provisions. But military action was possible, in principle, if the League members agreed (but agreement would require unanimous consent, which rendered this provision clearly ineffective in fact).

In its lifetime the League did settle 35 international disputes, of 66 considered. But the settlements – for example, in a Swedish–Finnish clash over a group of Baltic islands – depended on willingness of both parties to accept arbitration. Absent this – as in Japan's 1930s invasion of Manchuria – the League could only condemn in principle; nothing actually happened. Famously, in the 1930s, League efforts to protest Italian and German as well as Japanese military actions failed completely, as the world tumbled toward World War II.

During the 1920s member states made various efforts to repair the League structure – though nothing could compensate for the refusal of the United States to join in the first place. Countries like France – still worried about their vulnerability to German aggression, despite the Versailles Treaty – were particularly eager advocates of change; here was another case where mixed motives could contribute to peace suggestions. Thus in 1923 a proposal urged the formation of regional military agreements that would provide responses to aggression; but the idea got nowhere. Then a new Protocol was ventured – "for the Pacific Settlement of International Disputes" – which sought to assure states that reduced their level of armament that the League would offer protection against aggression. Signatories of the Protocol pledged "in no case to resort to war" and also to respect the judgments of the International Court in certain kinds of dispute. During the process of dispute resolution, the signatory states promised to take no military action and even to create a mutual demilitarized zone to prevent miscalculations. Any state which nevertheless went to war would be labeled the aggressor and then subjected to (vaguely defined) League sanctions; and if the League could not quickly decide who the aggressor was, it would require an armistice, whose violation would then be another act of aggression. And the Covenant talked clearly of setting up a joint military force to assist any state that was victim of aggression – though again, level of military contribution were not specified and League response was still contingent on a unanimous vote of members.

As a number of critics noted at the time, despite its additional efforts the League had not clearly managed to develop any real sanctions against an aggressor state. But the effort to define aggression, and to make it clear that aggression was unjust, was nevertheless intriguing in principle: no international body had ever gone so far in principle.

In fact, the whole discussion ultimately led to no concrete agreement. The British were opposed to accepting an unlimited obligation for arbitration. A Labour party leader disputed the notion of additional military expenditure in the interests of intermittent defense of peace, vaguely asserting that "our interests for peace are far greater" than this: "a machinery of defense is easy to create but beware lest creating it you destroy the chances of peace." Somewhat ironically, this kind of anti-military sentiment, another key current between the wars, complicated the discussion of effective international enforcement of peace. The British hoped instead that countries whose disputes were most likely to lead to war should engage with each other to accept arbitration and pledge not to move to armed conflict. The League was left essentially powerless when, in the 1930s, a number of key states decided that war was their best recourse.

Disarmament

The idea of controlling armaments in the interests of peace had gained ground in the later nineteenth century, and obviously the results of the world war gave further impetus to the idea that competition in weapons was a basic cause of conflict. Members of the League were in principle committed to the idea of arms control, and the League helped sponsor a number of key efforts until the whole process broke down in the mid-1930s.

The first big step was independent of the League. Naval competition resumed quickly after World War I, with both the United States and Japan building big ships. Britain still had the largest navy, but its ships were ageing, which gave it a new interest in limiting the whole competitive process. The United States was also newly wary of Japanese competition in the Pacific.

The result was the Washington Naval Conference of 1921, called by the American President and attended by several states including Britain and Japan. Japan was eager to use negotiations to gain greater international recognition, including acknowledgement of its new interests in northern China and Mongolia, while also limiting the U.S. naval buildup. Britain and the United States hoped to limit their own rivalry. As the conference began the U.S. intercepted some key Japanese messages to its negotiators, which helped them craft a set of limits that Japan would accept.

But the key points involved not just specific national goals, but the overwhelming international desire to avoid the kind of buildup that had contributed to world war, enhanced by the growing strength of the various national and international peace movements. The result was unprecedented.

For the conference did produce agreement. Japan accepted a 5:5:3 ratio for its battleships: the U.S. and Britain could maintain 525,000 tons in these ships, with 315,000 for Japan. France and Italy accepted lower levels. The size of the largest battleship was also limited, and ratios were established as well for the new category of aircraft carrier. As a result of the Five Power Naval Treaty (1922), the United States had to scrap a number of ships – 15 old ones, two new ones, and 13 under construction – and Britain destroyed even more. More warships were lost, as a result, than in any battle in history – though a few ships were turned into aircraft carriers.

Competition in battleship fleets actually ended as a result of the Treaty, a real change. Navies remained competitive, and mutually suspicious, and found other outlets – but here too some constraints applied for over a decade. Between 1927 and 1930, several countries raced ahead to build new cruisers, which had been limited in size (to 10,000 tons) but not in number. But a new London Naval Treaty in 1930 resolved this in turn, setting up a 10:10:7 ratio for the leading powers with regard to cruisers and destroyers; submarines were also limited for the first time, with parity among the three leading powers.

These gains were in many senses extraordinary – never before had major countries agreed to limitations in such a key military area. To be sure, individual countries, the U.S. in the lead, continued actively to build new ships within the framework, which maintained the competitive atmosphere. And many countries, though lesser powers, were not included at all, which might have been a problem for the future (the Soviet Union, most notably, was not invited to participate). And the whole arrangement came apart in 1936, when an increasingly militaristic Japan pulled out of the Treaty arrangements altogether, in the atmosphere of growing military rivalry more generally. Still, for a decade and a half, new ideas and arrangements really had been at work, providing some possible precedents for the future.

Disarmament efforts in the 1920s also applied to chemical weapons, which had been used in World War I with disastrous effects. The basic idea here was that weapons of this sort led to particularly awful deaths, and required special limits compared to other armaments. The League of Nations sponsored the Geneva Protocol in 1925, banning chemical and biological weapons. Many nations signed on, but with various reservations including the right to use such weapons against non-signatories or in defense were the weapons used against them. The United States, though a sponsor of the Protocol, did not sign at all, because of objections from the military and the chemical industry. Germany and Britain would develop chemical weapons widely in World War II, but refrained from using them for fear of retaliation in kind; but many countries developed chemical arsenals during the Cold War. In this area, as with navies, the 1920s set some important precedents, but tentatively and ultimately unsuccessfully.

The idea of disarmament did not die, even in the 1930s. The League of Nations began in 1925 to prepare a more general disarmament conference, and by 1931 this had received sufficient support actually to convene – in 1932. American President Franklin Roosevelt urged the conference: "If all nations will agree wholly to eliminate from possession and use the weapons which make possible a successful attack, defenses automatically will become impregnable and the frontiers and independence of every nation will become secure." Not only the United States, though not a League member, but also the Soviet Union participated in the discussions with some enthusiasm, as they unfolded in Geneva, Switzerland. Actual negotiations foundered on definitions of "offensive" and "defensive" weapons and on the resurgence of military tensions between France and Germany – the Germans wanted equal military stature, and the French believed that their only protection for the future lay in German military inferiority. Neither Britain nor the United States was willing to give France compensatory assurances. Then, under Hitler's new regime in Germany, the Germans withdrew both from the Conference and the League in 1933. Officially, discussions continued until 1937, but in fact they went nowhere.

Other efforts

Negotiations within Europe were sometimes seen as a way to address the failure of broader efforts at peace and arbitration. In 1925 a number of countries met at Locarno, in Switzerland, to try to provide new assurances of peace within the continent. Germany agreed to honor the borders of France and Belgium and to maintain a 50-kilometer demilitarized zone to the east of the Rhine River. But the Germans would not offer similar assurances to the East-Central countries, like Poland and Czechoslovakia, so the French signed separate defensive treaties with them. Tensions were patched over but not resolved, and of course it would be Nazi aggression against Czechoslovakia and Poland, in the later 1930s, that would bring on the European phase of World War II.

In 1928 the French managed to bring the United States to a wider conference on peace in Paris. The result, which included participation by a number of countries, was the Pact of Paris, or Kellogg-Briand Pact, named after the foreign ministers of the two initiating governments. The Pact pledged signatories "not to have recourse to war as an instrument of national policy, and to settle all disputes arising between them by peaceful means." The idea was to outlaw wars of aggression, though defensive action was still permissible. Fifteen countries initially signed on, and by 1934 the number had grown to 64. Japan, as well as all major European countries and the United States all participated. The Pact optimistically proclaimed that the result would "unite the civilized nations of the world in a common renunciation of war as an instrument of their national policy." The Pact certainly reflected the surge of peace hopes that so marked the 1920s, as well as a period of relatively friendly Franco-German relations; but it provided no mechanisms for enforcement, and in the long run it served primarily as a monument to hollow optimism.

Finally, in terms of major policy initiatives, France returned to the charge one last time between 1929 and 1932. The target here was a renewal of the discussion of military enforcement against violators of the peace. The French delegate argued, to the preparatory disarmament committee, that peace could only be assured if there were punishments against aggressors. An international association of airplane pilots declared their willingness to serve in a common air force for enforcing peace, rather than in national military units where they would be "executioners of war." Poland, appropriately nervous about its own security, urged an international army. Then in 1932 the French formally proposed a new international police force plus a multinational coalition to provide assistance to any state that was the victim of aggression. The biggest weapons – for example, ships over 10,000 tons – would be placed exclusively in the service of the international force.

Several countries welcomed these ideas in principle, though the British and Soviet delegates were cool (the Soviets feared that some Western power would dominate and so manipulate any international force to its own advantage). The French then pulled back, and proposed instead that the governments place certain specialized units in the service of the League: "these specialized contingents will be kept constantly ready for action."

But Hitler's rise, in the following year, put an end to all discussions of international policing. It turned out that no Western power was willing to take action against any of the initial German steps to remilitarize, and the idea of peace coercion would not really reappear until planning for a new United Nations began in 1944.

The policy initiatives of the 1920s and 1930s broke some really new ground, and advanced even more ambitious discussions. The fact that they ultimately failed, as major war resumed distressingly soon after the previous conflict, inevitably conditions historical interpretation. Governments did not really, permanently, change their stripes. One or two bad actors – in this case, Nazi Germany, Japan, and Italy – could ruin even the most widely accepted agreement, since the crucial issue of enforcement was never resolved. And the failure of the interwar efforts would have impact later on as well. It would encourage new efforts to address some of the limitations of the post-World War I initiatives, but it could also caution against reaching too far. Some of the most ambitious ideas of this brief decade plus have not been seriously taken up since that time. The legacy was decidedly mixed.

Peace ideas and peace movements

Alongside the key policy initiatives – supporting them and sometimes benefiting from them – a host of new nongovernmental peace efforts emerged in the wake of World War I. Old and new groups jostled for attention, and other entities, like the British Labour Party, participated strongly as well. The pursuit of peace clearly won new energy. A number of countries set up associations in support of the League, another channel for peace movements.

Overall, the surge of activity between the wars provided new, popular input into the policy process. World War I, and the spread of democracy, convinced many that diplomatic and military policy could not just be left to the experts. Nongovernment organizations had a role to play; this was one of the large framework changes during the interwar years.

At the same time, quite understandably, there was both overlap and confusion between explicit efforts to promote peace and a more general, unfocused sense of war-weariness – a dislike of war but without a particularly explicit commitment to peace. This kind of fatigue showed particularly in Britain and the United States, but it could condition reactions to peace organizations more generally.

Several new movements developed in the United States. Newly committed pacifists put together the National Council for Prevention of War (NCPW), in 1921, to support the naval disarmament conference. After this the NCPW became an increasingly strong lobbying group, coordinating peace efforts from women, youth workers, farmers, Christians, and others. It lobbied against military spending and against military training in schools and universities, while also advocating changes in educational curricula that would support peace more specifically. During the 1930s the group turned increasingly toward support for American neutrality should a new world war break out; this included participation in a new Emergency Peace Campaign in 1936–37, as German militarism heated up. Many women's groups continued to advocate for peace; from one came a renewed proposal, in 1925, that the government establish a Department of Peace (picking up on Benjamin Rush's original idea).

France produced new international leadership for pacifism. Marc Sangnier, a Catholic and veteran of World War I, vigorously advocated Christian pacifism. He instigated a series of 12 International Democratic Peace Congresses between 1921 and 1932, urging peace at the meetings and coining the phrase "disarmament of hatred." Sangnier devoted particular attention to improving Franco-German relations. He organized meetings of several dozen French youth with their German counterparts, based on peace and reconciliation. At one meeting, the German delegates took collections to help French regions that had been devastated by trench warfare; one woman even contributed her jewelry, which created quite a stir in France. Sangnier also set up the Volunteers of Peace, a scout movement, that he hoped would perpetuate the spirit of the peace congresses, combatting militaristic values with a pacifist youth culture, while also maintaining close ties between France and Germany.

German pacifism generated a number of important books. Lilly Jannasch, heading the Women's International League for Peace and Justice, urged her countrymen to accept responsibility for Germany's role in causing the war – she referred in fact to war crimes – as a basis for durable peace. Erich Maria Remarque wrote the most famous novel based on World War I, *All Quiet on the Western Front*, which became a major reference for pacifists because of its dramatic depiction of the horrors of war through the eyes of an army private. Other German artistic work explored the problems of war and disillusionment. Various private organizations supported peace efforts, including the goal of greater reconciliation with France. The German government itself, under the new Weimar Republic, also contributed to a peace effort particularly in education. Article 148 of the Weimar Constitution stressed the importance of truthfulness in textbooks, including avoidance of nationalist stereotypes and a positive presentation both of the achievements of other cultures and of the accomplishments of the League of Nations. In Germany and elsewhere many teachers' associations, as well as formal peace groups and women's organizations, promoted the revision of textbooks in the interest of greater international understanding and harmony; this was a major goal as well of the European branch of the Carnegie Endowment for International Peace, whose efforts continued.

Christian and labor pacifism flourished in Britain. A "No More War" emerged from the first wave, in 1921. George Lansbury presided over a new Peace Pledge Union, whose 1933 annual conference resolved unanimously to "pledge itself to take no part in war." The Labour Party, now the nation's second largest, did not accept systematic pacifism but did urge vigorous efforts toward peace under the League of Nations. Later in the 1930s, however, as Nazi Germany rearmed, the Labour party shifted to support rearmament. But Britain overall probably saw the most extensive peace movements, with the greatest popular impact. In 1935 a British group supporting the League took a poll, in which 11 million people participated with 91 percent favoring a strong international treaty that would reduce armaments. Similarly the Peace Pledge Union, opposed to war preparations of any kind, won 100,000 members by 1934.

Pacifists in the Soviet Union were initially tolerated, but then suppressed under Josef Stalin even as a pro-Soviet peace movement was encouraged abroad. All domestic groups were shut down, and a number of pacifists in the Tolstoy tradition were sent to prison camps. Pacifism was consistently active in Canada, in contrast. Several political leaders supported sanctions against states like Italy that became aggressors in the 1930s, while other figures urged the dismantling of state-sponsored military officer colleges in Canada itself.

As with British Labour, pacifists quite generally were sorely tested by the rise of fascist and Nazi militarism, including the bitter Spanish Civil War that began in 1936 as an active conflict between republican and fascist forces. Some pacifists clearly changed stripes in order to support resistance to fascism, while a few others maintained a more consistent stance in groups such as the War Resisters' International. A few, like Richard Gregg in Britain, tried to devise compromises that would feature campaigns of nonviolent resistance in the event of a fascist invasion.

Along with explicit commitments to peace, a host of political parties and individuals, without renouncing war in principle, simply tried to avoid commitments during this same period. Fatigue with war combined with the results of increasing political polarization. Thus France, in 1936, though politically republican, could not agree on any policy actively to assist colleagues in Spain because of divisions between left and right as well as the desire to shun any risks of engagement. The same avoidance strategy described even more durable reactions in the United States.

Isolationism

Beginning immediately after World War I, and in opposition to Woodrow Wilson's policies, a growing number of Americans and their leaders, particularly in the Republican Party, adopted a stance of isolationism: a desire to avoid deep engagements with the rest of the world, particularly in Europe. The impulse appealed to an old tradition in the nation, which held that standing clear of the tensions of the "old world" would help preserve regional peace. The nation had greeted the world war itself initially with a desire to avoid involvement, and this mood returned in 1919. The American Senate refused to join the League of Nations, and efforts by erstwhile allies, particularly France, to win American support in case of renewed German attack were uniformly rejected. Even the traditional policy of welcoming immigrants was reversed in the 1920s, as the nation imposed restrictive quotas. Save for the international economy, in which the country remained actively engaged, the hope was, globally, to stand largely alone. The goal was peace, but on a selective, purely national basis and without much attention to the complexity of issues that peace might entail.

Isolationist policies persisted in the 1930s, even as the world became more dangerous. The United States stood apart from even timid efforts to oppose fascist and Nazi aggression. Japanese moves in China were also ignored. The nation refused officially to acknowledge any territory the Japan had illegally acquired, but no action was contemplated. The obvious question – but it was not widely faced until the nation was finally drawn into World War II, in 1941 – was whether the short-term relief from international tensions justified the lost opportunity to work to stem aggression at a stage short of renewed global conflict. Non-involvement and peace-seeking reflected some similar impulses in the context of the times, but they were not the same.

When war did in fact break out in Europe, in 1939–40, the United States again held back. A number of pacifists maintained consistent positions in avoiding war altogether; one heroic congresswoman would even vote against war after the Japanese attack on Pearl Harbor. But isolationism trumped pacifism in defining initial response: somehow the nation should be able to stay out of these bloody entanglements elsewhere. It would take no small amount of anti-Nazi pro-Allied sentiment, along with the Japanese attack, along with manipulations by the government of Franklin Roosevelt to reverse this tide and win approval for American entry.

American experience with isolation raises important issues for both and contemporary historical interpretation. It offers, first, a fascinating case of continuity and change. Around 1800, when American leaders first sought some separation from European diplomacy, neutrality was a plausible policy, though even then the nation would be drawn into the 1812 war with Britain over Atlantic shipping. By 1939 the same impulse to distance the nation operated in a far more complicated context. Neutrality, which many isolationists urged as world war began anew, assumed that a possible German victory in Europe would not impact the United States. It assumed, further, that Japanese claims in the Pacific could somehow be accommodated, despite extensive American holdings in the region. By 1941, or at least 1945, most Americans had come to agree that the effort at isolation and neutrality had been a mistake. But what were the lessons going forward, as the United States emerged from World War II as the strongest world power? Was there a better path than non-involvement to defend peace, or was peace not a reasonable goal in the first place? In a sense, over 65 years later, the nation is still exploring the issue.

Peace movements outside the West

As before, the continued importance of the West in world affairs, particularly economic and military affairs, made European and United States policies and peace movements particularly prominent in the world at large. As before also, they did not in fact control the whole space. Japan became an active player in various kinds of peace strategies, most notably the disarmament moves, until militarism gained fuller ascendancy. Even beyond this, as various societies gained or sought to gain new space for initiatives outside full imperialist control, peace efforts proved to be a vital part of the process. Indeed, the rise of the new nonviolence movement in India was arguably the most important innovation in the whole field anywhere in the world between the world wars.

The Americas

Various regions made connections with earlier patterns or developed new ones: the revival and adaptation of traditions in several regions was striking. In Central America, for example, five key republics renewed the kinds of efforts that had surfaced in the later nineteenth century, though in this case with even more active United States sponsorship. In 1923 the General Treaty of Peace and Amity was signed, in which the signatories agreed not to recognize any regime imposed by revolution or *coup d'état*. The Treaty responded to civil unrest but also border conflicts between Nicaragua and Honduras. In addition to attempting defense of the political status quo, the Treaty set up a new regional court of justice, to handle disputes, and imposed limits on levels of military forces. The Treaty did not immediately end local tensions, but it did actually help the principal states of Central America maintain surprisingly small armies – by the general standards of the day. This tradition would affect developments after World War II, including the striking decision of Costa Rica, in 1948, to abolish its military altogether.

Peace efforts widened in the Americas during the 1930s. The United States was eager to promote good relations so that the Western hemisphere could stay free of the tensions consuming Europe and East Asia. With one fairly minor exception, the Chaco War, there were indeed no interstate conflicts of note during the whole period. Latin American leadership generated a new Anti-War Treaty of Non-Aggression and Conciliation in 1933, formulated by Carlos Saavedra Lamas in Argentina, a major peace leader during the period. This Saavedra Lamas Treaty, as it was sometimes called, condemned wars of aggressions and required peaceful resolution of disputes. The Treaty was signed by 14 Latin American governments and the United States, and it remained in force until replaced by the Pact of Bogota in 1948.

In 1936 the InterAmerican Conference on War and Peace took place in Buenos Aires, in response to the growing turmoil in Europe. The United States goal of stable relations was matched by Latin American hopes for a firm pledge of nonintervention from the giant neighbor to the north. The Conference emphasized the "common ideals of peace and justice" and their desire for a "purely American system tending towards the preservation of peace, the proscription of war, and the harmonious development" of cultural and economic relations. Full respects for mutual autonomy and independence was assured in principle; conflicts on the "American Continent" should find a "peaceful solution by means established by the Treaties and Conventions now in force." A new Convention for the Maintenance, Preservation and Reestablishment of Peace banned wars of conquest or intervention by one state in the affairs of another, while insisting that all disputes by settled by arbitration. Bolstered by arrangements of this sort, as well as regional power politics, the Americas did stand as a remarkably peaceful region (internal unrest aside) during the whole period and beyond.

Japan

Japan saw new peace activity, beyond government involvement in disarmament until 1936. It participated in some of the international currents of pacifism, including strong socialist interest in promoting peace. But there were distinctive efforts as well. A number of writers supported the League and its principles of peace, while hoping for more equitable treatment of their nation in the international system: a bit of tension was undeniable. Japan was thus urged to join the League but work against European and American imperialism. New peace leaders included retired businessman Shibusawa Eiichi, who set up the Greater Japan Peace Association before World War I, in conjunction with the

Carnegie Endowment for International Peace. A newer Japanese Council of the Institute of Pacific Relations, founded in 1925, supported League activities and served as a think tank devoted to peace, and particularly smoother relations with the United States. Key members, including one mid-1920s Foreign Minister, Shidehara Kijuro (who would be also a post-World War II prime minister), joined the Institute and worked against Japanese intervention in China.

As Japanese militarism increased during the 1930s, a revived current of Buddhist peace advocacy responded. A key early leader was Tsunesaburo Makiguchi, an educator deeply interested in individual and social wellbeing. This interest carried over into international relations, where Makiguchi early on urged the goal of bettering others and selecting paths that combined personal and humanitarian benefits: "it is a conscious effort to create a more harmonious community life." He converted to Buddhism in 1928, along with his colleague Josei Toda, and began to develop a grassroots movement aimed at founding a lasting peace. During World War II, Makiguchi attacked government militarism, and while it is not clear whether he directly opposed the war he was ultimately arrested for his lack of support, along with Toda and 20 other senior leaders of the new Soka Gakkai movement. Makiguchi died in prison in 1944, but Toda would carry on his work after the war, providing new voices for peace not only in Japan but internationally. Other groups developed as well. In 1936 an aeronautical engineer, Shinjo Ito, devoted his life to Buddhism, founding the Shinnyo movement, which derived, however, from a much older Japanese Buddhist tradition. The purpose was to make Buddhist principles available to a wide public, beyond the monastic movement, and to cultivate understanding of how these principles contributed to harmony and peace. Shinjo Ito and his heirs would be more fully associated with peace movements after World War II.

Gandhi

The most striking new ideas came from India, as Mohandas Gandhi, a successful businessman and lawyer, took a leadership role in India's resistance to British rule. Between the early 1920s and early 1940s, Gandhi led three major campaigns, all based on principles of nonviolence and the relationship between personal virtues and public values. Gandhi's effort was a broad one, focused on renewed spirituality – without adopting any single religion, Gandhi took ideas from many faiths (as well as from writers like Henry David Thoreau and Tolstoy) and routinely included Buddhist, Muslim, and Christian practices and rituals along with the primary emphasis on Hinduism. Gandhi struggled not only for Indian independence but for deep reform, including abolition of the caste system. Throughout, the devotion of nonviolence was primary: "We will be nonviolent; we will be truthful; we will be fearless; we will treat people of all religions equally."

Gandhi placed great emphasis on the traditional principle of *ahimsa*, or non-injury, that was so prominent in Hindu and Buddhist approaches to peace. He extended the idea beyond its opposition to killing and inflicting harm, calling for positive efforts to promote the happiness of others:

> In its negative form ahimsa means not injuring any living being whether by body or mind. I may not, therefore, hurt the person or any wrong-doer or bear any ill-will to him and so cause him mental suffering … In its positive form ahimsa means the largest love, the greatest charity. If I am a follower of ahimsa, I must love my enemy or a stranger to me as I would my father or son. This active ahimsa necessarily includes truth and fearlessness.

Between the world wars Gandhi's efforts focused mainly on the Indian situation, but his ideas began to spread more widely, with obvious implications for peace efforts as well as for civil disobedience movements elsewhere. Influence in South Africa reflected Gandhi's original work there, before his return to India. Gandhi's ideas also began to spread to the West.

And Gandhi himself was very conscious of how his ideas and approaches related to global peace. His own words make the connections clear: "I often feel helpless when I see the world in turmoil … [which] leads to grief and sorrow being inflicted on millions of innocent victims by a few who abuse the power of their convictions." "What difference does it make to the dead, the orphans, and the homeless, whether the mad destruction is wrought under the name of totalitarianism or the holy name of liberty and democracy?" "There are many causes that I am prepared to die for but no cause that I am prepared to kill for." Above all, Gandhi's insistence on the union between personal purity and the struggle for peace and justice set a demanding but inspiring standard for many generations to come.

Gandhi was killed, just after India achieved independence in 1947, by a Hindu nationalist who opposed his insistence on tolerance for Muslims – an ironic tribute to the power of his principles. Two days before his death early in 1948, Gandhi commented: "If I am to die by the bullet of a mad man, I must die smiling. There must be no anger within me. God must be in my heart and on my lips."

Munich: Giving peace a bad name?

In the long run, peace ideas and initiatives arising outside the West would have substantial impact, globally as well as in specific regions. As the 1930s ended the most crucial peace issues continued to center on Europe, simply because that was where the greatest danger lay – though the Japanese invasion of China had serious implications as well. It was in Europe, finally, that another complication arose, revealing the extent but also the weakness of the peace sentiment, coloring the balance between peace and war at the time and subsequently.

For the interwar decades drew to a close with a major effort at salvaging peace – but an effort which, in retrospect, seems indefensibly misguided. The focus is on the conference in Munich, in September, 1938, at which the leaders of Britain and France gave in to German demands for seizure of part of Czechoslovakia. Munich, for several generations of Europeans and Americans, would come to mean appeasement of an aggressive dictator – not the attractive city that it is in southern Germany.

Since coming to power in 1933, Hitler had worked steadily to undo the provisions of the Versailles Treaty that had hemmed Germany in and, probably, to prepare for a war that would allow Germany to seize wider stretches of Europe. Against the Treaty provisions, he had rearmed the nation – with no effective response from the Western powers. Earlier in 1938 he had managed to add Austria to Germany's territory. Then, later in the year, he prepared to move on a portion of Czechoslovakia – one of the new nations created by the Treaty, and a successfully functioning democracy – that had a large number of ethnic Germans who, he claimed, were clamoring to unite with the Fatherland.

Both Britain and, particularly, France had commitments to Czechoslovakia, and for a time war seemed inevitable. France, indeed, began to mobilize her army in September (after Czechoslovakia had done the same). But neither Western nation was prepared for war, so their leaders hastily organized a meeting in Munich – in which Italy's fascist leader also participated – where they gave in to Hitler's demand. The French prime minister, Edouard Daladier, hated the result, but he could not act without British support, and the British prime minister, Neville Chamberlain, was ecstatic, even staying an extra day in Munich to sign a one-page document that, he believed, assured peace between Germany and Britain. Hitler indeed made noises about consulting Britain in future, and working to iron out differences, without establishing any precise mechanisms.

The day after the Munich agreement German troops annexed the targeted part of Czechoslovakia, and then the following March took over the whole country. Again, no nation moved to oppose the aggression. Just a few months after that Germany invaded Poland and this, finally, roused Britain and France to declare war. Munich, obviously, had solved nothing, except to convince Hitler that he could make further moves with impunity. The agreement stands as a case study of unsuccessful appeasement.

Unfortunately, Chamberlain compounded the drama by returning to Britain and claiming that he had won "peace with honour" and indeed had rescued "peace in our time." The actual result, so soon leading to the destruction of an independent nation, made a mockery of these peace claims, compounding the ultimate belief that Munich provided one of history's really clear lessons: don't try to satisfy an aggressor through half measures, because this will simply provoke more aggression.

What is often forgotten is that it was not only Chamberlain who reacted oddly. The British public, in its majority, did too. Chamberlain was greeted with massive public gratitude and cheering crowds. The respected Manchester *Guardian*, though pointing out weaknesses in the agreement, gushed that the peacemakers:

have done something that has hardly ever happened before in history – the snatching of the world at the eleventh hour from a universal calamity, from a return to barbarism, from untold cruelty and misery ... The instinct of the peoples today to praise (even to the pitches of extravagance) the peace-makers is sound ... for however much civilization has seemed to slip back in the last few years, it is shown that peace is still the greatest hope in the hearts of men.

Clearly, the Munich accord tapped the deep belief in peace and probably the even more widespread desire to bypass war that had spread so widely during the interwar decades.

In the process the whole episode gave this kind of peace a bad name. Not only West European leaders, but also American politicians once the nation pulled away from isolationism, long believed that Munich provided an object lesson in what not to do. For decades after World War II, when Americans dealt with the Soviet Union during the Cold War, or even Middle Eastern opponents after 1990, the lesson of Munich was squarely before them, seeming to prove that military preparedness, not compromise, was the only way to go. Ultimately, Munich provides a test case in how to learn, but also possibly how not to learn, from history, for there is always the danger of becoming trapped by a historical analogy and losing flexibility in the process. Here, certainly, was a final legacy, a final complexity, in what the interwar period bequeathed to peacemakers for the future.

* * * * *

Viewed in retrospect, the 1920s and 1930s can play out as a classic tragic drama. Probably no two decades in world history had seen so much energy and idealism poured into peace initiatives. But another war ensued, even worse than the previous one in terms of global scope, death and devastation. Clearly, peace advocates still had not devised a strategy that could overcome governments that were willing to risk war.

So what were the lessons? Observers at the time and since have ventured various answers. What kinds of compromise make sense for peace? Arguably, more than the warring states had ventured during World War I, when opportunities for negotiation were deliberately shunned in favor of total victory – creating deep-seated ensuing resentments as a result. But arguably less than Munich – when pathetic compromise simply encouraged an aggressive state to take the next step. Where then is a middle ground? And another question from the period: how can fatigue with war be compared to more positive and energetic peace goals? Ultimately, for all the effort, the interwar period was defined more by avoidance than by bold steps for peace – though there were some new policies and ideas that ought surely to be preserved. But how could world society do better in future? The interwar period in this sense posed a stark and urgent question for the future.

Further reading

Catfield, Charles. "Peace as a Reform Movement." *OAH Magazine of History* 8.3 (1994): 10–14.

Degen, M. *The History of the Woman's Peace Party*. Baltimore, MD: Johns Hopkins University Press, 1939.

Farber, Dave. *Munich, 1938: Appeasement and World War II*. New York: Simon & Schuster, 2008.

Hoshchild, Adam. *To End All Wars: A Story of Loyalty and Rebellion, 1914–1918*. New York: Houghton Mifflin, 2011.

Moorhead, Caroline. *Troublesome People: Enemies of War, 1916–86*. London: Hamish Hamilton, 1987.

On pacifism

Barry, Gearoid. "'The Crusade of Youth': Pacifism and the Militarization of Youth Culture in Marc Sangnier's Peace Congresses, 1923–1932." In Neiberg, Michael S. and Jennifer D. Keene, eds., *Finding Common Ground: New Directions in First World War Studies*. Leiden: Brill, 2011, pp. 39–66.

Brock, P. and N. Young. *Pacifism in the Twentieth Century*. Syracuse, NY: Syracuse University Press, 1999.

Costin, Lela B. "Feminism, Pacifism, Internationalism and the 1915 International Congress of Women." *Women's Studies International Forum* 5.3/4 (1982): 310–15.

Howlett, Charles F., and Ian M. Harris. *Books, Not Bombs: Teaching Peace since the Dawn of the Republic*. Charlotte, NC: Information Age Publishing, 2010.

McCarthy, Helen. "Parties, Voluntary Associations, and Democratic Politics in Interwar Britain." *The Historical Journal* 50.4 (2007): 891–912.

Mock, Melanie Springer. *Writing Peace: The Unheard Voices of Great War Mennonite Objectors*. Telford, PA: Cascadia Publishing House, 2003.

Wittner, L. *Rebels against War: The American Peace Movement, 1933–1983*. Philadelphia, PA: Temple University Press, 1984.

On Japan

Akami, Tomoko. *Internationalizing the Pacific: The United States, Japan and the Institute of the Pacific Relations in War and Peace, 1919–1945*. London: Routledge, 2003.

Murata, Kiyoaki. *Japan's New Buddhism: An Objective Account of Soka Gakkai*. New York and Tokyo: Weatherhill, 1969.

Nish, Ian Hill. *Japanese Foreign Policy in the Interwar Period*. Westport, CT: Praeger, 2002.

On Gandhi

Docker, John and Debjani Ganguly. *Rethinking Gandhi and Nonviolent Relationality: Global Perspectives*. London: Routledge, 2007.

Fleischman, Paul R. and William Radice. *Cultivating Inner Peace: Exploring the Psychology, Wisdom and Poetry of Gandhi, Thoreau the Buddha, and Others*. Chicago, IL: Pariyatti Publishing, 2004.

On disarmament

Davies, Thomas Richard. *The Possibilities of Transnational Activism: The Campaign for Disarmament between the Two World Wars*. Leiden: Martinus Nijhoff Publishers, 2007.

Goldman, Emily O. *Sunken Treaties: Naval Arms Control between the Wars*. College Park, PA: Pennsylvania State University Press, 1994.

Goldstein, Erik. *The Washington Conference, 1921–22: Naval Rivalry, East Asian Stability and the Road to Pearl Harbor*. London: Frank Cass, 1994.

Kaufman, Robert Gordon. *Arms Control during the Prenuclear Era: The United States and Naval Limitation between the Two World Wars*. New York: Columbia University Press, 1990.

Kitching, Carolyn J. *Britain and the Problem of International Disarmament, 1919–1934*. London: Routledge, 1999.

McKercher, B. J. C. *Arms Limitation and Disarmament: Restraints on War, 1899–1939*. Westport, CT: Praeger, 1992.

On the League of Nations

Cooper, John Milton, Jr. *Breaking the Heart of the World: Woodrow Wilson and the Fight for the League of Nations*. Cambridge: Cambridge University Press, 2001.

Clavin, Patricia. *Securing the World Economy: The Reinvention of the League of Nations, 1920–1946*. Oxford: Oxford University Press, 2013.

Henig, Ruth. *The League of Nations: The Makers of the Modern World*. London: Haus Publishing Limited, 2010.

Housden, Martyn. *The League of Nations and the Organization of Peace*. Seminar Studies in History. New York: Routledge, 2011.

8 Peace in contemporary world history

A glance at world history during the past 70 years, since the end of World War II, shows an abundance of bad news. On the heels of the twentieth century's second major hot war came decades of Cold War struggles between the United States and the Soviet Union and their respective allies. This in turn brought several regional clashes, for example in Korea and Vietnam, and a relentless expansion of dangerous weaponry not only for the major protagonists but for many other states whose militaries were wooed by the great powers. Even aside from this core struggle, additional regional conflicts abounded, both before and after the Cold War ended: the Middle East featured several major wars involving Israel and then a brutal conflict between Iran and Iraq; many parts of sub-Saharan Africa became war zones; recurring violence simmers between India and Pakistan. And the list can go on.

Armaments levels drove up relentlessly. Most new states, formed as decolonization movements beat back Western imperialist control, assumed that they needed strong militaries and sought to purchase advanced weaponry. Nationhood and some military strength seemed indissolubly linked. United States commitment to steady advances in levels and lethality of weapons persisted, after the briefest lull following World War II: by 2013 the nation was spending over 40 percent of the world's military total, or more than the next 15 countries combined. This set a standard of power that could easily influence others. The advent of nuclear weaponry, from the end of World War II onward, added an ominous new element to the weapons race, with first Russia, then two other European countries, then China, India, North Korea, and Pakistan joining the "nuclear club" in ensuing decades, with capacity emerging also in Israel, Iran, and possibly elsewhere.

Yet, with all this, in part because of all this, there continued to be a vigorous history of peace, now on literally a global basis. Peace efforts resumed strongly as World War II drew to a close, with active efforts to benefit from the ideas and experiences of the interwar period but also to repair their obvious limitations. Nuclear weaponry quickly inspired efforts at control, and while they did not succeed in fully taming the beast, they did not entirely fail. New countries and individuals emerged to develop additional leadership in peace efforts – now including Germany and Japan. Key regions that had for so long served as hotbeds of militarism actually became peaceful – a huge step – with most of Europe acting as the poster child example. Peace ideas, in many countries, were now supported by new kinds of research, in areas like conflict analysis. On another front, the decline of imperialism and the rise of new nations from Africa to Southeast Asia, while unquestionably producing new possibilities for local conflict over borders or ethnic divisions, may also have removed an important spur to violence, while giving new voices for peace. It was no accident, for example, that India, once independent, ultimately established a Gandhi Peace Prize as one of its contributions to new relationships around the world. Finally, other general developments, including new commitments to democracy but also possibly the rise of consumerism, had potential bearing on peace results as well.

The obvious fact was that, despite all sorts of threats, the worst kind of war that could have occurred, after World War II, has not occurred. This is no guarantee for the future, and it involves a number of factors besides intentional peace movements – but the movements have been involved. More precisely still, there was some evidence, by the first decade of the twenty-first century, that collective violence in general was declining worldwide, and again intentional activities, by peacekeeping bodies, volunteer groups, plus public opinion more widely, had something to do with this new pattern.

Peace has not triumphed. It cannot yet compete with violence for headlines. But the unfolding of peace interests over the past several decades – building clearly on precedents not just from the interwar period but from older religious and philosophical traditions – is an important part of the contemporary story. In this chapter we look at the most formal peace institutions and policies, on an international scale – including of course the United Nations and its contrasts and connections to the earlier experience of the League. We also more briefly explore some larger shifts in the global framework that may have a bearing on peace, though in ways that are harder to assess than is the case with formal policy initiatives. The unifying thread here involves changes in the international context for peace, in policy but also public and political environments. The following chapter then examines regional patterns, including the striking innovation of outright demilitarization. Then we turn to peace ideas, movements, and scholarship where again the trends pick up on earlier experiences but add significant innovation.

Advancing a new (and improved?) global framework

Various moves after World War II sought to improve opportunities for peace, often seeking explicitly to address problems that had emerged in the wake of World War I. Developments were long skewed by the rapid emergence of the Cold War. Rivalries between the Western and Soviet blocs even prevented a grand peace conference, in the style of Vienna or Versailles. Settlements with Germany and Japan emerged piecemeal. This unsystematic approach may have had some unexpected advantages. Many Allied powers, for example, were eager to punish Germany, and indeed the country was divided into occupation zones among France, Britain, the United States, and the Soviets, and the capital city of Berlin was split as well. But the punitive approach soon gave way to attempts to use Germany as a player in the Cold War. The Russians allied with partners in East Germany (the German Democratic Republic), while the Western nations helped to rebuild West Germany (the Federal Republic). Thus German resentment, a key problem after World War I, was at least substantially diverted, and a balance of power approach reemerged. Germany remained tense for many years, divided as it was (until 1990 and the Cold War's end) between Soviet and Western alliances, and war threatened at several points. But it never came, as both sides realized the potential costs of outright conflict and exercised a perhaps surprising amount of self-restraint.

New approaches to peace more generally were certainly colored by the Cold War. We will see in several domains a more hesitant approach before 1990, as bitter superpower rivalry complicated the possibility of international agreement, and patterns in the more recent past half-century. Nevertheless, even during the Cold War substantial innovations occurred, and many of them set a clear framework for the acceleration of effort after this conflict ended.

War crimes

The idea of war crimes followed very loosely from classic debates about just versus unjust wars – but the idea of actively punishing the perpetrators of unjust wars, beyond sheer defeat, was obviously more novel. The Geneva Conventions of the late nineteenth century set a context in which some individuals could be accused of violating standards, for example in the treatment of prisoners of war. After World War I the new German government did in fact try a few army officers for war crimes.

But it was in the wake of World War II, and the fairly obvious aggressions by Nazi Germany and by the military regime in Japan, that the idea of international trials for war criminals came into its own. In Germany, the victorious powers in 1945 cited the Geneva Convention but also other international codes dating back to the early twentieth century as the basis for charging various leaders with fomenting war, mistreating civilians and prisoners and attempting to exterminate various ethnic and religious groups. An international panel heard the German cases in Nuremberg, beginning in late 1945. A key conclusion was that planning or instigating a war of aggression was a crime under international law. Several whole leadership groups were declared criminal, and punished. A separate trial opened in Tokyo in 1946, again under international auspices. Several Japanese officials were executed, particularly for severe mistreatment of prisoners of war.

The approach was controversial. Cold War politics caused both sides to exempt some German scientists from war crimes prosecution, so that their knowledge could be deployed for weapons development in the new conflict. No one from the Allied countries was brought to trial, despite massive bombings of civilian targets. An Indian jurist, serving in the Tokyo trial, actually withdrew on these grounds – the procedures were too inequitable, smacking too much merely of revenge.

But the idea of war crimes, and their prosecution as a means of deterring bad behavior in the future, did not die. Geneva Conventions were reaffirmed and expanded in 1946. Then a new agreement, in 1977, focused on further protections for civilian populations during wartime. Special reference was made to women and children, and military actions against infrastructure – such as food or water supplies – that might affect civilians were now regulated in principle. Many countries signed these new agreements, but there were notable abstentions (even to the present day), including India and the United States.

Then in the 1990s, with the Cold War over and attention focused on new regional disputes and some massive atrocities against civilian ethnic groups, the war crimes prosecutions resumed. The United Nations set up special courts to try war criminals in the bitter conflicts that had accompanied the dissolution of Yugoslavia, in the Balkans, and also the perpetrators of genocide in Rwanda. The United Nations also began exploring methods to prevent individual countries from protecting war criminals.

The most sweeping new measure was the establishment of a new International Criminal Court, in 2002. The goal was a permanent tribunal to prosecute individuals for war crimes and other crimes against humanity. The Court was also to have jurisdiction over crimes of aggressions (though this category was not to come into play until 2017). Within a decade 119 countries had signed onto this process, including most of Europe and all of Latin America, half of the nations of Africa – though some key nations, headed by the United States, held out against this kind of international oversight. In its early stages the Court actively sought opportunities to bring accused war criminals, from several regions, to trial.

As with the Geneva Conventions earlier, the war crimes approach had complicated implications for peace. The approach did not seek to ban war, though the extension of efforts to criminalize aggression potentially moved in that direction. No great-power leader was brought to trial, though many in the international community believed that the policies of some American leaders, in invading Iraq in 2003, were at least potentially actionable. It was not clear that potential international sanctions actually deterred violence, for example in attacks on civilians, in areas of great tension in Africa or elsewhere: the worst offenders seemed to ignore the possibility of punishment. Still, the attempt to introduce international regulation and criminal procedures in the interest of limiting behavior in war was an interesting contemporary response, a clear sign of a willingness to innovate.

The United Nations and peacekeeping

Discussion of a new United Nations began fairly early in World War II. An international declaration, by the Allied powers, proclaimed as early as

January, 1942, the intent to form this new organization, with the goal of providing a more reliable system for global security; Britain and the United States had referred to the plan the year before. American President Franklin Roosevelt made the expectations clear in his 1942 State of the Union address: "We of the United Nations are not making all this sacrifice of human effort and human lives to return to the kind of world we had after the last world war. We are fighting today for security, for progress, and for peace, not only for ourselves but for all men." Conferences including not only Britain but also the Soviet Union, during the later stages of the war, confirmed the plans.

Wartime leaders deliberately intended the new organization to differ from the old League, particularly when it came to promoting peace, and the differences applied both to framework and structure. In terms of framework, the United Nations immediately stood apart because of the full, and initially enthusiastic, participation of the United States. Non-Western nations were also more clearly represented, and over time, with decolonization and the creation of many new nations, this representative quality only increased.

Structurally, the big issues involved creating the ability to act against aggression, in contrast to the League's endemic paralysis. The United Nations from the outset included a 15-member Security Council, which was in turn meant to bear particular responsibility for keeping the peace. "The Security Council shall determine the existence of any threat to the peace, breach of the peace, or act of aggression and shall make recommendations, or decide what measures shall be taken … to maintain or restore international peace and security." Security Council members were always available, in contrast to the situation with the League when international crises often arose when it was not in session. Also in contrast to the past, the United Nations did not require a unanimous vote for action. The Security Council had the power to investigate any situation threatening international peace; recommending procedures for peaceful dispute resolution; calling upon other member nations to impose economic, communications and/or diplomatic sanctions on an aggressor state; and – in a clear departure from the inconclusive interwar debate on this subject, enforcing its decisions militarily or by any means necessary.

Even with all the innovation, compromise was still essential. The UN founders agreed that there should be five permanent members of the Security Council – the United States, Britain, France, China, and the Soviet Union; and any one of these members could veto a Council resolution. The great powers still did not want to accept dictation by a majority of all member governments, and of course the permanent membership list was also biased toward the West. Use of veto power significantly hampered UN ability to handle Cold War issues, since either the US or the Soviets stood ready to defend particular national issues. And it also affected other policy areas, such as the approach to Israeli-Arab relations, with the United States frequently employing its veto on behalf of Israel.

Still, it early became clear that the new United Nations was not simply different on paper; it was really prepared to act in certain circumstances. Between

1948 and 2013, the United Nations would undertake 68 peacekeeping missions (with 15 still in effect in 2013). Several hundred thousand troops from member nations served in these operations, with 3,116 casualties during the whole period 1948–2013. Over time, the United Nations clarified its procedures for military action, seeking to improve its command structures and reducing the amount of time any given force would serve.

The process began in 1948, though cautiously. The United Nations Truce Supervision Organization (UNSTO) was the first peacekeeping venture, in which unarmed military observers went to Palestine to supervise a UN-brokered settlement between Israel and its Arab neighbors (Egypt, Syria, Jordan, and Lebanon). Over time, UNSTO would monitor a number of ceasefires, after renewed wars (1956, 1967, 1973), as it became the UN's longest-running mission, observing and investigating border clashes or other violations. Then in 1949 a similar observer group was sent to monitor border relations between India and Pakistan, in the disputed Kashmir region; this group, also, continues to operate.

During the 1950s, when UN operations overall were deeply affected by the United States-Soviet conflict, a major effort did respond to French and British attack on Egypt after the Egyptian seizure of control over the Suez Canal. While the Security Council could not act because of the veto provision, the General Assembly urged military withdrawal and, back by US and Soviet pressure, the European nations did pull back. During the 1960s the UN sent a mission to oversee the withdrawal of Belgian forces from the Congo and to seek to restore order in that former colony; ultimately, 20,000 personnel were involved. This was the first instance in which actual military force was used – to end the secession of one province – as opposed to more general peacekeeping.

New interventions greeted renewal of hostilities between Israel and Egypt, in 1973, with the ultimate creation of a larger buffer zone under UN control. Another mission intervened in fighting in Cyprus between Greek and Turkish Cypriote communities, with a ceasefire also involving brokered negotiations with Greece and Turkey. The project explicitly referred to "preserving international peace and security." Again, this mission continues to operate in maintaining a buffer zone. Another UN force went to Lebanon in 1978, to promote the withdrawal of an invading Israeli force. Military action was not involved, even as the UN encouraged an "immediate end" to hostilities; the project highlighted observation and humanitarian aid. The UN peacekeeping operations won a Nobel Peace Prize in 1988, as the organization consistently worked to reduce armed conflict and maintain appropriate neutrality between contending parties.

Peacekeeping efforts greatly accelerated in the early 1990s, as Cold War barriers to action disappeared. With this came increased reliance on the dispatch of actual military forces, rather than mere observer groups. Between 1988 and 1993 13 new operations were launched; in 1992 the number of deployed military and police personnel rose from 11,000 to 52,000. Costs rose to $2.8 billion per year, and deaths of UN personnel also increased. This was a period of great expectations, as the UN was seen as a vital contributor to a new and more peaceful world order. During the 1990s as a whole, 120 member nations contributed troops, police and/or observers, with an average of 76 participating each year – an unprecedented global commitment to peace efforts.

In the process, the UN also became increasingly involved not just in classic confrontations between states, but in internal civil wars. It became harder to assure that the belligerent parties had consented to the operation, which increased both danger and risk of failure. UN forces were often, still, involved in trying to monitor ceasefire agreements, but with less assurance that all the parties would abide by the settlement.

A major operation involved Somalia, in 1992, where the UN and the Organization of African Unity tried to broker a peace in a bitter civil war. Humanitarian aid figured prominently, but the UN also mounted a force made up of contingents from 24 countries to secure relief centers militarily, so that aid could be distributed. The organization also sought to arrange a peace, among 14 different internal political movements, and then for two years (until the force was withdrawn in 1995) tried to assure law and order.

More substantial effort still went to former Yugoslavia, where a number of regions split off amid mutual hostility. A mission went to Bosnia and Herzegovina in 1995, with the goal of reconstituting police activities, after a peace agreement, with particular attention to reducing internal ethnic violence. The mission continued to operate until 2002, when its duties were taken over by a European Union police group. Also in 1995 the UN sent a unit to various parts of the Balkans in a preventive capacity, trying to inhibit violence before it started. The idea of a preventive military force came from the former leader of the Soviet Union, Mikhail Gorbachev. In this specific case, the goal was to observe conflicts on the borders of new states, like Macedonia, that might undermine stability in the region. By the end of 1995 the UN had set up 24 permanent observation posts on the Macedonia-Yugoslav border, with 40 patrols daily. Overall, the most ambitious UN efforts to maintain or restore peace in this troubled region were not successful. Only a United States–European force, called the "coalition of the willing," managed to curb aggression from Serbia, with substantial use of air power. The UN's peacekeeping reputation suffered greatly from its failure, and activities slowed down in consequence for several years.

Several more recent activities were arguably more carefully planned, and faced less substantial local obstacles. A 1998 mission to Sierra Leone, in Africa, became one of the largest ever, with 17,000 troops at its height, ending a civil war and restoring substantial peace. The mission was concluded seven years later. In 1999 another major effort attempted to enforce a cease fire in Congo, among six Border States. The effort enjoyed partial success, though violence in several parts of the Congo continued.

By 2013, 15 UN peacekeeping operations were in effect, with over 109,000 personnel. The range of peacekeeping has obviously expanded, to embrace additional regions but also to include a broader definition of peace, involving internal strife as well as more classic wars or potential wars. Greatest growth of activity has focused on implementing a settlement (either between states, or among contestants in civil strife) agreed upon by the parties involved. This can include not only enforcement of a ceasefire, but also humanitarian efforts, destruction of local weapons, and training of new police or military units. Discussions of peace efforts by UN officials have also expanded, for example to include the idea of intervention before the escalation of conflict. This kind of interest, for example, supported an "Agenda for Peace" initiative in 1992. Peace consolidation, correspondingly, has broadened to include not only preventing new violence but also assisting in creating a functioning administration and police force.

Obviously, currently as in the recent past, UN efforts have had mixed results. The most blatant limitation has involved conflict situations where the UN simply could not gain effective entry. UN observer missions to Syria, during the bitter civil war that raged from 2012 onward, were uniformly denied effective access and did no real good as the fighting raged on. Assessment of the UN role in reducing overall levels of collective violence in recent years, correspondingly, remains controversial.

It is also important to note the UN efforts have frequently combined with or encouraged other coalitions on behalf of peace. While the UN itself failed in the Balkans, its activities brought attention to the region and served as a prelude to the "coalition of the willing." UN collaboration with the Organization for African Unity has also been significant on a number of occasions.

The "international community" also continued to try to improve the framework for peace: the effort remained a work in progress, particularly as conventional wars declined and attention turned to regional civil strife. In the wake of the failure to stop bloodshed in places in Rwanda in the 1990s, a doctrine called "responsibility to protect" (R2P) gained new attention. The idea was sanctioned by a meeting of United Nations member states in a "world summit" in 2005. The argument here was that governments should protect their citizens against collective violence – directed for example at particular religious or ethnic groups – but that if they fail the international community has a responsibility to step in militarily – though only if authorized by the Security Council. The doctrine worked well in spurring international observer teams for political hotspots such as the new nation of South Sudan; groups from China, Norway, the Arab League, the African Union, Russia, and the United States fanned out, with Security Council backing, to monitor conditions, successfully preventing violence. But the new concept had its own limits: public opinion in many countries might shy away from the risk and expense of contributing to international efforts, and vetoes in the Security Council could also restrict the capacity to respond.

Finally, for all the mixed record, it is important to remember how unprecedented this kind of international action is – long discussed, as part of peace ideas and proposals, but never before undertaken. Impressive as well has been the willingness of so many states, on various occasions, to contribute troops and financial support on behalf of peace, often in regions in distant parts of the globe. Membership in the United Nations was supposed to include agreement to supply military forces, but the commitment was arguably observed far more often than might have been expected. Motivations for participation vary. Some countries, like Canada, that have sent many troops may be seeking greater international prestige on the strength of a special peace role; others, like Pakistan (one of the largest sources over time) may benefit from financial support and training opportunities for otherwise overextended military forces. Motives, in other words, vary. And the biggest countries, like the United States, have less frequently been involved, partly because of distaste for serving under an international commander; partly because many regions would fear unacceptable levels of big-power interference. Overall, for all the complexity, the fact is that many countries, of various types, have been willing to pitch in, and their genuine interest in enhancing peace must not be discounted.

The International Court

In 1945–46, The United Nations replaced the old Permanent Court of International Justice with a new International Court of Justice, though the basic mandate remained much the same. The idea, still, was to have an international unit available to help with dispute settlement, to prevent the intensification of conflicts that might, down the line, burst into violence. Members of the Court are now selected by the UN and the Security Council. As before, submission of disputes depends on the willingness of the parties involved, and this can vary greatly. Many treaties, among different nations, now contain a clause specifically providing for conflict resolution by the Court, though increasingly many treaties set up their own arbitration procedures. By 2011, 66 countries had accepted the Court's jurisdiction automatically in certain types of cases, though of the major powers only Britain had agreed to this approach. To encourage submission of cases, the Court can add a judge from a contending country, along with its usual staff.

Willingness to use the Court varied as well. In the initial decades after World War II, industrial nations were the main participants – for example, the United States and Canada, in an effort to settle a disagreement over their mutual maritime boundary in the Atlantic. With time, however, developing countries have shown increasing confidence in the Court as a mechanism for dispute resolution. In the mid-1980s the Court ruled that the United States had violated international law in a covert war in Nicaragua. This antagonized the US, which withdrew from compulsory arbitration in 1986, but it emboldened some other nations. (The US also used its Security Council veto power to prevent enforcement of the Nicaragua decision, which had ordered payment of reparations.) Overall, the number of cases handled by the Court has not been massive, and some of its judgments have not been accepted by one of the parties involved. In principle, the UN Charter calls for Security Council enforcement of decisions, but this has not usually occurred. Still, a number of conflicts, particularly between adjacent countries like Tunisia and Libya, or Greece and Macedonia, have been adjudicated with at least some success. Clearly, the Court continues to serve a recurrent supporting function in the organizational structures available to promote peace.

New efforts to limit weaponry

The idea of limiting armaments through international treaties was obviously not new, given the important precedents set in the 1920s. A need for renewed effort, however, became increasingly apparent, particularly as Cold War rivalries pushed the level of weaponry up steadily, particularly in the United States and the Soviet Union, but also in a number of allies.

The focus now was on nuclear weaponry and associated missiles and other delivery systems, not on naval forces. The United States briefly maintained exclusive nuclear capacity, after dropping two bombs on Japan in the final phases of World War II. In a crucial if probably inevitable decision, it declined to abandon its nuclear capacity or to place it under international supervision, in the immediate postwar era. Soon the Soviet Union joined the United States in the world's "nuclear club," and during the Cold War decades both societies built a capacity to destroy each other, and the rest of the world, several times over. Britain, France, China, India, North Korea and Pakistan developed nuclear weapons in ensuing decades.

A number of groups and individuals spoke out against nuclear weapons soon after World War II ended. These included established peace organizations and older communities, such as the Quakers in the United States. Public opinion in a number of Latin American countries, such as Venezuela, reflected growing fears about the potential for a new and now nuclear world war, as the early stages of the Cold War unfolded. Asian opinion was also roused, with leaders like India's first prime minister, Jawaharlal Nehru, speaking out explicitly against atomic weapons. Opinion in Japan, understandably, quickly mobilized, with the credentials of having alone experienced nuclear attack. By 1948 large anti-nuclear demonstrations were occurring in places like Norway, seemingly remote from direct involvement with the new arms race. Communist parties, spurred by Soviet leadership bent on constraining the United States, also promoted anti-nuclear agitation. Obviously, how much all of this reflected an interest in peace, as opposed to a more specific set of fears, was not entirely clear; but the result was a surge of global activity of substantial dimensions.

Nuclear testing

Conferences to address the nuclear threat first focused on weapons testing. Experimenting with weapons obviously contributed to the arms race, but also spread dangerous chemicals in the atmosphere.

By the mid-1950s a good bit of the global concern about the nuclear threat coalesced around opposition to nuclear testing. A 1954 American atomic test in the Marshall Islands, in the Pacific, scattered radioactive fallout on a Japanese fishing vessel, killing one crew member and hospitalizing many – a new focus for global outrage. Again, scientists in many countries, including some experts in the Soviet Union, and various Christian groups mobilized increasingly. By this point 86 percent of the Japanese public disapproved of American tests, and massive meetings occurred along with new organizations like Gensuikyio, the Japanese Council Against Atomic and Hydrogen Bombs. Buddhist groups chimed in, reflecting earlier religious traditions along with contemporary concerns. Large anti-testing movements also developed in Australia and New Zealand, concerned about the use of Pacific Ocean sites for testing. An Australian leader spoke of the "absurd risks" of testing and the spread of weaponry, arguing that people either "reach the point of self-destruction or organize for peace." By this point, the French were also testing weapons in the Sahara, which roused protests in Egypt. Many women's organizations and youth groups raised their voices in Europe and the United States, speaking particularly on behalf of public health; and explicit anti-nuclear organizations formed in a number of countries. Marches and petitions added to the pressure, and in the early 1960s a new International Confederation for Disarmament and Peace sought to provide some loose coordination to the various organizations involved. Several countries, including Japan but also Sweden, specifically renounced the possibility of ever acquiring nuclear weapons.

The United States held out against the pressure for some time, arguing often that the whole test ban movement was a communist plot to weaken the American military. But ultimately the chorus was irresistible: President Dwight Eisenhower, in 1958, noted the power of world opinion to "oblige the United States to follow certain lines of policy." That was the year in which the government declared a moratorium on testing, followed in 1963 with an explicit test ban treaty with the Soviet Union. This step, ending above-ground testing for good (as the newer nuclear powers carefully developed underground facilities for their own programs), was the first move in an effort to control the new weapons risk. With this, however, organized public opinion trailed off, as the most visible threat receded.

Attempts to control the nuclear option

Disarmament discussions did not end with the test ban, and a variety of players and policies continued to be involved, also representing many different parts of the world. A number of scientists, on both sides of the Cold War divide, voiced growing concern about the dangers of continued nuclear competition. In the mid-1950s a group of American scientists, including Albert Einstein, urged new restraint:

> We have to learn to think in a new way. We have to learn to ask ourselves, not what steps can be taken to give military victory to whatever group we prefer, for there no longer are such steps; the question we have to ask ourselves is: what steps can be taken to prevent a military contest of which

the issue must be disastrous to all parties." In 1957, following up, an initial conference of scientists from many countries occurred in Pugwash, in eastern Canada, launching a series of Pugwash conferences that spurred new and more far reaching negotiations to limit nuclear weaponry. Scientists in this spirit began urging a full renunciation of force; the American Linus Pauling argued that nuclear weapons require that "war be given up, for all time. The forces that can destroy the world must not be used.

A number of petitions were presented to the United Nations, and larger popular anti-nuclear movements formed.

The Soviet Union and the United States, actively building up their nuclear arsenals, also began to compete in putting forward arms control proposals, partly because of a genuine fear that competition could lead to outright conflict, partly to woo undecided elements of world opinion. Soviet Premier Nikita Khrushchev, in 1959, filed a proposal for "General and Complete Disarmament" at the United Nations. President Kennedy spoke at the UN as well, stating that "Mankind must put an end to war, or war will put an end to mankind." The U.S. Department of State formed a new Disarmament Administration, which worked with its Soviet counterpart to establish principles for actual discussion, though recurrent tensions, including a crisis over Soviet missiles in Cuba, delayed negotiations beyond the test ban agreements. The United Nations General Assembly passed a resolution against nuclear weapons in 1961, though no enforcement was possible.

By the 1960s, more systematic efforts to curb nuclear weapons began to move out in three closely related directions. First was an intriguing attempt to limit the number of nations that had any direct access to the weapons. The second approach involved wider regional commitments to shun nuclear weapons, either directly or through arrangements with any of the nuclear great powers. And third, the leading nuclear powers agreed to limit or even cut back their arsenals.

The idea of controlling nuclear weapons proliferation centered on a belief that having too many nuclear states would magnify the risks of actual utilization, through possible miscalculation, unauthorized use, or escalation of regional tensions. The idea of a non-proliferation treaty was launched in 1958, by the Irish foreign minister Frank Aiken. An actual treaty was opened for signature in 1968, with Finland the first state to sign. Other countries gradually joined in, including several major Arab states in 1988–89. Then acceptance became almost universal after the end of the Cold War and of South African apartheid. In 1992 France and China accepted the treaty, the final agreed-upon nuclear powers to do so. In 1995 the treaty itself was extended indefinitely. Argentina and Brazil joined in 1995 and 1998, respectively, and Cuba, and final non-nuclear power to hold out, agreed in 2002.

The treaty had three major premises. First, obviously, was the commitment by most of the world's nations not to pursue a nuclear weapons program, with only five nations – the Security Council permanent members, the United

States, Russia, China, France, and Britain – allowed to maintain an arsenal. The hope was that these nations would not attack each other, because retaliation would be so dreadful: the doctrine here was called Mutually Assured Destruction, or MAD. Second, the nuclear states themselves agreed to work on arms limitation. And third, the nuclear states promised to help others in developing peaceful uses of nuclear energy. An inspection operation was established by the United Nations to monitor the terms of the treaty, and particularly to help distinguish between energy development and weapons.

There were some precedents for this kind of arrangement, particularly in the interwar naval treaties that had recognized inequalities among nations in the numbers of warships that were allowed. Still, the acceptance of these commitments and international monitoring reflected the unprecedented concern about the nuclear potential. As the world had never before developed such dangerous weapons, so it had never before so widely agreed to keep them under control.

The effort had several flaws. A few nations simply did not sign on, and developed internationally unauthorized nuclear programs: this included India, Pakistan and probably Israel (which refuses to release information about its nuclear efforts). With United States help, India's program gained greater international recognition after 2008, though several nations expressed active concern about this kind of precedent for expansion. North Korea signed the treaty but by the later 1990s proceeded to develop weapons anyway, and then renounced its treaty participation in 2003. Huge disagreements surfaced early in the twenty-first century about Iran's nuclear program, which the nation claimed was directed toward energy use but amid many doubts and a clear Iranian reluctance to allow international monitoring.

There were also violations or possible violations by the "agreed" nuclear nations themselves. China may have provided nuclear information to Pakistan, which was illegal under the treaty. The United States kept nuclear weapons in Turkey and in several West European countries, via secret agreements in the North Atlantic Treaty Organization (NATO), which was initially formed as the basic Western Cold War alliance. The United States government claimed that, since the weapons remained under its control, this was not a treaty violation, but there were many concerns about regional use.

But the treaty, and the sentiments behind it, had real impact. A number of governments, that could fairly easily have mounted weapons programs, did not do so. South Africa became the only country actually to dismantle an existing program, in the 1990s. Central Asian and East European republics, formed after the collapse of the Soviet Union but in which many Soviet nuclear installations had been located, signed the Non-Proliferation Treaty in 1993, and transferred or destroyed most of the weapons in their territory – with assistance from the United States and Russia.

Regional arrangements were important as well, and sometimes preceded national adhesion to the larger non-proliferation effort. This was the second step toward greater control. An Antarctic Treaty in 1959 was the first regional accord. A Treaty in 1967 (the Tlatelolco Treaty) created an Agency for the

Prohibition of Nuclear Weapons in Latin America and the Caribbean; here too, Cuba was the last state to join in, in 2002. In 1971 a new Association of Southeast Asian Nations (ASEAN) formed, declaring the region a zone of peace and explicitly committing to freedom from nuclear weapons development. In 1996 most African nations signed a Treaty for the Nuclear Weapons Free Zone in Africa (the Pelindaba Treaty), setting up the Commission on Nuclear Energy of the Organization of African States as the enforcement agency. A wider Southeast Asian treaty (the Bangkok Treaty) was signed in 1995. A South Pacific nuclear-free zone was created by the Treaty of Rarotonga in 1985, including many island countries but also Australia and New Zealand, with the five "agreed" nuclear nations cooperating.

Finally, though much more slowly than the non-nuclear majority of nations wished, the United States and the Soviet Union entered into direct agreements, amid great mutual suspicion about cheating and considerable interest by the militaries in both countries in maintaining the maximum possible nuclear arsenal. Strategic Arms Limitation Talks (SALT) extended from 1969 to 1979, predicated on a dominant belief in both countries that actual nuclear war was not a viable option and that therefore the risks of such war should be curtailed. SALT I agreements, by 1972, involved a mutual pledge not to expand the number of strategic ballistic missiles. Another agreement forbad the creation of defensive systems against missiles – the idea here was to keep both countries equally vulnerable, as a means of assuring that in fact neither would attack. This treaty had no initial terminus, but the United States withdrew in 2002 in order to develop defensive systems. But with the Cold War ending, a number of important new negotiations expanded agreement in other areas, particularly toward actually cutting back weapons levels. Leaders of the two countries in 1986 actually discussed full nuclear disarmament, but this proved far too ambitious. On a more limited basis, a 1987 agreement was the first actually to require destruction of some existing weapons – a major category of ballistic missiles. The Strategic Arms Reduction Treaty (START) in 1991, a product of nine years of negotiation, set levels of the major kinds of missile systems and the number of nuclear warheads – cutting United States long-range weapons by 15 percent, Russian by 25 percent. Subsequent START treaties, in 1993 and 2010, then set even lower limits, not only on missiles but on long-range bombers. While tensions between the two military giants sometimes increased, and while both sides retained enough nuclear weaponry to destroy each other several times over, a commitment to try to keep the nuclear option under control seemed fairly durable.

Other efforts

While primary attention focused on nuclear limits, other weapons systems also came under partial international control, in some cases reviving or amplifying older League of Nations agreements like the chemical weapons measure of 1925. At the height of the Cold War, limits on chemical and biological arsenals were widely ignored, as many countries developed new supplies; along with the great powers, many smaller nations found chemical weapons cheap and easy to produce, in contrast to the more complicated nuclear devices. But the idea that chemical and biological threats were particularly dreadful and menacing persisted, calling forth renewed international attention. In 1968 the United Nations Disarmament Commission initiated a ban on chemical and biological weapons. The General Assembly finally completed the Chemical Weapons Convention in 1992, which almost all the world's nations quickly accepted. Under the treaty, and under separate international inspection, large numbers of weapons were gradually destroyed, with countries with the largest stockpiles, like the United States, Russia, and ultimately Libya leading the way. Iraq, which had used chemical weapons against its Kurdish minority, also joined the process after the overthrow of its longtime dictator, Saddam Hussein. But several key countries, including Syria, Egypt, and North Korea, had not signed on, creating the potential for renewed tension over this aspect of arms limitation. Syria did however agree to new measures in 2013.

United Nations efforts, finally, linked broader disarmament goals with the peace efforts of the international body. The General Assembly set up a Disarmament Department in 1982 (it would undergo several name changes), to support the establishment and enforcement of disarmament. The agency worked on standards for reducing conventional weaponry, while monitoring the observance of several disarmament treaties. It also brokered disarmament arrangements after the end of conflicts, including internal civil strife. Overall, disarmament became a pervasive mechanism in reducing the chances of war or limiting its impact in contemporary world history.

Weapons limitations efforts were not, of course, a full commitment to peace, though some of the regional nuclear-free arrangements were linked to wider pledges to avoid war of any sort. They did respond to widespread public concern – reflecting the variety of peace movements that operated in many countries after World War II, and a new power of public opinion to impose some constraints on official policies. And they did contribute to the fact that, for at least 70 years after 1945, the nuclear genie was kept in the bottle, however fragile the new arrangements might seem.

Changes in the framework: Democracy and consumerism

Along with the formal efforts toward peace or toward reducing the danger of war at the policy level, a number of other transformations in global affairs had a potential impact on conflict and conflict resolution. We have noted the importance of decolonization, in the three decades after World War II. The rise of newly independent nations created new instabilities in some cases, where internal unrest challenged the legitimacy of new governments and border tensions arose; this was particularly true in parts of Africa, but it played some role in Middle Eastern instability and in India-Pakistani relations as well. But decolonization also reduced imperialist rivalries among the leading industrial powers, particularly in Europe and Japan, and it addressed key nationalist aspirations in many places, reducing the danger of confrontation.

Ongoing globalization was another double-edged sword. Many historians and social scientists argue that the pace of globalization began to accelerate immediately after World War II, despite Cold War divisions. The range, speed and intensity of contacts among different parts of the world advanced rather steadily. Technology played a key role here. Jet travel, becoming widely available by the 1950s, was a factor here; so were new methods of communication, ultimately including satellite transmission and cell phones, plus the Internet. Never before could so much information or so many goods and people move so rapidly and in such volume around the world. Organizational arrangements provided a second spur to globalization. The post-World War II settlements involved concerted efforts to set up new global financial and economic institutions, like the International Monetary Fund, that would reduce the dangers of economic depression and damaging national rivalries and provide smoother guidance to economic growth and stability. Under these umbrellas, other new global organizations began to spread rapidly. Multinational corporations, based mainly in industrial nations like Germany, the United States, or Japan, fanned out widely, linking different regions of the world more tightly while taking advantage of special opportunities in labor costs or regulatory climate to locate particular production activities toward maximum profit. By the 1960s international nongovernmental organizations (INGOs) also began to proliferate – Amnesty International, for example, began operations in 1961 – seeking to provide more global connections around issues such as human rights, women's rights, or environmental protection.

The network of globalization encouraged new flows of people across borders, as migration increasingly focused on groups from less developed countries seeking work in the industrial world. It greatly deepened cultural contacts of various sorts, from international gatherings of scientists to the spread of consumer culture from centers such as the United States or Japan. Under UN-affiliated groups like the World Health Organization, health policies were increasingly coordinated toward reducing the spread of new epidemic diseases. The overall network was striking. Striking also were the decisions by key countries to abandon earlier hesitations and participate more fully in global relationships. The United States jettisoned its previous isolationism. In 1978 the People's Republic of China reversed course and began to open widely to international contacts; Russia made the same choice in 1985, as the hold of communism began to decline in Eastern Europe.

Advancing globalization could be a force for peace. Efforts to reduce economic rivalry and provide assistance to nations in economic difficulty obviously had peace as well as prosperity as a goal. New cultural connections could directly promote peace. We have seen that growing contacts among physicists in the United States and the Soviet Union, by the 1960s and 1970s, contributed quite directly to discussions of nuclear arms limitation. More broadly, new contacts might encourage greater understanding and sympathy for diverse peoples around the world.

But globalization could also cut the other way. While the process of globalization moved ahead fairly steadily, it was not always popular. Many people feared growing competition for jobs, as multinational corporations located production wherever they deemed advantageous. Cultural globalization roused resentment. Many religious leaders feared the insidious effects of Western consumer culture, which seemed highly sexualized and crassly materialistic. Others simply worried about the challenge to traditional regional or national identity, as global fashions and food styles spread so widely. In one international poll early in the twenty-first century, 72 percent of all respondents professed dislike of cultural globalization. Globalization could, in other words, fuel new tensions and even contribute to violence, as in the rise of certain forms of terrorism. And the speed of global contacts made the impact of even regional conflicts more important to all international players: to take an obvious example, it became harder for the West or Asia to overlook tensions in the Middle East, when dependence on oil exports increased steadily.

Two other developments, taking shape particularly from the 1960s and 1970s onward, both with links to globalization, bore a possible relationship to peace, perhaps less ambiguously than globalization itself. The undeniable (though not universal) spread of democracy was one key step. The expansion of consumerism was another. Neither of these developments took root because of a new commitment to peace, but both, in the eyes of some observers, might be genuinely conducive to it. And of course, in a number of countries, the two developments coexisted, possibly reinforcing their mutual impact.

New types of consumerism simply involved a growing interest in material acquisitions beyond the minimum of survival, and a growing desire to judge one's success in life, and one's family achievements, in part by consumer standards. The phenomenon involved buying new kinds of products in new settings, such as department stores or shopping malls; it involved an increase in spectator activities, watching athletic or musical performances either directly or on television; it embraced a growing interest in the newest fads.

Mass consumerism was not new. It had developed in the West from the eighteenth century onward, though it reached new levels after World War II as prosperity expanded. Japanese participation in new levels of consumerism, though a bit hesitant, dated from the late nineteenth century. But there was no question that consumer interests and capacities began to spread more widely, particularly around the turn of the new century when economic growth turned the corner in places like China, India, Mexico, Brazil, and Turkey. The fall of communism in Russia opened further consumer opportunities there as well. The rapid growth of the middle class, in these countries and beyond, was expressed in part in consumerist activities.

And here was the connection that some observers claimed for peace: as more and more people expanded their consumer interests but also their consumer success, they would become increasingly resistant to policies that threatened war. For, unquestionably, war and consumerism did not go together: the costs and destruction of war clearly indicated otherwise. Just as nineteenth-century economists had urged that the growing priority of business success might deter war, so now it became possible that consumer preferences might plan an ever greater role, discouraging guns, as a classic saying goes, in favor of butter. One American journalist put the proposition this way: no two societies that both had McDonald's restaurants have ever declared war on each other. The idea was not McDonald's per se, but the priorities that accompanied these kinds of global food and fashion standards.

The proposition was difficult to prove, because mass global consumerism is such a new phenomenon. We will see that growing Asian consumerism has not prevented new military rivalries between Japan and China (though not at all anything like outright war). The United States has managed to conduct significant foreign wars without disrupting domestic consumerism, at least directly. And consumerism is not uniform. The undeniable growth of an Indian or Chinese middle class comes amid great poverty in other sectors, particularly in the countryside. Some nations Africa or Latin America have not been able to make the turn to widespread consumerism at all. So even if the consumerist peace argument is right, it does not assure stability. Still, the claim is interesting, and worth monitoring in future.

Global consumerism also links to the continued growth of international sports competitions. Though interrupted in World War II, the Olympic movement resumed strongly from 1948 onward, only occasionally affected by tensions between the United States and the Soviet Union. Great national effort went into these athletic competitions. Cold War competitors participated strongly, as did China by the 1980s. The result clearly expressed national pride and rivalry. Did it also help divert from actual military rivalry – as the modern Olympics founder had hoped? Certainly the Olympics were increasingly supplemented by other competitions, such as World Cup soccer. And all of these efforts were viewed ultimately literally by billions of people, as satellite communications linked television services. The role of international sports in peace promotion is impossible to quantify, and some might argue that by confirming loud national pride sports might promote militarism, not retard it. But the equation remains intriguing.

The final big development potentially linked to peace was the expansion of political democracy. Systems based on wide voting rights and some real opportunities for choice among parties and candidates had fluctuated wildly in global currency during the twentieth century. Many societies chose against democracy by the 1930s, as we have seen. The post-World War II period and decolonization briefly encouraged democracy – important systems were durably installed in Germany, India, and Japan – but many new regimes proved fragile and toppled quickly. The Cold War pitted arguments for or against democracy.

But by the 1970s, democratic forms unquestionably began to gain ground, if not uniformly. Between that point and the 1990s, virtually the whole of Latin America converted to democratic systems, after a long period of emphasis on authoritarian or military regimes. Democracy spread to new parts of Asia, including South Korea, the Philippines and Indonesia. By the 1990s sub-

Saharan Africa began to participate, with important new regimes not only in post-apartheid South Africa, but also Nigeria, Kenya and elsewhere; by the early twenty-first century about half of all African nations were democratic. The fall of communism in Russia opened great new opportunities for democratic change in East-Central Europe and, at least to an extent, in Russia itself. Regionally, the principal exceptions to the democratic trend were the People's Republic of China, where a democratic movement was put down in 1989, and many nations in the Middle East and central Asia. It remained true that by the first decade of the new century democracy had become the world's most common form of government.

At least during the flush of excitement following the end of the Cold War, and as democracy was spreading, some social scientists speculated that the rise of democracy was also a major step forward toward greater peace. Democracies, the argument ran, would not declare war on each other. The assumption here, obviously, was that ordinary people, and political leaders who knew they were responsible to ordinary people, would never deliberately choose war. Either they valued peace or at least they knew the burdens and horrors of war: they would not choose it. Just as peace groups between the wars had contended that decisions about war and peace should not be left to an isolated elite, so the hope now was that, with political control resting more clearly with a voting public, war would not be seen as an option. One commentator noted, a bit ambiguously, "the fact that 'peace' seems to be breaking out in many parts of the world."

As with consumerism, the claims about democracy may not yet have been fully tested. No major war, in recent decades, has in fact pitted one democracy against another – but the timespan is too short to claim definitive validation of the proposition. And we know that democratic publics, both now and in the past (as with ancient Athens) can in fact become excited about patriotic values or a taste for action – the principle of popular aversion to war, though immensely attractive, can be challenged. In 1982 Argentina (then a governed by a military dictatorship) seized the British-controlled Falkland Islands (the Malvinas, to the Argentines). Britain responded quickly by sending a military expedition, amid widespread popular enthusiasm and support. This was not democracy against democracy, and it did not entail a probable risk of a major conflict: but it was certainly a democracy eagerly backing military action. (Peace was ultimately restored, with very little actual violence, though the issue of control has not been definitively resolved.) Observers were in fact surprised by the rush of belligerent British nationalism. Against this, there are other recent cases in which public opinion has resisted war – for example, in European response to the impending invasion of Iraq in 2003, though in this case many leaders went ahead despite popular opposition. Finally, the fact that some major societies are not democracies complicates contemporary analysis. Frequent recent conflicts in Africa have mainly involved non-democracies, for example.

As with consumerism, democracy as a source for a significant new approach to peace remains well worth considering and monitoring. The claims are interesting, but both in theory and in fact they are not yet easy to assess definitively. It remains true that a number of general shifts in the global environment may affect prospects for peace in ways that differ from the past. In this sense, they need to be combined with evaluation of the results of policy initiatives such as United Nations peacekeeping efforts or the struggle for arms control.

* * * * *

Important changes occurred in the promotion of peace after 1945. Deliberate innovations emerged at the policy level, though of course there were still important continuities from the past including hesitations about how much to commit to the international enforcement of peace. Limitations on disarmament recalled some of the struggles of the 1920s, though focused now on very different weaponry. Again, change and its impact need serious attention, but neither should be overemphasized.

Continued complexity showed in other ways too. The regional map of peace and war changed significantly after 1945 – but very diverse reactions to peace priorities continued to prevail from one area to the next. On the whole, the list of additions to regional peace commitments expanded, with some striking conversions to reconsiderations of military roles and goals. Other regions, however, confirmed or even expanded military activities. The map of regional differentiation on nuclear weapons was revealing in this regard: Latin America, Southeast Asia and the south Pacific, and Africa proved deeply committed to avoiding nuclear weapons development, as were other individual nations such as Germany and Japan. But other regions, including the Middle East, South Asia, and the great powers in Europe and North America, presented a more mixed picture. There was a fairly general desire to avoid nuclear war, but also major regional disagreements on how to achieve this. More broadly still, regional definitions of peace, and how best to preserve the peace, continued to vary. Finally, change occurred within the period, in terms of regional priorities and policies. This, too, maintained regional complexity even amid the context of globalization. There would be no single global contemporary history on peace and war.

Further reading

On the United Nations

United Nations Peacekeeping Operations website. Available online at www.un.org/en/peacekeeping/operations/past.shtml.

Cede, Franz and Lilly Sucharina-Behrmann. *The United Nations: Law and Practice.* The Hague: Kluwer Law International, 2001.

Goulding, Mark. "The Evolution of United Nations Peacekeeping." *International Affairs (Royal Institute of International Affairs 1944–)* 69.3 (1993): 451–64.

Plesch, Dan. *America, Hitler and the UN: How the Allies Won World War II and Forged a Peace.* London: I.B. Tauris, 2010.

Sinai Joshua. "United Nations' and Non-United Nations' Peace-Keeping in the Arab-Israeli Sector: Five Scenarios." *Middle East Journal* 49.4 (1995): 629–44.

Volger, Helmut. *A Concise Encyclopedia of the United Nations*. Leiden: Martinus Nijhoff Publishers, 2010.

On nuclear weapons

Bellany, Ian, Coit D. Blacker, and Joseph Gallacher. *The Nuclear Non-Proliferation Treaty*. London: Frank Cass, 1985.

Cirincione, Joseph. *Bomb Scare: The History and Future of Nuclear Weapons*. New York: Columbia University Press, 2007.

Hymans, Jacques E. C. *The Psychology of Nuclear Proliferation: Identity, Emotions and Foreign Policy*. Cambridge: Cambridge University Press, 2006.

Joyner, Daniel H. *Interpreting the Nuclear Non-Proliferation Treaty*. Oxford and New York: Oxford University Press, 2011.

Kissinger, Henry A. and Gordon Dean. *Nuclear Weapons and Foreign Policy*, 2/e. New York: Council on Foreign Relations by Harper, 1957.

Thee, Marek, ed. *Armaments and Disarmament in the Nuclear Age: A Handbook*. Stockholm: Almqvist and Wiksell International, 1976.

On peace issues and the Olympics

Miller, David. *The Official History of the Olympic Games and the IOC: Athens to London 1894–2012*. Edinburgh: Mainstream Publishing, 2012.

Young, David C. *A Brief History of the Olympic Games*. Malden, MA: Blackwell Publishing, 2004.

See also

Croft, Stuart. *Strategies of Arms Control: A History and Typology*. Manchester: Manchester University Press, 1996.

Friedman, Thomas L. *The World is Flat 3.0: A Brief History of the Twenty-First Century*. New York: Picador, 2007.

Gantzel, Klaus Jurgen and Torsten Schwinghammer. *Warfare since the Second World War*. New Brusnwick, NJ: Transaction, 2000.

Stearns, Peter N. *Consumerism in World History: The Global Transformation of Desire*, 2/e. New York: Routledge, 2006.

9 Regional approaches to peace

The comparative challenge

Where have all the soldiers gone? This was the title of a major study on post-war Germany, highlighting the extraordinary conversion of this nation from strong military tradition to a policy of demilitarization and a popular culture to match. Demilitarization was imposed by the victors in World War II, not only on Germany but on Japan as well. But the results were arguably far more sweeping and durable than might have been imagined. Here were two societies that drew their own lessons from the world war, and actively sought a different kind of future, for themselves and ideally for the world at large. Demilitarization also occurred, more spontaneously but in conjunction with earlier traditions, in parts of Central America. Beyond national demilitarization, several of the societies involved became new global leaders in advocacy for peace.

In contrast to demilitarization, many societies in the postwar world assumed that maintaining or developing a strong military was a standard part of state building. Tradition and the Cold War framework, along with internal rivalries within key regions, both supported this trend, but there were important new entrants into the ranks of military leaders.

Between these two poles, many societies tried to navigate toward clearer priorities for peace, or at least greater control over military options. During the Cold War, a number of important nations sought to carve out a neutral approach, not abandoning military commitments but seeking to avoid entanglements that might lead to conflict. By the 1990s, and in part because of the Cold War's end, even more societies began quietly to reduce military establishments.

New regional coalitions emerged, seeking to use partnerships to reduce disputes – in some cases, trying to overcome centuries of violence and instability. Yet additional regions – most obviously, in Latin America – confirmed older commitments to peaceful relationships.

The mixture was complicated. It involved different levels of interest in peace but also dramatically different decisions about how best to promote peace. Was more military the answer – peace through strength and preemptive action? Or was the newer model of outright demilitarization a better route? Globally, there was no single answer, either in 1945 or in 2014.

Demilitarization

By 1948, three countries were committed to a new policy of demilitarization, two initially because of their defeat in World War II, but one voluntarily. This was clearly not the most common policy approach, at this point or since. Nor was it entirely new – victors in other wars, including World War I, had forced substantial destruction of weaponry and reduction of military personnel on defeated powers. But the postwar approach to demilitarization turned out to go farther than precedent suggested, somewhat surprisingly creating new attitudes more than new resentments.

Japan

The groundwork for Japan's demilitarization rested not only on defeat in war, but on several subsequent years of American occupation during which the old military apparatus was fairly thoroughly dismantled. Many returning soldiers were angry at the wartime military and its officer corps, blamed for dragging the nation into a ruinous war for selfish, militaristic reasons. This new perception, as well as American pressure, produced a striking founding document for the postwar government.

Article 9 of a new constitution, issued in 1947, obliged the nation not to maintain "war potential" nor recognize the "right of belligerency" – Japan should not have large military forces nor undertake any aggressive action. The language was sweeping:

> Aspiring sincerely to an international peace based on justice and order, the Japanese people forever renounce war as a sovereign right of the nation and the threat or use of force as a means of settling international disputes. In order to accomplish [this] aim, land, sea and air forces, as well as other war potential, will never be maintained. The right of belligerency of the state will not be recognized.

Military leaders were banned from cabinet posts, and of course many top officials were tried for war crimes. Several business conglomerates that focused on weapons production were disbanded, and militarism was purged from the teaching profession and the education system. Though pressed by American occupation, these various demilitarization measures won wide, though not uniform, popular support. Loss in war and the searing experience of atomic attack on two key cities, along with the new demilitarization campaign, convinced many people that military power was no solution to key human problems. While disagreements quickly surfaced over specifics, all the major political parties agreed in rejecting any return to militarism. The socialists, though a minority, actually favored unarmed neutrality.

Demilitarization was soon tested by the Cold War. Fairly quickly, the United States began – more than a bit ironically – to press Japan to strengthen its military, as an ally against Soviet strength in East Asia. The Japanese government itself accepted long-term American bases, particularly on the island of Okinawa, even after formal occupation ended. This American presence both excused Japan from wider military efforts, offering American protection against external attack, and served to press the Japanese to do more in the military arena than the new embrace of anti-militarism might imply. Japan was locked into the American side of the new Cold War conflict, to the dismay of many who hoped that Article 9 would create the nation as a new "peace state." While socialist objections never prevailed, the existence of strong anti-war popular sentiment continued to constrain the government in going too far toward developing new military forces. The effective compromise was the firm embrace of the security arrangements with the United States, to meet the perceived Soviet threat, while maintaining low military spending and primary focus on economic growth.

The 1950s, and the nearby Korean War, did see the development of a small new military force – the so-called Self-Defense Forces, including a new air force, ratified by legislation in 1954. Japan now sought to combine continued, if loose, commitment to Article 9 with what its leaders now called an inherent right to self-defense. Military forces existed, but were still to be kept to a minimum. No external military action was permitted, though in principle the boundary between self-defense and "belligerency" was hard to determine. An accompanying legislative measure prohibited the use of Japanese forces overseas, another sign of the ongoing pressure against any full remilitarization. And of course there was a firm commitment not to develop nuclear weapons, though the nation clearly had the necessary scientific and technical capacity. Finally, new legislation strictly regulated the sale of arms overseas, with a ban on sales to countries in or near conflict zones. During the whole Cold War period, frequent popular concern about United States Cold War moves – not only the operation of bases in Japan, but other aggressive moves such as nuclear testing – helped confirm widespread opposition to significant military expansion.

Demilitarization came under unexpected new pressure after the end of the Cold War. While the Soviet threat had ended – which supported those Japanese voices that sought an end to American bases – there were legitimate and immediate new concerns about the aggressive stance of North Korea and the rise of greater Chinese military power. Elements that had long sought a more active military stance gained new voice – including those in political leadership that had continued, despite international concern, to honor the memory of Japan's World War II forces. Specific debate revolved around Japan's role, or lack thereof, in new international military operations designed, at least in principle, to promote greater world peace and security. Could Japan now send significant military forces to support United Nations peacekeeping operations or anti-terrorism efforts such as the American-led invasion of Afghanistan? Some compromises did emerge: the Japanese provided troops for peacekeeping in Cambodia, in 1992–23, and also as part of UN efforts along the borders of Israel; a new International Peace Cooperation Law loosened restrictions. But the troops overseas were placed under strict constraints, carrying only side-arms as weapons, as a bow to the continuing strength of anti-militarist sentiments. In support of American anti-terrorism efforts, the Japanese sent mainly humanitarian contingents and logistical support. There was some new openness to expansion: Japanese forces supporting the 2003 invasion of Iraq were focused on reconstruction efforts, not active military patrols, but they were allowed to carry heavy weaponry for the first time – though under strict rules of engagement which prohibited their use unless they came under fire. And these ground troops were withdrawn quickly, in 2006, in part because of the ongoing public concern about overseas military engagements.

By 2013 Japanese commitment to demilitarization continued to be a moving target. In 2011 the government relaxed the ban on weapons sales to other countries, though the new contours were not entirely clear. A new prime minister, in 2013, was firmly committed to a more vigorous statement of Japanese nationalism, while new military tensions surfaced over ownership of some small, rocky islands in the Pacific which both China and Japan claimed. At the same time, widespread public commitment to Article 9 and the values it embraced in the whole area of anti-military policy remained strong, continuing to condition any ongoing debate.

Germany

German demilitarization launched with timing and motivation very similar to those present in postwar Japan. In many ways the process went even farther in Germany, with less subsequent contestation, making today's unified Germany probably the least militarized of all industrialized states. In most respects, Germany has come to represent what one United Nations agency has defined as a "peace culture" that "rejects violence and, instead, seeks solutions to problems through dialogue and negotiation," while working as well to identify and resolve sources of conflict well before they burst into open hostility.

Allied arrangements imposed major limitations on German military activity in a series of agreements beginning in 1945. As in Japan, significant foreign forces were located in Germany, and here too substantial American bases still remain; these bases, in what became West Germany, helped defend from attack, but also helped oversee what the limited German military activity that did develop. The goal was, as a US declaration proclaimed in 1945, "to prevent Germany from ever again becoming a threat to the peace of the world." Not only were German forces disbanded and several leaders put on trial; as in Japan considerable attention was also devoted to dismantling relevant industrial capacity. All military clubs and organizations were "completely and finally abolished," and educational as well as political systems were recast in order to stifle militarism as well as Nazi ideas.

The new West German constitution of 1949 forbad citizens from participating in "belligerent actions," while recognizing that "no person shall be compelled against his conscience to render military service as an armed combatant."

Again as with Japan, the efforts of the occupying forces were greatly aided by a widespread conviction among the German people, that war and militarism had led the nation down a disastrous path.

Full demilitarization was reconsidered under the spur of the Cold War, and both East and West Germany (the Democratic Republic and the Federal Republic) were allowed to develop limited military forces. For West Germany, United States pressure clearly supported more rapid military effort than either the government or the wider society was willing to endorse. Even with limits, considerable public opinion was opposed, with the slogan *"ohne mich!"* or "without me" a rallying cry for former soldiers and younger men who were hostile to any military service. The new army faced recurrent underfunding as well as an insufficient number of recruits, with only slightly more than half the projected number of troops raised by 1956. As in Japan, the attractions and rewards of building a new and dynamic civilian economy clearly outweighed military goals. Here is a case where the growth of an active consumer economy constituted a clear alternative to older interests. A famous West German peace movement poster, in the 1980s, featured pictures of two soldiers dead in World War I and World War II, contrasted with a contemporary smiling youth in a fashionable turtle-necked sweater: the slogan ran, "He wants peace, he wants disarmament, and actively campaigns for it."

Structural limitations were also imposed, to make sure that the military would never again contest civilian authority. Soldiers and officers were first and foremost citizens, not representatives of separate military values.

Experience was surprisingly similar in communist East Germany, where it proved hard to recruit new soldiers and where a combination of widespread pacifism, fear of renewed war, plus greater interest in economic development limited military attractions. Some East Germans expressed Christian hostility to any actual combat, while others cited the fear of later being treated as a war criminal if they engaged in action. The number of conscientious objectors grew rapidly.

By the 1960s and 1970s, though most clearly in West Germany, a growing popular culture identified with demilitarization. The process may have gone further than in Japan, if only because of greater German willingness, even at the top leadership levels, to acknowledge the horrible atrocities the nation had committed during World War II. Protests against aspects of the Cold War were widespread, with many demonstrations against nuclear weaponry and against American bases and missile sites. Literally hundreds of thousands of people were recurrently involved. In both East and West Germany, important movements also arose to urge a peaceful end to the division of the nation itself. Several East Germany movements directly aimed at destroying military capacity of any sort, under titles like "Swords into Plowshares" or "Create Peace without Weapons." Organizations in both countries protested later Cold War moves, most obviously the Vietnam War but also the 1979 Soviet invasion of Afghanistan or United States action against Guatemala. Despite Cold War barriers, considerable communication developed among peace activists in the

East and West Germany. Peace ideologies expanded beyond the effort to avoid death and physical devastation, to highlight the psychological damage done by fears of war and violence. Peace should be social and personal, external and inward, with the very real concerns that Germany could become the center of a Cold War nuclear conflict underlying this extension. Here was one reason that a culture of German demilitarization retained greater strength than its Japanese counterpart: it was fueled not just by World War II memories but by ongoing diplomatic conflicts and fears.

The end of the Cold War and the rise of new sets of regional tensions created new challenges for German policy and culture, with the country now reunified (1990). The collapse of Yugoslavia led to agonizing issues for the nation, concerning participation in military intervention. Here was new strife very close to home, where military action could be seen as a contribution to peace; but the insistence on preserving a low-profile military took precedence. Only in 1999, amid great debate, did the German air force participate in actions in the Balkans, the first major foreign combat mission since 1944. Later on, Germany would also refuse to participate in European military action to support a rebellion in Libya. But the nation did send military forces in cooperate in the invasion of Afghanistan, and also in several United Nations missions in Africa.

Meanwhile, alongside new debates, military limitations continue. Conscription for the military was ended in 2011, creating a smaller but more professional force. Military spending has gone down steadily – in real terms, the reduction was almost 33 percent between 1990 and 2001, and as a percentage of Gross National Product the change was even more substantial. By the early twenty-first century, Germany had become a key part of a definite peace zone, and while the end of the Cold War contributed to this, actions by the German government and public had played a key role. Many Germans proudly boasted of their conversion to a genuine "civilian" nation, in which nonmilitary goals took clear priority. Even more than with Japan, self-imposed limits continued to differentiate Germany from many other contemporary states where the priority of military capacity is concerned.

Costa Rica

Demilitarization in this Central American nation, dramatically proclaimed in 1948 and steadfastly maintained thereafter, was obviously a different matter from the process in Germany and Japan. The nation was under no external pressure to demilitarize. It had not lost a war. In a general sense it was part of the regions for which the United States felt some responsibility, but it faced no threats that required active military protection; indeed, the potential for American intervention was part of the region's historic problems. Indeed, the United States found Costa Rica's new policy somewhat contradictory to its growing belief that all states should want to have a military establishment and that ideally the establishment should have links to the neighbor to the north. As with Germany and Japan, though for different reasons, the United States applied some pressure to change course, though without real result. Finally, this was a small country, with no active militarist tradition – another contrast with the defeated powers from World War II.

Nevertheless, the 1948 move, announced unexpectedly by beleaguered President José Figueres, was striking. On December 1 the President took a sledgehammer to the walls of the massive Bella Vista military fort and announced the banning of the Costa Rican military. The following year the military was constitutionally abolished, and the nation launched a commitment to demilitarization that has lasted to the present day.

Latin America, including Central America, had long been a surprisingly war-free region. Only three major wars have occurred since independence early in the nineteenth century, and war deaths overall have been far lower than in almost every other world region. Most states historically retained only small military establishments, by the standards of many other countries. To be sure, small militaries sometimes reflected weak states more than peaceful interests; there were downsides to the pattern. And militaries, though usually not designed to conduct external wars, were sometimes larger than they needed to be for purely police functions, which led to recurrent political takeovers and military, or militarily supported, authoritarian regimes. But violence among states was not an endemic problem.

Costa Rica had experienced a brief dictatorship in the early 1920s, with an effort to grow the military as a means of regime protection. But the dictatorship crumbled, partly under United States pressure, and an abortive border war with Panama further discredited the military. The nation reverted to a relatively small, though noticeable, military establishment. Public opinion was ashamed of the brief flirtation with greater military power and higher spending.

During the late 1940s Costa Rica experienced substantial internal unrest. Figueres himself became president thanks to the activity of a band of mercenaries from neighboring countries. Very quickly the regime was in serious trouble, with disputes between conservatives and communists, United States disapproval, and covetous ambitions from neighboring dictators. In terms of historic precedent, this might have been the moment to try to build up the military in hopes of propping up the government, but Figueres decided on the opposite approach.

It was the Minister of Security, Edgar Cardona, who proposed not to strengthen the security apparatus but to abolish the armed forces. He later said he told the President:

> "Look, Mr. President, the press is attacking us and the minister of education for spending too much money on education; we should spend even more. We can tell them that it is necessary to spend money on education in the country, and with the abolition of the army we can spend ever more … Let us abolish the military, for with a civil guard we have sufficient security." Figueres thought for a while, and he said yes, it seemed like a great idea.

The move encountered little protest, for again there was no great military tradition to defend. The policy was new, but it could seem appropriate and not particularly radical in the Costa Rican context. Figueres was able to get mercenary forces from other countries to leave, as part of shutting down the military apparatus, though in some cases it took a few months. He was able to appeal to the Organization of American States for support and potential intervention should a neighboring country attack. And the lack of a separate military left his conservative opposition without any means to overthrow the regime or reverse the demilitarization project. No major sector of public opinion defended the military, so there was really no contest.

The result was arguably as dramatic as the move itself. Over ensuing decades, there was no military to disrupt internal politics or contribute to civil unrest. Politicians and elites had to learn to appeal for votes to gain or maintain power, and this gave them incentive to provide education, civil rights, and jobs to the citizenry – and this was facilitated as well by the absence of any defense budget. Costa Rica had far more development funds than its still-militarized neighbors in the region, and began to stand out in consequence.

Cold War pressures, developing after the new policy was installed, and particularly the rise of a communist regime in Cuba in 1959 led to some new external criticism. The United States began to argue that only a state with an army could guard against communist subversion, and pressed the Costa Rican regime hard. As one politician noted, "We received great pressure from the United States so that we would form a modern army here. They wanted to give us equipment and training and everything. We said no." In 1981 the US ambassador to the United Nations accused the Costa Rican President of communist subversion, and insisted that further American economic aid – Costa Rica was facing a debt crisis at the time – would be predicated on re-creating a professional army. She added, "Costa Rica is not a viable country, because it has no military." Here too, Costa Ricans resisted.

Until after 2000, furthermore, the country stood out in the region, where military regimes continued to pop up. Honduras, which earlier in the twentieth century had maintained a smaller military than Costa Rica, briefly debated demilitarization in 1954. Then the United States offered Honduras a new military pact. Some sectors of public opinion were resolutely opposed, on grounds of no apparent need:

> it makes us laugh because Honduras has never fought with anybody and has no one to fight with … and to think that we could be invaded by the Russian Soviets, this causes even more laughter because truth be told … it is easier to believe that we will be invaded by those that are now making treaties to protect us.

But the nation went ahead with the deal, and soon military leaders were claiming "if you want peace, prepare for war … The armed forces are necessary to oversee the order and tranquility of the country."

Costa Rica maintained its course. With the political, economic and possibly even psychological benefits of demilitarization, it grew at a faster rate than its neighbors, reduced poverty, and diversified the economy – enhancing a strong democratic system in the process. In 2001 the then president visited South America, arguing that elimination of the armed forces was a "great blessing," because it ended the existence of a separate military caste and the threat of political takeover, while lowering "this enormous and unproductive military expenditure." He urged Uruguay to transfer military resources to education, job creation and health: "The countries of Latin America should eliminate their armies because we are poor and we need these resources to develop human capital." Officers in his audience bristled, but many in the crowd cheered. On another occasion, speaking to the United States Congress shortly before receiving the Nobel Peace Prize, President Oscar Arias summed up his country's experiment:

> I belong to a small country that was not afraid to abolish its army in order to increase its strength. In my homeland you will not find a single tank, a single artillery piece, a single warship, or a single military helicopter. In Costa Rica we are not afraid of freedom. We love democracy and respect the law ... We have made considerable progress in education, health and nutrition. In all of these areas are levels are comparable to the best in Latin America. Although we are poor, we have so far been able to reach satisfactory social goals. This is largely because we have no arms expenditures and because the embedded practice of democracy drives us to meet the needs of the people. Almost 40 years ago we abolished our army. Today we threaten no one, neither our own people or our neighbors. Such threats are absent not because we lack tanks, but because there are few of us who are hungry, illiterate, or unemployed.

* * * * *

Demilitarization and the accompanying popular culture did not constitute the common path in contemporary world history. It differed also from other independent policies, like Swiss or Swedish neutrality, aiming at peace in somewhat different fashion. The approach was a key part of contemporary regional diversity. But it also, informally, would win wider attention after the Cold War ended, even without quite such explicit commitments as Japan, Germany and Costa Rica had displayed. It was not, on other words, merely a recent oddity.

Regional efforts

Many parts of the world sought regional agreements to promote peace. In the case of Latin America, a regional pattern already existed, but it was refreshed at several points. For other areas involved, the effort was far more novel. And some parts of the world were not able to make a serious or comprehensive effort. Ongoing distrust between China and Japan, for example, prevented an effective collaborative initiative for peace in East Asia, at any point after World War II – though there was no major outright conflict in the area following the end of the Korean War. Organizational initiative was another arena in which regional developments varied widely.

Innovation – putting ideas into practice

Europe

Without question, though somewhat surprisingly given the experience of the 1920s and 1930s, the most important regional innovations occurred in Western Europe. Here was one of the great historical centers of war – for all the imaginative discussions of peace – and yet, after 1945, no outright wars occurred at all. The Cold War, for all its tensions, may have contributed to this result: many Western nations banded together, under American guidance (some would say, domination), because the Soviet threat seemed greater than any local conflict.

But the real key was a wide resolve, on the part of many leaders and larger political parties, to change historic hostility into a new commitment to peace and collaboration. Relatively gentle treatment of Germany, and then the larger process of German demilitarization, played a role here. Organizational efforts, however, were more important still.

Under American leadership the North Atlantic Treaty Organization (NATO) was formed, to provide collective security against the Soviet Union and its allies. This was a military organization, but it also helped reorient some of the traditional goals of purely national military establishments. Further, after the Cold War ended, NATO established a new subgroup called the Partnership with Peace, which worked actively with a number of East European nations, now outside the Russian orbit, to create more peaceful military and civil structures. Some of these countries were later directly admitted to NATO.

The most important initiative, however, and the one most clearly open to a new priority for peace, involved the various European economic organizations that grouped key countries together. One of Europe's future leaders, Jean Monnet, put the case clearly as early as 1943, when he was fighting against Nazi occupation: "There will be no peace in Europe, if the states are reconstituted on the basis of national sovereignty ... The countries of Europe are too small to guarantee their peoples the necessary prosperity and social development. The European states must constitute themselves into a federation."

The postwar focus was on better economic coordination, that would lead to greater prosperity, but even more to the reduction of national economic rivalries and to a level of mutual interaction that would clearly take precedence even over wider historic tensions. Associations in Europe did not focus on rhetorical commitments to peace and mediation, but to active economic and other ties that would reduce aggressive nationalism and make war increasingly inconceivable. Integration of Germany into a successful European structure was the key goal, in close connection with its longtime French opponent. But Italy and the Low Countries were included from the outset, and ultimately the

inconceivable – unbelievable

European effort would expand to include virtually all of Western and Central Europe and then, after the Cold War, most of East-Central Europe as well. The Europeans also ultimately intervened in the clearest internal regional trouble spot, the nations that emerged from the former Yugoslavia, though by 2013, while peace had been restored, this was still a work in progress.

For the core nations, initial efforts involved a Coal and Steel Community (1951), to coordinate policies in heavy industry, and then a more ambitious Common Market to create a larger trading zone, along with freer migration of labor. Ultimately, the European Union formed, with a host of common regulations, widespread student and educational exchange, even (for many countries) a common currency in the euro. This was the association that ultimately spread to embrace virtually the whole continent west of Russia, Belarus and Ukraine.

The evolution of the European effort faced a number of challenges and setbacks, but the goal of creating beneficial ties that would replace older military tensions never wavered. What finally became the European Union was focused on peace on the continent, while contributing to global peace more generally. One of the founders of the Coal and Steel Community, Robert Schumann, clearly stated that the goal of what might seem a rather prosaic economic arrangement was "peace, to give peace a chance." And while peace within Europe and reduction of aggressive nationalism constituted the most obvious point, the founders also saw their efforts as a promotion of peace in the world more generally – where European rivalries had caused so much damage in previous decades. In the same vein, in 2012, the European Union won the Nobel Peace Prize for its role – now over six decades – in effectively promoting "peace and reconciliation." Old enemies had become surprisingly durable and harmonious collaborators. National boundaries that had long been heavily fortified virtually disappeared.

From the 1970s onward, European leaders in fact increasingly referred to their states as "civilian" powers, focused on economic and social advanced with relatively little attention to military matters.

The Americas

Collaboration for peace was probably better established in the Americas than in any other part of the world. It historically had blended genuine Latin American preference for avoiding war and extensive external military commitment, with United States interest in exercising substantial control over American affairs. In broad outline, this pattern continued after World War II. A few new complexities intruded, particularly with the establishment of a communist regime in Cuba in 1959, but it was also true that no major war broke out in the hemisphere. Regional coordination partly accounted for this achievement.

In 1947 most of the nations in the Americas signed a new Inter-American Treaty of Reciprocal Assistance, or the Rio Pact. Its central principle involved a pledge that an attack on one signatory would be regarded as an attack on all; intervention from outside the region would not be tolerated, in what came to be known as the "hemispheric defense" doctrine. Basic motivation came from the United States, which hope to seal the Americas against any communist threat as the Cold War began to take shape.

Then in 1948 an international conference in Colombia agreed to form the Organization of American States (OAS), to replace the older Pan American Union. Goals of the new group included "strengthening the peace and security of the continent" and "preventing possible causes of difficulties and ensuring the pacific settlement of disputes that may arise among the member states." The pact also included a commitment to limit conventional weaponry, in order to free up resources for economic development. Over time, the OAS did work effectively to support peace agreements in several countries, after civil strife, while working to resolve the few remaining border disputes (Peru/Ecuador, where an old border dispute was resolved in 1998, and Guatemala/Belize). The Organization took a lead in removing land mines that had been deployed in some member states.

United States disapproval of the new regime in Cuba complicated the united front, as American leaders persuaded the OAS to exclude Cuba. Many member states were unhappy with this tension, and after 2009 a new effort was made to arrange for Cuba's readmission.

Other problems intruded. The United States refused to back Argentina in the conflict with Britain over the Falkland Islands, arguing that Argentina had been the aggressor; to most Latin American states this seemed to make a mockery of the Rio Pact. The United States sought assistance in the War on Terror after 9/11, invoking the same Rio Pact, but only four Central American countries actually joined in. Mexico withdrew from the treaty in 2002, in part to avoid participation in the upcoming invasion of Iraq. Several other countries ended their membership later on, again in disputes over United States policy.

In 2008 a new Union of South American Nations created their own regional security council, to provide for mutual defense and adjudication. Headed by Argentina, Brazil and Chile, this new group sought much closer coordination, on the model of the European Union. Mutual security should be provided by the new organization, and the goal of peaceful relations was vigorously maintained. The Union in fact successfully mediated an intense dispute between Venezuela and Colombia, in 2010.

Overall, tensions over United States–Latin American relations were not fully resolved, as various treaty arrangements and organizations were deployed. But there was no risk of major violence, and the principle of mutual agreement to resolve disputes won consistent support. Aside from a few recurrences of United States intervention in Central America, and a number of outbreaks of internal strife, the region remained a war-free zone.

The Non-Aligned Movement

A different kind of associational peace effort emerged in the 1950s and 1960s, based on economic and political conditions rather than region. As the Cold War developed, a number of countries, many of them newly created with the retreat of imperialism, sought to establish their essential neutrality in the conflict: they resisted choosing sides between the West and the Soviets and they worried about the excessive influence of the great powers. Many also believed that a large non-aligned bloc would help modify Cold War tensions, reducing the chance of global war. Resistance to foreign military bases was a key part of the approach, as a specific way to limit the dangers of the Cold War. In 1955 the government of Indonesia organized a conference for African and Asian states, including several Asian communist leaders but also the president of Yugoslavia. The influence of the Indian Prime Minister Jawaharlal Nehru was considerable, around assurances of mutual non-aggression and peaceful coexistence. The conference issued a declaration on "promotion of world peace and cooperation." A more formal non-aligned conference then occurred in 1961, where the Non-Aligned Movement (NAM) was actually founded. The organization continues today, with 120 member states and a number of observers.

Nations that joined the movement promised respect for the United Nations and a commitment to settle all international disputes by peaceful means, while refraining from any acts of aggression or uses of force against another nation. Not surprisingly, by 1983 NAM proudly proclaimed itself "history's biggest peace movement," and indeed winning such wide support for the core principles was an impressive achievement. The organization did not actually settle many disputes, but rather served as a sounding board for the concerns of many of the world's poorer countries. The end of the Cold War diluted NAM's purposes, though there was still considerable opportunity to criticize excessive Western economic power or United States military interventions and anti-terror tactics.

Regional organizations in Asia and Africa

We have seen that an Association of Southeast Asian Nations, formed in 1967, worked to promote a "zone of peace, freedom and neutrality in the region." Early on the organization helped resolve hostilities between Indonesia and Malaysia. With the huge exception of the Vietnam War, which also involved Laos and Cambodia, the region has been quite peaceful, and careful relations among ASEAN member states has played a role here. Vietnam and its neighbors joined the Association after the war's end. In 1976 the Association orchestrated a Treaty of Amity and Cooperation, designed to emphasize peace amid a growing number of boundary disputes. The Association also worked to improve mutual trade and deal with refugee problems.

The Organization of African Unity formed in 1963, as many new nations were emerging from European colonial control. The group proclaimed a commitment to mutual noninterference. It was reconstituted as the African Union in 2001, with renewed interest in promoting peace in the continent, and with a clearer mandate to take active measures to preempt or end wars among members, and also to prevent genocide. Members of the African Union periodically contributed troops to United Nations peacekeeping efforts on the continent. A Peace and Security Council was formed in 2004.

Another group espousing peace and cooperation was the Commonwealth of Nations, formed among Britain and most of its former colonies, particularly in Africa and Asia. A founding Singapore Declaration, in 1971, actively espoused world peace and support for the United Nations, and these principles were repeated in the Harare Commonwealth Declaration in 1991. "We believe that international peace and order, global economic development and the rule of international law are essential to the security and prosperity of mankind."

The Arab League was one of the oldest regional associations, formed in 1945. In its early years the League professed its devotion to peace and to non-violent resolution of conflicts. The League did not include some key states in the region, such as Israel, and even among Arab members its operation was not consistently effective. Renewed interest in promoting peace developed after 2000, with various peace plans for dealing with issues such as interventions in Lebanon. In imitation of the African Union, a Peace and Security Council emerged in 2006.

Finally, in the wake of the collapse of the Soviet Union, a loosely structured Commonwealth of Independent States united most of the newly independent central Asian and East European successor nations, along with Russia itself. A 1994 Collective Security Treaty pledged all members to abstain from force, and the Commonwealth also coordinated some military arrangements. The Commonwealth was not able to prevent some serious conflicts among several member states, including Russia and Georgia, where a military clash broke out in 2008.

* * * * *

Some regional associations were far more active and effective than others, and the impact of key organizations on actual conditions for peace varied greatly as well. Even so, the proliferation of organizations pledging peace and mutual respect was a significant new development. In several regions, associations provided services that helped resolve conflict and reduce a sense of risk; both could contribute to a greater commitment to peace. In some cases, partial demilitarization built on the security assurances that regional associations provided. Also significant, at the other extreme, was the fact that a number of key regions lacked any associational effort or saw organizations emerge that focused more exclusively on issues such as trade and economic development, rather than a larger peace mandate. Again, the world's regional map remained exceptionally diverse, and the range and limits of association efforts added to the variety.

The riddle of the United States

The United States was unquestionably the world's leading power, economically and militarily, during the decades after World War II, a period sometimes labeled as part of an "American Century." After World War II the nation particularly relied on its air power, supplemented by a large navy and by a substantial standing army. This level of strength gave the nation an unusually important role in determining options between peace and war. We have seen that the United States moved decisively away from isolationism, toward a far more active engagement in the postwar world, in the Cold War, and this continued in the quarter-century since the Cold War ended when the nation, as some observers claimed, became "the world's only remaining superpower." Not surprisingly, if only because of size and position, the nation did not easily fall into any of the regional categories we have already explored. The question obviously was: where did peace now figure in the American equation? The answer is surprisingly difficult to determine, because the nation indulged in several strategies, depending to some extent on context and timing. While most Americans usually saw their nation as a force for peace, a minority recurrently disagreed, and certainly there were varied opinions around the world. Hence, an important American riddle.

Pax Americana

One line of argument saw the United States as an ardent supporter of peace, as part of its mission and self-interest alike. Certainly, as we will see in the next chapter, the nation harbored a variety of eager and energetic peace movements. It served as a center for peace research, mounting some of the first academic programs in conflict analysis, for example. Older Christian movements, some new impulses in youth culture during the 1960s, the new scientific concern about nuclear armaments – a number of forces could provide vigorous American peace advocacy, with influence on government policy and with international outreach as well.

Beyond this, mainstream policy itself often seemed to be a force for peace. The term *Pax Americana*, derived from earlier patterns of Roman or Mongolian peace, was sometimes introduced to describe an international peacekeeping role. The North American continent itself remained peaceful, and had been so since the mid-nineteenth century American Civil War and the territorial struggles with Mexico. Remarkably stable relations with Canada continued to describe the longest unfortified frontier in the world. The term *Pax Americana* was first employed, in fact, in 1894 to describe the extension of American control throughout the continental United States, under conditions of democracy and legal order.

We have seen that the United States frequently sought to defend peace, or at least to prevent outside interference, on both the American continents. The expulsion of Spain from Cuba and Puerto Rico in the Spanish–American War of 1898 left the United States the clearly dominant power in the Western hemisphere, and while it frequently intervened in the affairs of other American states, sometimes dispatching military forces particularly in Central America, it was certainly eager to keep the region free from wider conflicts and rivalries.

Some Americans claimed a larger peace mantle at the end of World War I, under the banners of Woodrow Wilson's idealism. Writer Roland Hugins praised the nation's pure ideals:

> The truth is that the United States is the only high-minded Power left in the world. It is the only strong nation that has not entered on a career of imperial conquest ... There is in America little of that spirit of selfish aggression which lies at the heart of militarism ... We have a deep abhorrence of war for war's sake ... this political idealism, this strain of pacifism, this abstinence from aggression ... has been manifest from the birth of the republic.

The claims were interesting, but of course the United States partially abdicated a high-minded global goal when it turned to isolationism.

The concept *Pax Americana* particularly applied to the nation's new role after World War II, when it actively promoted peace in a number of regions besides the New World. "World's policeman" was another term frequently used to describe the nation's desire to keep order in many places, to prevent conflicts that might damage American as well as local interests. Critics might also use the *Pax Americana* term, but with emphasis less on the peace part, more on a level of global assertion that reminded some of an ambitious latter-day version of imperialism.

Peace interests, backed by military force, showed in many ways, in addition to the long-established role claimed in the Americas. The United States worked explicitly for peace in Western Europe after the end of World War II, supporting economic development and eagerly encouraging the steps toward greater European unity. It offered protection from any Soviet threat, but it also actively adjusted disputes among European countries themselves. The nation also offered defense of Japan and South Korea, protecting its own interests as against communist expansion but also helping to maintain peace in the region after the settlement of the Korean War. It also supported peaceful relations among nations in Southeast Asia. And while it was not successful in creating stability in the Middle East, it frequently intervened to encourage negotiations between Israel and its neighbors. Finally, the United States took a lead in many of the new international economic and monetary institutions that sought to reduce economic disputes and promote widespread international trade.

In 2000 a think tank issued a document entitled *Rebuilding America's Defenses* that put the best possible gloss on the *Pax Americana* ion a post-Cold War era:

> The American peace has proven itself peaceful, stable and durable. It has, over the past decade, provided the geopolitical framework for widespread economic growth and the spread of American principles of liberty and democracy. (But) even a global Pax Americana will not preserve itself ... What is required is a military that is strong and ready to meet both present

and future challenges; a foreign policy that boldly and purposefully promotes American principles abroad; and national leadership that accepts the United States' global responsibilities.

To be sure, there have been other versions of American peace. In the early 1960s John F. Kennedy argued for a peace that would not be "enforced by American weapons of war":

> I am talking about genuine peace, the kind of peace that makes life on earth worth living, and the kind that enables men and nations to grow, and to hope, and build a better life for their children – not merely peace for Americans but peace for all men and women, not merely peace in our time but peace in all time.

At the end of the 1970s, Jimmy Carter sounded similar hopeful notes during his presidency and afterwards:

> War may sometimes be a necessary evil. But ... it is always an evil, never a good. We will not learn how to live together in peace by killing each other's children. We have no desire to be the world's policeman. But America does want to be the world's peace maker.

Most supporters of American enforcement of peace did not use quite such high-flying language, which legitimately recalled the earlier idealism of Wilson or Secretary of State Kellogg. Too much idealism risked seeming impractical or naïve, particularly after the experiences of the interwar period. Most advocates and critics of the American peace focused squarely on American power and enlightened self-interest. This was the tone of both Democratic and Republican party platforms up to 2001: peace, but military strength first. That did not mean, however, that these arguments about a special national role were incorrect.

The problem was that the United States could not in fact always maintain peace. It intervened only rarely and often indecisively in African struggles. It could not tame the Middle East. It could not reconcile India and Pakistan; it could not figure out how to discipline North Korea. American participation in United Nations-led peacekeeping efforts, as opposed to involvement in its own initiatives and alliances, was also sparing.

Military actions

At least as important as the peace rhetoric was the fact that, as an enforcer, the United States had unusually frequent recourse to war, and while it always surrounded war with noble intentions, the nation did not always seem focused on doing all that might be possible to preserve peace in various parts of the world. During the Cold War aggressive American action was spurred by a great fear of communist expansionism; it was also supported by the lessons American leaders drew from Munich, and a resultant belief that responding to hostility early was a vital means of avoiding a larger conflagration later on. A similar approach underlay leadership in a war against Iraq, in 1990, with the Iraqi leader sometimes portrayed as a latter-day Hitler. Following the Cold War, some of the same reactions were then applied to efforts to stem terrorism, particularly after the 9/11, 2001, attacks on New York and the Pentagon. The result was a recurrent level of military intervention and outright war abroad, that may not always have been necessary – disputes on that score continue – and that certainly roused widespread foreign criticism, including criticism in the name of peace. American military bases expanded literally around the world during the Cold War, and the network was largely maintained even after 1990. Between Cold War and frequent regional conflicts, the United States was arguably involved in maintaining war-readiness over an exceptionally long period of time – literally for decades after 1945; and this experience could take its own toll, leading some to see war or threat of war as a normal state. The nation also became the world's leading supplier of arms to other countries.

President Dwight Eisenhower highlighted the change in the national approach to the military in a farewell address in 1961, patterned after George Washington's address over a century and a half earlier and touching on some similar themes. The Republican President, a former military commander, stressed the importance of a strong military establishment in keeping the peace – "our arms must be mighty, ready for instant action, so that no potential aggressor may be tempted to risk his own destruction." But he warned also of the vast armaments industry alongside a huge permanent military, seeing these as "new to the American experience." "We must guard against the acquisition of unwarranted influence … by the military-industrial complex … Only an alert and knowledgeable citizenry can compel the proper meshing of the huge industrial and military machinery of defense with our peaceful methods and goals …" The President ended by urging further disarmament and a continuing quest for peace, hoping that "in the goodness of time, all peoples will come to live together in a peace guaranteed by the finding force of mutual respect and love."

Recurrent wars were the most obvious symptom of the new American approach to world affairs. The American public largely supported at least the initial stages of the nation's involvement in regional wars, and the fairly steady buildup of military expenses, armaments and personnel. In both Korea and Vietnam (1950s and 1960s, respectively) there was a widespread acceptance of a need to push back communism. The invasion of Afghanistan soon after the 9/11 attack seemed a proper response, given a need to attack the terrorist base; and while almost a third of the American public was opposed to the 2003 invasion of Iraq, the majority was either favorable or acquiescent. Whatever the wider views about the desirability of peace, it did not seem the most important short-term priority.

With time, however, support for the wars usually faded. We will deal in the next chapter with the important opposition that arose to the Vietnam War, where peace rhetoric figured prominently. In Vietnam, but also in the wars of the early twenty-first century, public fatigue with inconclusive results, cost, but above all the death toll among American troops turned the tide. Beginning with Vietnam, television reporting and careful media tallies of the dead and wounded affected public opinion as never before. A poll taken three years into the Iraq war, asking Americans how many deaths were tolerable in war, elicited zero as the most common answer, with 500 the most frequent maximum among Americans willing to contemplate casualties at all. War fatigue and the new distaste for casualties did limit American military exposure in practice, generating new caution for more than a decade after Vietnam and projected for a period after Iraq and Afghanistan. But weariness was not the same as a positive evaluation of peace, and it did not clearly generate a high priority for nonmilitary options.

And American leaders did divise new responses to public concerns. The nation's military became increasingly aware of the need not only to minimize American losses, by relying heavily on bombardments from the air for example, but also to mask those deaths that did occur. During the early stages of the Iraq war bodies were brought back to the United States at night, to limit media coverage, and particularly to prevent sorrowful photographs. Elaborate praise of the sacrifice of troops and veterans also helped maintain some popular support. And American wars, though costly, rarely directly limited consumer options (in contrast to the rationing programs of World War II). By 2010 use of automated drone airplanes to attack suspected terrorists further limited the kind of "harm's way" engagement that ultimately stirred domestic opposition. The United States was perfecting what some people called low-stakes aggression, by avoiding much burden on the core society back home.

With these tactics, the United States was able to intervene militarily on a number of occasions, with innumerable lesser actions adding to the five major post-1945 wars*. The conflicts may have been in the interests of peace, at least by keeping war and violence far from American shores. But they hardly constituted the only possible strategies, as it frequently turned out (most obviously in Vietnam) that massive military engagement led to few durable results.

Pursuit of a heavy military investment strategy proceeded nevertheless. American military spending dipped briefly after World War II, only to reverse with the advent of the Cold War, and again modestly in the early 1990s, only to reverse again with the new terrorist threat after 2001. Here, substantial public support seemed secure; no large or consistent political debate challenged the effort to outspend all other major nations by a huge margin, maintaining considerable capacity for the nation as world's policeman. By 2012 direct military spending consumed well over 4 percent of the total Gross National Product (in contrast to 2.2 percent in China or Britain). Whether this kind of preponderance was necessary, whether it was most conducive to larger goals of greater world peace warranted debate: there were strong arguments on both sides. But this was a debate that, in the American context, did not clearly emerge.

* Korea; Vietnam; Gulf War; Afghanistan; Iraq.

By the early twenty-first century, indeed, and particularly with the widespread fear of terrorism, peace references tended to decline in the dominant American political rhetoric, in favor of a focus on security and the need for constant readiness. In the 2012 presidential debates, for example, the word peace was used only once. The Democratic Party platform in both 2008 and 2012 called for an end to the wars in Iraq and Afghanistan, but did not establish peace as a positive aspiration; Republicans in 2012 talked of peace in the Middle East also the Balkans, but also made it clear that continued attack on terrorists along with overall military strength were the main goals. This was a far cry from the abundant references to peace that had described the Eisenhower or Kennedy administrations or that surfaced again for several years as the Cold War drew to a close.

And so the United States did not participate in the widespread movement away from military investments in the quarter-century after 1990 and the Cold War's end. Of course other societies maintained important arsenals. China increased military spending as its economic base improved, though at obviously lower levels, and Japan responded by some steps toward remilitarization. Middle Eastern states remained heavily armed, as did individual nations like North Korea. Nevertheless, despite important peace traditions and previous precedents, the distinctive American position was noteworthy, a vital complexity in the mix of regional patterns.

Reducing the military

For against the military commitments of countries like the United States, an impressive number of regions participated in military shrinkage in the post-Cold War world. The trend reflected other budget priorities, but also a reduced sense of military threat. At least in some cases, the result was a further reduction in the risks of war. There was no major new case of outright demilitarization (though Panama abolished its military in the wake of the U.S. invasion in 1989), but many countries in fact approached the levels maintained by German and Japan – spending at 1 percent of Gross National Product or below.

New Zealand was a case in point. The country renounced any association with nuclear weaponry in 1986, reducing military ties with the United States in the process. Then in the 1990s the country decided on what it called "minimum credible force," with only about 4,000 troops – highly trained and professional – for the purpose of defense along with participation in United Nations peacekeeping forces.

South Africa made a dramatic turn in 1994, after the end of apartheid. The South African National Defense Forces were cut back to a purely defensive mission, the budget slashed to 1.2 percent of Gross National Product. The result caused criticism, for the navy and air force deteriorated rapidly, but the policy was maintained. Most other southern African nations followed suit, reducing military spending rapidly and arguably creating a new regional peace zone.

The trend affected several parts of Latin America. With the advent of a democratic system, replacing authoritarian and military rule, and in the wake of the Falkland Islands defeat, Argentina reduced its budget to 1 percent of GNP. After more democratic regimes replaced military rule, and as internal civil strife subsided, both El Salvador and Guatemala rapidly pared down their military levels – encouraged by the United Nations as monitor of local peace agreements which set formal targets for spending reductions. El Salvador in 1992 began to replace older officers and to introduce a new and more democratic spirit into the army while also changing the training system. Civilian rule was emphasized in a new constitution. Armed forces doctrine was redefined to stress "the prominence of human dignity and democratic values, respect for human rights, and subordination to civilian authorities." Troop levels were cut by 50 percent, the military budget by more than half – or from 3.4 percent of GNP to 0.8 percent by 2009. Equally important was the adoption of new functions for the military, in combatting crime and in providing humanitarian assistance in cases of natural disasters – with a major increase in public support responding to the change. El Salvador also began to participate in several UN peacekeeping initiatives, for example in monitoring the border between Iraq and Kuwait. Patterns in Guatemala followed somewhat similar lines, including participation in international peacekeeping efforts. Some scholars argued that Latin America more generally was turning from a kind of peace the resulted from weak states and poor military preparedness, toward a positive commitment to more active peace goals and dispute resolution, with greater regional stability resulting as well.

Finally, many European nations followed a similar pattern in reconsidering military levels as part of their evolution as "civilian" states. Many of the Scandinavian nations, but also the Low Countries and Spain cut military budgets, believing that the threat of war had receded and that funds were better spent on other issues. The idea of keeping a military force capable of aggressive action clearly receded. While a German-style peace culture did not spread uniformly, at the policy level many countries were now essentially adopting the German approach.

* * * * *

Changes of this sort continued to redefine the world's regional map, in terms of peace goals and strategies. The growth in the number of states committed both to small military forces and to the growing emphasis on humanitarian and global peacekeeping goals was impressive, but of course other nations and regions continued to take a somewhat different approach. Would the new trends persist, and possibly embrace an even larger number of countries? This was a great question, as globalization increased mutual awareness and arguably made regional conflicts more dangerous. Overall, globally, military spending had dropped to 1.7 percent of GDP by 2012, down from 5 percent a few decades earlier.

Further reading

Pax Americana

Barrett, Graham. "Imagining the Pax Americana." Available online at www.theage.com.au/articles/2003/04/16/1050172646729.html (accessed August 2013).

Ebeling, Richard M. "The Dangers and Costs of Pax Americana." Available online at www.fff.org/freedom/fd0212b.asp (accessed September 2013).

Party Platforms and State of the Union Addresses. Available online at www.presidency.ucsb.edu/index.php (accessed August 2013).

Rubenstein, Richard. *Reasons to Kill: Why Americans Choose War*. New York: Bloomsbury, 2010.

On peace in various world regions

Agius, Christing. *The Social Construction of Swedish Neutrality: Challenges to Swedish Identity and Sovereignty*. Manchester: Manchester University Press, 2006.

Busrus, Rajesh M. *South Asia's Cold War: Nuclear Weapons and Conflict in Comparative Perspective*. New York: Routledge, 2008.

Hallward, Maia Carter. *Struggling for a Just Peace: Israeli and Palestinian Activism in the Second Intifada*. Gainesville, FL: University Press of Florida, 2011.

Kacowicz, Areie Marcelo. *Zones of Peace in the Third World: South America and West Africa in Comparative Perspective*. Albany, NY: State University of New York Press, 1998.

Porto, João Gomes, and Ulf Engel. *Africa's New Peace and Security Architecture: Promoting Norms, Institutionalizing Solutions*. Farnham: Ashgate Publishing, 2010.

Salomon, G. and B. Nevo, eds. *Peace Education: The Concept, Principles, and Practices around the World*. Mahwah, NJ: Lawrence Erlbaum, 2002.

Smith, Michael E. *Europe's Foreign and Security Policy: The Institutionalization of Cooperation*. Cambridge: Cambridge University Press, 2004.

Wolpert, Stanley A. *India and Pakistan: Continued Conflict or Cooperation?* Berkeley, CA: University of California Press, 2010.

On militarism/demilitarization throughout the world

Black, Jan K. *Sentinels of Empire: The United States and Latin American Militarism*. New York: Glenwood Press, 1986.

Bowman, Kirk S. *Militarization, Development and Democracy: The Perils of Praetorianism in Latin America*. University Park, PA: Pennsylvania State University Press, 2002.

Dinan, Desmond. *Ever Closer Union: An Introduction to European Integration*, 4/e. Boulder, CO: Lynne Rienner Publishers, 2010.

Franko, Patrice. "De Facto Demilitarization: Budget-Driven Downsizing in Latin America." *Journal of Interamerican Studies and World Affairs* 36.1 (1994): 37–74.

Harries, Meirion and Susie. *Soldiers of the Sun: The Rise and Fall of the Japanese Imperial Army*. New York: Random House, 1991.

Horst, Tord and Høivik Aas. "Demilitarization in Costa Rica: A Farewell to Arms?" *Journal of Peace Research* 18.4 (1981): 333–51.

Hook, Glenn D. *Militarization and Demilitarization in Contemporary Japan.* London: Routledge, 1996.

Isacson, Adam. *Altered States: Security and Demilitarization in Central America.* Washington, D.C.: Center for International Policy, 1997.

Köchler, Hans, ed. *The Principles of Non-Alignment: The Non-Aligned Countries in the Eighties – Results and Perspectives.* London: Third World Centre, 1982.

Lamb, Guy. "Reflections on Demilitarization: A Southern African Perspective." *International Peacekeeping* 7.3 (2000): 120–36.

Solimano, Andrés. *Colombia: Essays on Conflict, Peace, and Development.* Washington, D.C.: World Bank, 2000.

Stearns, Peter N., ed. *Demilitarization in the Contemporary World.* Champaign, IL: University of Illinois Press, 2014.

Stivachtis, Yannis A., Chris Price, and Mike Habegger. "The European Union as a Peace Actor." *Review of European Studies* 5.3 (2013): 4–17.

Thomas, Darryl C. and Ali A. Mazrui. "Africa's Post-Cold War Demilitarization: Domestic and Global Causes." *Journal of International Affairs* 46.1 (1992): 157–74.

Ward, Robert E. and Yoshikazu Sakamoto, eds. *Democratizing Japan: The Allied Occupation.* Honolulu, HI: University of Hawaii Press, 1987.

Williams, Philip J. and Knut Walter. *Militarization and Demilitarization in El Salvador's Transition to Democracy.* Pittsburgh, PA: University of Pittsburgh Press, 1997.

See also

Vaidya, Ashish. *Globalization: Encyclopedia of Trade, Labor and Politics.* Santa Barbara, CA: ABC-CLIO, 2005.

10   Peace ideas and peace movements after 1945

Never before had there been as much diverse thinking and activity directed toward peace as developed in the framework set by the end of World War II, decolonization, and the Cold War. Older peace influences, including religious commitments, developed new vitality and novel outlets. The influence of Gandhi's legacy showed strongly in many places. Contemporary peace endeavors built strongly on the past. Yet there were major innovations in ideas and strategies as well, including new efforts in research and education. Widespread popular responses to some new threats formed an important part of the picture as well, whether the issue was nuclear weaponry or the broadly criticized plans for American invasion of Iraq in 2003.

Peace and anti-war movements surfaced almost everywhere that sufficient freedom existed for voluntary groups to form. Indeed, the surge formed a crucial part of the larger spread of Non- Government Organizations (NGOs), which provided new voice for diverse groups and, at times, significantly influenced governments themselves. The wide geography of peace activity and the emergence of initiatives separate from the West were key changes in their own right. No brief analysis can do justice to the range of activities involved. Energy and idealism, and sometimes fear as well, combined on many fronts.

Questions about impact and significance inevitably arise. Obviously, a number of peace movements failed in their purpose, at least in the short run. Peace activists in Israel, despite impressive effort, did not capture the majority of the public. Massive international protest against the 2003 campaign in Iraq did not stop the invasion. But there were successes as well, and many cases in which peace efforts directly contributed to international action or regional reconciliations. Some experts argued, particularly as democratic political systems spread, that a new kind of public involvement was entering the peace process by the early twenty-first century. We will also see that new kinds of expertise were involved as well.

Traditional sources, new voices

The lessons drawn from World War II and then the tensions of the Cold War gave new life to many longstanding arguments and strategies for peace, though in some cases there had been hints of new vitality between the wars. Philosophers in many academic institutions, at least in the Western world, returned to questions about just and unjust wars, reviving older thinking but sometimes adding new dimensions such as the contemporary concern for human rights: was it legitimate to use war to attack abusive states? Several American philosophers now vigorously argued in the affirmative. But criteria by which wars could be judged unjust remained important in the discussion as well, and several new military actions were widely condemned on this basis.

More important than philosophy was the new vigor of religious movements directed toward peace. Linked to religion was the legacy of Gandhi's thinking on nonviolence, which spurred important movements toward social justice but also toward peace. Conscientious objection, another traditional staple, took on new meaning as well in several contexts. Peace history generated an active legacy in the contemporary period.

Major religions

Christianity provided many new spurs to peace thinking and peace organizations, based on earlier principles now juxtaposed with contemporary problems including the nuclear threat. Catholics took a more vigorous role. Popes issued many statements in favor of peace, often addressing specific tension points such as, for example, the dangerous divisions in Korea. Pope John Paul made peace a highlight of his message on the advent of a new millennium, in 2001: "To everyone I affirm that peace is possible. It needs to be implored from God as his gift, but it also needs to be built day by day with his help, through works of justice and love." Catholic action in the United States was considerable. During the 1950s individual lay leaders, like Dorothy Day, and several organizations fought hard against the national commitment to nuclear weapons, in some cases refusing to participate in civil defense drills designed to protect against attack. They were accused of civil disobedience, but actually helped rouse greater popular support for efforts to limit the nuclear threat.

Protestant involvement was also considerable. It included Quaker groups, which continued a systematic opposition to war: "We utterly deny all outward wars and strife ... for any end or pretext whatever." Quakers were actively involved in humanitarian relief efforts and mediation attempts in many conflict sites. Individual Quakers took an active role in other organizations. It was a Quaker convert and former navy commander who helped form the Committee for Non-Violent Action in the United States, which held non-stop vigils and deliberate disruptions at nuclear-related government facilities across the United States. But mainstream Protestant groups also became more involved. The World Council of Churches, an international Protestant body formed in 1948, issued many statements against war, setting up a "justice, peace, and creation" commission designed to promote racial harmony, environmentalism and nonviolence. The Council worked hard on causes such as "peace journalism," trying to introduce greater balance into press accounts which often, in its judgment, overemphasized war. The Council declared the first years of the twentieth century the Decade to Overcome Violence, seeking common action in defense of peace; activities including an annual International Day of Prayer for Peace, supporting churches in war zones and helping them to "promote non-violent resolution of conflicts, reconciliation and forgiveness."

Buddhists also stepped forward smartly, from centers in Japan and elsewhere but often with far flung international operations in a variety of countries. Exiled from Tibet after Chinese communist occupation, the fourteenth Dalai Lama became a major spokesman for peace. He constantly advocated for greater rights for his country, though always on the basis of nonviolence, hoping that Tibet could become a zone of peace. More generally he urged that war "should be relegated to the dustbin of history."

Buddhist peace activity flourished in postwar Japan. The Soka Gakkai movement expanded rapidly. It opposed the use of nuclear weapons as "criminal" under any circumstances, and called on young people around the world to work for their abolition. The effort became a cornerstone of larger peace efforts. From the late 1950s onward a new leader, Daisaku Ikeda, preached an international message, while also infusing an array of educational institutions with the priority of peace on the basis of Buddhist principles. "We must take on the larger challenge of transforming the currents of history from destruction to construction, from confrontation to coexistence, from divisiveness to solidarity ... while ensuring that all that we do contribute to the larger objective of a global society or peace and creative coexistence." Peace, and its basis in mutual support and understanding, become the "social mission of religion in the twenty-first century." On more specific issues, Ikeda argued passionately against nuclear weapons and a systematic reduction in military spending, and also worked hard for reconciliation between China and Japan. Buddhist efforts of this sort were also noteworthy for pointedly including peace references from many religious and philosophical traditions, not just their own.

Islamic efforts at peace, stemming from this religious tradition, were admittedly sometimes overshadowed by minorities preaching violence, but they were very real. In fact, many Islamic thinkers and organizations, in different parts of the Islamic world, built on the religion's earlier traditions – traditions that had persuaded Gandhi himself to note lthat "the basis of Islam is not violence, but is unadulterated peace. It regards forbearance as superior to vengeance. The very word 'Islam' means peace." But more than tradition was involved: involvements in varied conflicts and the continuing vitality of the faith, and its many specific sects, produced important new commitments to peace.

A number of examples make the point clearly. Early in the twenty-first century the current leader of the Ahamdiyya Muslim Community (a sect that began in the late nineteenth century, and now embraces millions of Muslims) launched the International Peace Symposium. He followed with a Muslims for Peace initiative that, among other things, works on interfaith dialogs, particularly with Christian and Jews, in the interests of peace. Hazrat Ahmad emphasized the equality of all people under Islam, with no prejudice or discrimination: "This is the key and golden principle that lays the foundation for harmony between different groups and nations, and for the establishment of peace."

A variety of Sufi movements clarified their own commitments to peace, in places like Bangladesh and Southeast Asia. Here too the emphasis was on tolerance and compassion, and the brotherhood of all peoples. Sufi leaders in Turkey and the Balkans often work actively with other faiths, such as Christianity, in the interests of regional peace. As a Sufi mystic put it in 1986, "We should not carry a sword in our hands ... we should not arm ourselves with guns; we should be armed with contentment. We should not put our trust in battles; we should have trust in God ... These are the true weapons of Islam." In the same spirit, many Muslim leaders in India committed to nonviolence, often explicitly embracing the legacy of Gandhi, and specifically for peaceful relations with Pakistan.

Based in Turkey, another Muslim movement, under the inspiration of Bediuzzaman Said Nursi, picked up the theme of nonviolence, working actively with Christian and other groups to promote peaceful relations. In the strife-torn Balkans, in the 1990s, yet another group built on the Gandhian theme of nonviolence, establishing the Kosovo Civil Disobedience Movement on the basis of complete pacifism. Various nonviolent protest organizations also spread in Iran and Iraq, including the La'Onf organization whose name means "no violence" in Arabic.

Many Palestinian movements worked actively in the interests of peace, often collaborating with Jewish colleagues. Mubarak Award set up a Palestinian Centre for the Study of Nonviolence in 1983. In 2001 an Interfaith Encounter Association, with substantial Muslim leadership, developed a number of Israeli-Palestinian working groups.

Obviously, key aspects of the Islamic peace approach matched interests from other religions in working increasingly in an interdenominational framework. In 2002, for example, a summit among Christian, Muslim, and Jewish leaders in the Middle East, in Alexandria, Egypt, produced a Declaration of Interfaith Coexistence, committing to peace and condemning violence. Meetings of this sort worked hard to emphasize shared elements among the major religions, rather than points of dispute, while confirming a mutual priority for peace. Similar coalitions could be found in Europe, North America, and elsewhere, often embracing Buddhist and other groups as well as the Abrahamic faiths. In 2005–6 for example, the Buddhist, Japanese-based Shinnyo-en movement brought Christian, Muslim, and Jewish youth together in the Middle East, as a part of a Paths of Peace program, while actively organizing interfaith efforts in the Unites States and elsewhere. The importance of tolerance and a priority for peace broke down traditional religious boundaries in a growing number of activities and organizations.

The nonviolence legacy

We have seen that Mohandas Gandhi worked out an increasingly explicit strategy of nonviolence in the struggles for Indian independence from Britain in the decades between the wars. He translated his ideas into opposition to war itself with growing fervor once World War II broke out. "Concern for humanity is inconsistent with the recklessness with which [war mongers] shed human lives." "I have reasoned out the doctrine of the sword, I have worked out its possibilities and come to the conclusion that man's destiny is to replace the law of the jungle with the law of conscious love."

Gandhi's ideas had a profound influence on the American civil rights leader Martin Luther King, Jr., who also placed them in the context of Christian peace thinking. King's strategy of nonviolence applied particularly to the struggle for equal rights for racial minorities in the United States, guiding a major movement during the 1950s and 1960s along with many other leaders. But he fully understood the relevance of the approach to issues of war and peace, particularly when confronted with his nation's growing involvement in Vietnam during the 1960s. He found the damage to the Vietnamese people from American military action unacceptable, but this led him to even wider comments on the war-centered approach: "A nation that continues year after year to spend more money on military defense than on programs of social uplift is approaching spiritual death." He worried that the United States was turning away from social justice at home, for example in the efforts to reduce poverty, to become "the greatest purveyor of violence in the world." "Today the choice is no longer between violence and non-violence. It is either non-violence or non-existence."

Gandhi's ideas, amplified now by the Reverend King, had considerable influence also in the struggle against apartheid in South Africa. Nelson Mandela's commitment to nonviolent strategies was somewhat less systematic than that of his exemplars, but he carefully espoused a policy of peace and reconciliation once apartheid was finally demolished. "If you want to make peace with your enemy, you must work with your enemy. Then he becomes your partner." Mandela's vision for Africa, more broadly, was a vision of peace. Not surprisingly, these views helped engender the marked turn against militarism and military spending in the mid-1990s that characterized not only South Africa but the several neighboring states.

Commitments to nonviolence also spread in Asia. In 1986 the Nonviolent Peaceforce emerged in the Philippines, aiming at effecting political change as a popular movement newly challenged a dictatorship. The Peaceforce continued to monitor local conditions, enforce ceasefires, and report any recurring human rights abuses. Nonviolence movements also surfaced in places like Burma, Mongolia, and South Korea, where they sometimes linked with Christian or Buddhist groups. They encountered varying degrees of success, but they undeniably provided a new approach, aiming largely at local or regional disputes rather than larger global issues. We have seen that nonviolence, including explicit references to Gandhi's legacy, permeated many Islamic movements for peace and justice, especially from the 1980s onward.

Ideals of nonviolence motivated peace efforts in many other situations, including Palestine, even when they were overshadowed by more militant approaches. The combination of tradition and contemporary example created an important new force in recent world history that would inspire and guide peace thinking in a variety of regions.

Conscientious objection

Religion had long linked closely to individual protests against war in the form of conscientious objections to military service. Here too, new developments connected to older patterns. We have seen that conscientious objection surged in some countries after the war, such as West Germany, becoming a key index of cultural change. Conscientious objection of sorts would also characterize massive protests by young men in the United States against the Vietnam War, though because the refusals centered on this war, more than wars in general, formal legal status was not achieved; as a result, many fled to Canada or Sweden to avoid the draft.

An important new development centered on the gradual enshrinement of conscientious objection as a human right. The issue was not mentioned directly in the 1948 Universal Declaration of Human Rights, though there was a reference to freedom of conscience. In 1974 a UN official said that another right might be added, "The Right to Refuse to Kill." An international group of War Resisters urged more explicit commitment, noting that some nations continued to argue that it is a moral duty to serve the military. Other rights organizations, including Amnesty International, agreed, and in 2006 a UN committee judged, though not unanimously, that conscientious objection was an extension of the right of conscience. Even earlier, in 1998, the High Commissioner for Human Rights issued a document confirming that not only was conscientious objection a basic right, but that "people already performing military service may develop conscientious objections" – they should not be excluded from the right.

The overall importance of conscientious objection actually declined, in fact, as the use of a military draft declined. Many countries found that a smaller, professionally trained force was better than mass conscription, while also avoiding confrontation with a wider public opinion that objected to a service requirement. Massive evasion of military service during the Vietnam War convinced the United States to move in this direction, in 1973. With fewer requirements, people with a moral objection to war could now simply refrain from participating.

Mass protests

Contemporary history was dotted with an unusual phenomenon: mass demonstrations and other agitation against a war or prospect of war. These occasions reflected religious and nonviolence themes, but also other concerns about moral conduct and security. They certainly built on the growing array of peace groups that were forming in many places, and they contributed to the groups in turn. Moral outrage could be a force in its own right. The protests sometimes influenced policy directly, sometimes not; but they did constitute a new element in decisions about peace and war.

Nuclear weapons

Three outbursts were particularly interesting and important. We have already dealt with elements of the protests that swelled over uncontrolled nuclear tests and nuclear weaponry, during the late 1950s and through the 1960s. Emotions ran particularly high in Europe, Japan and the United States, but there were echoes in many regions. Testing served as an initial focus, but after the test ban was concluded attention turned to levels of nuclear arsenals more generally. In 1957 the National Committee for a Sane Nuclear Policy (SANE) formed in the United States, spurred by a variety of peace and health activists. They won support from many prominent scientists plus Hollywood stars like Marilyn Monroe. SANE put pressure on political candidates, to restrict presidential war powers. It organized large women's groups, including a 50,000 Strike for Peace campaign worldwide.

Protests were widespread in Britain and elsewhere in Europe. A Campaign for Nuclear Disarmament held yearly rallies and meetings, under the slogan "we must protest if we are to survive." Key groups maintained tens of thousands of members, extending in the 1990s. In Germany, anti-nuclear protest helped form the new Green Party, in 1983, which included nonviolent opposition to nuclear weapons and missile delivery systems slated for Germany. Mass protests against United States plans to extend missile sites continued through the 1980s. Obviously, this prolonged wave of agitation did succeed in pressing governments to enter into new arms control arrangements, so this was not idle furor; equally obviously, the most sweeping demands, for example for a full end to nuclear arsenals, were not successful.

Vietnam

The drawn-out war in Vietnam was the second target of widespread popular anger, during the later 1960s. Initially featuring a French struggle against an anti-imperialist movement, the conflict gradually drew in the United States, in what some would say was rather haphazard process; but by the middle of the decade the Americans were engaged in massive military operations, giving and taking serious losses. The new role of televised news gave developments in Vietnam vividness, and an international audience, that had never before occurred. American involvement began with widespread public support (only 24 percent opposed, in a 1965 poll); but by 1973 the vast majority had turned against the effort.

By the mid-1960s anti-war groups were already mobilizing in the United States against the war. One group proclaimed, "We shall encourage the development of [various] nonviolent acts, including acts which involve civil disobedience, in order to stop the flow of American soldiers and munitions to Vietnam." Many young people began declaring conscientious objection or evading the draft in other ways, and a surprising number of Vietnam veterans began openly campaigning against the war. Images of American troops deliberately or accidentally injuring Vietnamese civilians steadily amplified the anti-war torrent.

But it was students, in the United States and Europe, who made the war a clear target of popular protest. Campus rallies and teach-ins opposed American involvement, as peace goals became central to the rising tide of youth unrest. A number of leading intellectuals joined in, but student numbers really swelled the ranks of dissent. One rally in Washington, DC had 100,000 participants. A number of protesters shot flower petals from cannon, toward the Pentagon, with slogans like "flower power" and "make love not war." Opposition to American involvement figured prominently in the student risings in France and Germany in 1968; 10,000 students joined a university sit-in in Berlin, explicitly against the war. Violent street protests against the war occurred not only in Germany but also in London and Rome. There were also reverberations elsewhere: a Latin American tour by American astronauts was disrupted on several campuses by students shouting "Murderers, get out of Vietnam." Student protests surged in Australia as well. Popular culture support included Beatles songs like "Give Peace a Chance" or Cat Stevens' "Peace Train." Without question, despite huge divisions for and against youth protest plus the distraction of other youth protest targets, the anti-war surge contributed ultimately to the American decision to launch negotiations to end hostilities. There were other lingering effects, including opposition to army training programs on a number of American college campuses. The link between youth culture and peace would gradually loosen, but the combination had proved quite powerful for a key period.

Iraq

The final mass movement for peace, on an even more global basis, occurred in anticipation of the American invasion of Iraq in 2003. The setting was quite clear, as the administration of President George W. Bush publicly outlined its case against the Saddam Hussein regime, particularly around the presumed possession of "weapons of mass destruction." (What the full motives were in deciding American action continue to be debated; it turned out of course that the weapons did not exist.) On February 15 2003 the largest anti-war demonstration in the history of the world took place. Hundreds of thousands of people marched in London – some estimates claimed 2 million, in what may have been the biggest outpouring ever in the United Kingdom. Scottish protest was equally vigorous, centering in Glasgow. Massive protests erupted in Germany and Italy. Huge marches occurred in Spain, while 300,000 paraded in Athens. Many American cities were involved, with hundreds of thousands of protesters. Big demonstrations also occurred in Australia, which had promised some troops to the effort. Great crowds assembled in Japan and South Korea, with significant protests also in Russia, Mexico, Indonesia, and Turkey. In Seoul, South Korea, 2000 Buddhists said prayers for the Iraqis who would be killed. A precise tally is impossible, but it is clear that over 25 million people voted with their feet that day, around the world, in a magnificently coordinated action facilitated by the unprecedented power of the Internet. Youth elements loomed large in the protest, but there were also large contingents of older people. Families brought children, believing the bearing witness would be important for them. Anti-war union locals mobilized workers, particularly in Western Europe and Australia, but middle-class presence was strong as well. Masses of people truly found the prospect of this war – a "war of choice," not a clear effort at self-defense – repellent.

The protest capped months of building outrage. Demonstrations had begun the previous fall, in Italy, Japan, Australia, India, and elsewhere. In Switzerland 20,000 gathered to urge the parliament to protest the war. In Paris, marchers dumped bottles of Coca-Cola, as a symbolic gesture against unilateral American action. Large groups also gathered in the Middle East and Southeast Asia, where Muslim populations were large. International polls showed over 90 percent of the world opposed to the war, at least without United Nations approval, with ranges between 80 and 95 percent in Russia, Japan, and many parts of Europe. A host of ad hoc organizations fanned the flames. These included some of the venerable anti-nuclear groups that had formed several decades earlier, plus the Quaker Society of Friends, International, but there were also a number of newcomers stirred by this particular occasion. As always, a number of media figures participated, in Hollywood and elsewhere.

Inevitably, in an outpouring of this sort, a host of motives were involved. Some protesters were against war, period. Others worried about this particular war, which seemed unnecessary – or as one British demonstrator put it, in classic language, "unjust." Some focused on the probable American reliance on bombing, and the deaths this would cause. Muslims were concerned about Muslim victims. But concern for peace was quite real, as with an Italian marcher who stated quite simply, "we wanted to demonstrate that a different world was possible." The pope himself used the occasion to renew a commitment to peace. Whatever the precise set of goals, there was no question that emotions ran high: many people talked of being "angry," "upset" or "anxious" at the prospect of another conflict.

In the short run, the protests failed: the invasion occurred. Yet anti-war opinion limited the number of allies the United States could persuade to join in. It may have encouraged the substantial resistance to American occupation, within Iraq, after the war had ended. And it certainly colored a longer aftermath, in which people, in the United States as well as elsewhere, continued to be suspicious of unnecessary military involvements and, more specifically, American motives. The skepticism massively complicated a proposed American venture against Syria, in 2013, when even the British Parliament, long a reliable ally, declined participation. It was becoming harder to persuade people to tolerate certain kinds of wars.

Massive outpourings against war remained unusual. It was hard to sustain a widespread commitment to peace at this level of active engagement. Still, the phenomenon was significant as well as novel. It signaled some very new fears about certain kinds of war, but also a more active public engagement in defining just versus unjust wars – moving from abstract discussions of principle to new uses of street demonstrations and global petitions. Popular outcry unquestionably added a vital ingredient to policy determinations, a clear sign of innovation in contemporary world history. Were ordinary people more interested in peace than ever before, or simply better able to find means of expression, or both?

Scholarship and teaching

At virtually the opposite pole from mass demonstrations, another set of innovations involved the emergence of various kinds of research, teaching and outreach devoted to the pursuit of peace. Scholarly involvement was not of course brand new. Philosophers had debated peace and war for centuries. Many intellectuals began to contribute their voices on behalf of peace causes during the nineteenth century. Efforts to use education to promote peace, or to change education away from aggressive nationalism, characterized many peace endeavors particularly after World War I. But the post-World War II era was distinctive nevertheless, in the emergence of new interdisciplinary centers studying peace and conflict, researching methods of conciliation, and then seeking to apply lessons in classrooms and through academic outreach. The effort had global scope, even though the leading centers clustered in the wealthier countries. It might connect with other peace impulses, including religious motivations and Gandhian nonviolence. But the overall framework was new.

A host of new educational initiatives emerged. In the United States, Betty Reardon, at the Teachers College of Columbia University, developed new programs in peace education, with emphasis on training other educators. Her goals were sweeping: the ultimate aim of peace education is "the formation of responsible, committed and caring citizens who have integrated [peace] values into everyday life and acquired the skilled to advocate for them." Quaker groups in the United States and Britain opened new education centers, focusing on materials designed to help people cope with conflict, in Europe and various parts of Latin America. In 1980 a new University for Peace was launched in Costa Rica, with some backing from the United Nations. Its intention was "to help lessen obstacles to world peace and progress." The University hosted students from more than 100 countries, and established branches in Ethiopia, South Korea and elsewhere. Also in 1980 the United Nations itself launched a new program in "disarmament education." Here the purpose was ambitiously defined as "any form of action aimed at limiting, controlling or reducing arms, including unilateral disarmament initiatives and, ultimately, general and complete disarmament under effective international control. It may also be understood as a process aimed at transforming the current system of armed nation states into a new world order of unarmed peace, in which war is no longer an instrument of national policy." UN efforts in this area continued in subsequent decades, producing educational materials of various sorts.

The most systematic innovation, however, focused on a combination of new types of research on peace and conflict, soon combined with education and outreach. The interwar period had seen changes in scholarship, most notably in applied psychology, directed toward trying to figure out why people might turn to violent confrontations, though the focus was more on labor disputes than on international relations. This basis combined with the growing concerns about nuclear warfare to generate a more explicit scholarly agenda, centered on conflict and quickly including a variety of disciplines.

Early work centered both in the United States and Europe. A psychologist, Ted Lentz, set up a new Institute for Peace Research in St. Louis, in 1945. Kenneth Boulding, at the University of Michigan, began to examine conflict from the standpoint of economics and social psychology, establishing a new Center for Research in Conflict Resolution that would last for 20 years. His work quickly combined with efforts by various scientists and mathematicians to use game theory to model conflict situations. The group formed a new *Journal of Conflict Resolution*, in 1957. On the European side, a new Peace Research Institute was launched in Oslo, Norway, in 1959. Johan Galtung, a Norwegian social scientist, tried to define different categories of peace, from negative types of compromise to more positive engagement, and to use these models to improve mediation techniques. For some time European researchers tended to emphasize a more holistic approach to peace issues, regarding American efforts as somewhat mechanistic, focused on specific techniques of conciliation rather than a more embracing notion of positive peace; but this gap would ultimately close.

Other disciplines began to join in. Again in the United States a movement toward alternative dispute resolution began among lawyers, during the 1970s. Various scholars began to collect data on the numbers and patterns of conflicts and collective violence, often with regional analyses attached. Sociologists began to play a growing role in relevant research as well, while humanists worked on the roles of storytelling and historical representations in conflict.

In 1983 several scholars, from Britain as well as the United States, joined to form a new Institute for Conflict Analysis and Resolution, at George Mason University. The Institute shied away from specific references to "peace," lest decision makers in Washington dismiss the effort at too idealistic; these would be added in only during the 1990s. But the Institute served as a next step in interdisciplinary research, and also established the first degree programs in the field, at the master's level. John Burton, a British scholar joining the Institute, brought an interest in trying to address deeply rooted social conflicts, where mediation techniques alone would not suffice. Overall, the goal of the new Institute, and increasingly of the larger field, centered on combining theoretical work with practical example, and on blending research, teaching and actual conflict resolution practice.

Research approaches obviously continued to evolve, particularly after the end of the Cold War refocused attention to regional, ethnic, and religious conflicts. Conflict scholars tried increasingly to differentiate not only among types but also stages of conflict, with intervention strategies more closely adapted to the situation involved. New concerns, like disputes over environmental issues or feminist agendas, added in as well.

Further divisions opened in a field that was still defining itself. Some practitioners in the United States cooperated closely with government organizations, like the State Department, often working to settle local disputes or build new civic structures in the aftermath of American military interventions, as in Vietnam or, later, Iraq, and Afghanistan. Other experts viewed these efforts with skepticism, preferring to work on conflicts as more independent agents. Practitioners outside the United States were sometimes particularly suspicious of the motives of some of their American colleagues, worrying that they preferred to serve the national power structure more than the interests of the oppressed. Other disputes were more strictly scholarly, around how best to define conflict or the role of violence.

The most important points involved the steady expansion and geographic extension of this increasingly professional field. By 2013 there were over 100 academic programs in the United States alone, with commitments developing at places like the University of San Diego and Notre Dame. Here and elsewhere religious traditions sometimes entered in, as not only several Catholic institutions but also Eastern Mennonite University (with a Center for Justice and Peacebuilding) established major operations. Again, the combination of older peace traditions with new opportunities was striking. *Pax Ludens* was a group in the Netherlands doing international relations simulations for purposes of peace building. In Israel the University of Tel Aviv offered degree programs at several levels. In New Delhi a Nelson Mandela Center opened at an Islamic university. A larger Seeds of Peace movement, founded in 1993, trained people in conflict resolution in over 27 countries, with emphasis on trouble spots such as India and Pakistan, Cyprus, and the Balkans: "we know that it is possible to redirect human passions, even calls for revenge, toward the positive goal of creating peace."

The result of these new opportunities for research and education was, clearly, the growing emergence of trained professionals ready to work in NGOs or, sometimes, governments in the interest or promoting peace. The academic centers themselves actively engaged in outreach. The program at George Mason for example conducted negotiations among various factions in the Sudan, or between contesting parties in Georgia and Azerbaijan, or among different religious groups in Israel, Palestine, Jordan, and Syria. Even more important was a flood of graduates from programs of this sort (often from a variety of different countries), ready to guide and serve the growing variety of peace activities, armed with formal knowledge of peacemaking and its complexities. It was a combination of popular concerns but also the newly available professionalism that helps explain the lively array of groups and movements that, in turn, provided the final component in approaches to peace in contemporary world history. Less measurable was the impact of wider social programs on a larger swath of public opinion, but here too some change may have occurred.

Organizations for peace

Literally thousands of peace organizations have sprung up around the world over the past half-century. Some, obviously, build directly on the new research and teachings centered on peace, and are closely linked to academic activity. Others work more on advocacy, trying to propose new peace policies or monitoring situations that may threaten peace. Still others focus more specifically on mobilizing support or conducting direct action for peace, including acts of civil disobedience. Many groups are durable, having lasted for several decades, others respond to shorter-term crises or opportunities. Some groups enroll many members, or draw from elite groups or celebrities, others are small or humble. The fact is that there is no systematic catalogue of the range and nature of peace organizations, and while we can try to divide them into different functional types even here the boundary lines are blurry. The main points are that the scope and number of peace activities and the geographical range of such activities are greater than ever before in world history. This reflects the flowering of peace thinking and concerns (including the opportunities to build on older peace traditions), the new levels of anxiety about the dangers of war, and the variety of specific peace problems that have dropped up since World War II.

Innovation also reflects other developments. Increasing democratization, in many societies, encourages popular organizations around all sorts of issues, including peace. Growing self-consciousness among population sectors like youth and women promotes particular approaches to peace, though there were some precedents for this, particularly in the association of women and peace, earlier in the twentieth century. New communication technologies undoubtedly help: using the Internet and social media has made it much easier than ever before to form grassroots organizations or to mobilize around particular crises.

The surge of peace groups reflects an intriguing combination of what scholars like to call the "local and the global." International influences run strong, benefiting as well from the new communications technologies: many countries have offshoots of United Nations support organizations, or feminist-derived peace activities. Religious movements seek new global audiences: important Buddhist peace centers have emerged in the United States, for example, based on Japanese sponsorship. As noted, peace activities have clearly benefited from the larger network of International NGOs. Yet local roots are also vital. Taiwan established a "Peace Memorial Day" in 1995 (celebrated in February), along with a cluster of peace parks: the goal was to atone for a 1947 government attack on civilians, though the resulting peace themes could have wider and more contemporary applications.

Interest fluctuates, to be sure. Between 1988 and 1992, by one calculation, the number of peace groups worldwide dropped by 35 percent, due to declining fears of nuclear war (thanks to the end of the Cold War) and also political settlements in Central America. But then new regional conflicts, concern about uses of American power and other issues generated a new set of activities.

Except where rigidly authoritarian regimes predominate, there is no part of the world and no crisis area that has not seen the emergence of new peace organizations. Thus in 2005 a group of private citizens in India and Pakistan helped launch an initiative called the Peace Bus, to help people in Kashmir, on both sides of the military border, get together with relatives and, hopefully, reduce the tensions involved. Peace organizations flourished in many parts of Africa. In 1984, for example, the Nairobi Peace Initiative-Africa was founded, as a pan-African institution aiming at providing conflict mediation, training and capacity building, research and humanitarian outreach, aimed of course at promoting peace throughout the continent. A PeaceWomen project, affiliated with the United Nations, set up conferences in many parts of the world to involve women in peace efforts and generate research on topics relevant to peace. It also sponsored regional affiliates, such as a group in Ghana, West Africa that sought to mobilize African women for peace causes. Again, the range and variety were dazzling, and remain so today.

Initiatives to promote peace in Israel and Palestine reflected the intensity of conflicts in the region, but also the desire to generate solutions. Literally hundreds of relevant groups sprang up, in the area and abroad, working on various aspects of reconciliation and policy. A number of United States philanthropists brought Israeli and Palestinian youth together, for example in summer camps. The Alternative Information Center was set up near Jerusalem in 1984. It was one of the first joint Palestinian and Israeli organizations within Israel, and often drew police attention from the government because of its opposition to Israeli occupation of arguably Palestinian territory. On yet another plane, the Machsom Watch was set up in 2001, for women only: the Watch sends observers to checkpoints between Israeli and Palestinian territories to monitor abuses and the free flow of people and goods, or lack thereof; it publishes regular reports on line. The goal is nonviolent action to press the government in the interests of greater justice and peace. Another group, Women in Black, organized in 1988, in Israel but with an international membership: members hold weekly silent vigils for peace, wearing black clothing. Still another group, the Peres Center for Peace (founded by a former president of Israel) works on direct Israeli-Palestinian interaction, seeking to reduce tensions and form a more peaceful younger generation through shared activities. Thus it sponsors technology research by teams of students from a Palestinian and an Israeli university; it supports fashion industry collaboration, with Israeli stylists visiting various Palestinian textile factories; it teams with a Spanish football club to organize soccer clinics for 2000 Israeli and Palestinian youth, as part of the club's larger "Peace Tour." A host of groups, finally, undertake scholarly activities and outreach around the widely discussed "two state" solution, that seeks to resolve conflict through the establishment of separate Israeli and Palestinian states. And the list goes on.

Other conflict regions saw an organizational response. Sri Lanka was long locked in a struggle between the government and separatist Tamil ethnic groups, involving a great deal of internal bloodshed. Concerned about the level of violence and what they saw as international neglect, a group of citizens formed the Campaign for Peace and Justice. This multi-ethnic organization sought to monitor atrocities on both sides of the conflict (though particularly those it claimed were perpetrated by the government). It used social media to call international attention to the violations, hoping to induce more active United Nations intervention. It also provided more direct humanitarian relief to those in the war zones.

Yet another set of efforts tried to involve governments in new peace commitments, through organizational initiatives on an international scale. Early in the twenty-first century the Solomon Islands became the first government to set up a Department of Peace. Nepal joined in soon thereafter, and in 2009 Costa Rica converted its Ministry of Justice into a Ministry of Justice and Peace, hoping that more explicit promotion of peace would encourage nonviolence locally and globally alike. Costa Rica quickly arranged for an international conference, to promote Peace Departments in other countries. Supporting the initiative, the Dalai Lama endorsed with effort:

> Peace is not something which exists independently of us, any more than war does. Those who are responsible for creating and keeping the peace are members of our own human family, the society that we as individuals participate in and help to create. Peace in the world thus depends on there being peace in the hearts of individuals.

It was not clear whether other countries would join this tentative new movement, but by 2013 32 nations were considering the possibility. Legislation for a Department of Peace was routinely introduced to the United States Congress, though with no concrete results. The movement for a department in Canada – as one Canadian Senator put it, "the department would develop a coordinated and coherent paradigm for sustainable peace across all government units" – roused greater enthusiasm.

The surge of voluntary organizations, such as Paths for Peace, combined with United Nations interests to establish an annual international Peace Day (September 21), beginning with a General Assembly resolution in 1981. While hardly a massive success, the Day did rouse various peace and religious groups to significant public observances.

While not part of this quasi-official initiative, the Alliance for Peacebuilding – an umbrella United States organization – illustrated the diversity of strategies peace organizations could adopt. The group linked a variety of civic organizations across the country. It supported educational efforts, with close relationships to academic centers in the conflict resolution field. An annual conference brought local leaders together to discuss current peace issues and reconciliation strategies. The Alliance worked hard to bring its concerns to the attention of groups like the State Department and the governmental Institute for Peace. But it was also available for quick response to current threats: thus in 2013 a proposed American military strike against the Syrian government brought quick calls for a peace conference instead, with former President Jimmy Carter providing a leading voice to the initiative.

Countries more remote from the global fray nevertheless had their own rich diet of peace institutions. New Zealand, for example, a country that increasingly developed a sense of identity around peace initiatives, featured a Peace Foundation that, in turn, loosely coordinated a host of separate efforts. Two universities sponsored undergraduate degrees in conflict resolution. The National Center for Peace and Conflict Studies offered master's and doctoral degrees, while providing advice to public and private institutions on reconciliation approaches. A branch of a French Catholic movement, the *Pax Christi*, provided another facet. A United Nations association and a youth counterpart focused strongly on peacekeeping, while New Zealand also boasted an affiliate of the Women's International League (the group that dated back to 1915). A Disarmament Center in Christchurch operated out of a private home, but sought to spur the government in this domain. The Global Peace and Justice Center in Auckland sprang up in response to the wars in Iraq and Afghanistan. And here, too, the list goes on.

South Korea, confronted with greater regional potential for conflict, has its own rich roster. Foreign organizations work on peace in the peninsula, including an American Quaker group, an initiative by concerned US veterans of the Korean War, and a New Zealand Korean Peace Committee. Interestingly, Korean Buddhism played little role, in contrast to its Japanese counterpart: emphasis rested on individual contemplation and spiritual improvement. But anti- nuclear activities spurred various organizations, and then in the twenty-first century widespread opposition to the American-led invasion of Iraq created new interest in peace themes. Among Koreans themselves, Solidarity for Peace and Reunification of Korea (SPARK) concentrates on reconciliation with North Korea and withdrawal of American military forces. Nodutal is a Korean community development organization seeking the peaceful reunification of the peninsula. Nautilus, based in Seoul, works on regional, Northeast Asian issues, including efforts against nuclear proliferation. Women Making Peace is a specialist organization, formed in 1998, conducting research on regional peace from a feminist perspective. A Peace Network tries to build a framework for open exchanges of opinions between North and South.

Examples could be multiplied, but the basic point is clear: Most countries, by the early twenty-first century, offer a diverse array, easily comparable to the pattern in South Korea or New Zealand, reflecting particular local issues but almost always with connections to various international movements and support agencies. Active membership is often small, but there are opportunities to rouse larger campaigns when specific threats arise. The global expansion of grassroots efforts clearly explains the bewildering number of specific labels, but serves directly as one of the key markers of contemporary change. Overall, the unprecedented range of peace organizations combines a number of sources: concern about the dangers of war and violence in the contemporary world; the spur provided by the growing number of peace "experts" and academic programs; the new voices generated by local opportunities and international sponsorship. Mobilization for peace has become a global resource.

* * * * *

The great question beyond the undeniable proliferation of groups and movements, was: so what? What did this new level of popular and scholarly activity accomplish? And what might be some realistic hopes for the future?

Obviously, there were many failures and limitations. While the impressive array of reconciliation groups in Israel and Palestine may have helped to temper violence, they did not produce lasting peace. Conflict resolution techniques worked in some cases but not in all: some of the worst conflict settings in Africa, in places like Sudan and the Congo, provided vivid examples of the constraints.

But specific strategies and a broader awareness of a peace option could have effects. Popular mobilization did ultimately influence nuclear policy, even if risk remained. Peace initiatives have affected the way foreign policy is conducted, in many societies – including the United States. They provide unprecedented support for specific peace agreements, in places like the Balkans or post-conflict zones in Africa, helping to insure more than on-paper settlements. Some scholars contend that the results, in combination with the United Nations initiatives and other strategic forces, including the various pressures toward reduction of military budgets, add up to a new linkage between participatory democracy and the goals of peace.

One other complexity must be noted. Many peace groups, including some of the most active local organizations, stand for peace but also justice, often defined in terms of human rights. The dual commitment often makes sense, but it can raise questions about priorities. Is nonviolence the chief goal, or can a group advocate military solutions when human rights abuses persist – possibly along lines of the Responsibility to Protect idea? Must democracy be established, by force if necessary, before peace is secure? Growing peace activism inevitably generated new debates.

Overall, the surge of peace ideas and initiatives is relatively recent, by the slow-moving standards of world history overall. It builds on prior precedent, but it adds a variety of interesting innovations. It may be too soon to tell how the mixture is working – though as we will see in the Epilogue some bold spirits think we may have entered a new era. At the least, it seems fair to say that awareness of options other than war and military response is more active, with more opportunities for expression, than ever before on a global basis.

Further reading

Abu-Nimer, Mohammad. "Religious Leaders in the Israeli-Palestinian Conflict: From Violent Incitement to Nonviolence Resistance." *Peace & Change* 36.4 (2011): 556–80.

Avruch, Kevin. "Does Our Field Have a Centre? Thoughts from the Academy." *International Journal of Conflict Engagement and Resolution* 1.1 (2013): 10–11.

Bell, Christine and Catherine O'Rourke. "The People's Peace? Peace Agreements, Civil Society, and Participatory Democracy." *International Political Science Review* 28.3 (2007): 293–324.

Chakrabarty, Bidyut. *Confluence of Thought: Mahatma Gandhi and Martin Luther King, Jr.* New York: Oxford University Press, 2013.

Ikeda, Daisaku. *Compassion, Wisdom and Courage: Building a Global Society of Peace and Creative Coexistence.* Tokyo: Soka Gakkai International, 2013.

Kriesbert, Louis. "The Conflict Resolution Field: Origins, Growth, and Differentiation." In Zartman, I. William, ed., *Peace Making in International Conflict: Methods & Techniques.* Washington, D.C.: United States Institute of Peace, 2007.

Stearns, Peter N *Global Outrage: The Origins and Impact of World Opinion from the 1780s to the 21st Century.* Oxford: Oneworld Publications, 2005.

On peacebuilding

Bell, Christine and Catherine O'Rourke. "The Peoples Peace? Peace Agreements, Civil Society, and Participatory Democracy." *International Political Science Review* 28.3 (2007): 293–324.

Chenoweth, Erica and Maria J. Stephan. *Why Civil Resistance Works: The Strategic Logic of Nonviolent Conflict.* New York: Columbia University Press, 2011.

Jensen, Lloyd. "Negotiating Strategic Arms Control, 1969–1979." *The Journal of Conflict Resolution* 28.3 (1984): 535–59.

Nehring, Holger. *The Politics of Security: Protests against Nuclear Weapons and the Early Cold War.* Oxford: Oxford University Press, 2013.

Richmond, Oliver P., Roland Paris, and Edward Newman. *New Perspectives on Liberal Peacebuilding.* Tokyo: United Nations University Press, 2009.

Sheehan, James. *Where Have All the Soldiers Gone? The Transformation of Modern Europe.* New York: Houghton Mifflin, 2008.

On Islam and nonviolence

Pal, Amitabh. *"Islam" Means Peace: Understanding the Muslim Principle of Nonviolence Today.* Sana Barbara, CA: Praeger, 2011.

Sayilgan, Zeyneb, and Salih Sayilgan. "Bediuzzaman Said Nursi's Ethics of Non-Violence: Implications for Christian-Muslim Relations Today." *Dialog: A Journal of Theology* 50.3 (2011): 242–52.

Shank, Michael. "Islam's Nonviolent Tradition." *Nation* 292.20 (2011): 24–5.

Epilogue

Analysis of peace in world history suggests a cup half empty or half filled. On the one hand, impressive visions and strategies to assure greater peace dot the human experience. The aspiration is clearly a fundamental part of the global story, despite its neglect in most history books. People arguably have at least as natural a peace impulse as an impulse to war. And major societies have achieved long periods of peace, in part at least through explicit goals and deliberate arrangements.

Yet the historical cup is clearly unfilled. No major society has managed to definitively banish war. Even demilitarized societies today keep debating the topic. Every large claim, including recent ones about a war to end all war or even simply peace in our time, has proved hollow. Motives for conflict run strong. Many states develop an active stake in war, or in methods and institutions that make war difficult to avoid.

World history suggests, then, that efforts to produce peace will continue to surface. But it also suggests that it might be foolish to expect permanent success.

But some peace advocates in the present day, in the United States but also in many other societies, believe or at least strongly hope that some components now exist that might allow more decisive departures from the past – in part of course because wars over the past century have proved to be unusually dreadful, in terms of brutality and loss of life. They argue that we now have a growing array of trained professionals who put peace first, and who can help societies more generally turn away from violence. They note for example that a number of fragile states, newly recovered from war or internal strife, now sign up specifically with conflict-prevention groups, hoping to learn new ways to include former foes in a common purpose. They see ways to incorporate peace commitments into other fields, such as economic development or even water management – areas that, without active advice, can easily generate potentials for dispute.

The peace experts argue as well for the importance and promise of education. They see the possibility of incorporating mediation techniques into school curricula. Why, they contend, cannot peace building become as popular with contemporary youth as environmental sustainability has become? Why can't peace advocacy take its place alongside the promotion of human rights, pressing citizens and governments alike to shun war in favor of other means of resolving conflict? After all, growing consciousness of human rights has clearly created at least some improvements in conditions in many societies; can we not aspire to a similar agenda for the promotion of peace?

As we have noted, there may in fact be a real tendency, at least for the moment, for a growing number of states to shun war, preferring to privilege other goals. Violence increasingly involves transnational criminals, more than government actors – hardly a promise of utopia, but a suggestion that change is possible. Can peace become a more standard expectation on the part of ordinary citizens, so that war is viewed not as a normal recourse but as a clear sign of failure?

For there is some evidence, though it is both varied and quite recent. A number of kinds of violence may be declining, and some authorities argue that this may be one of the most important, but least appreciated, developments in human history. No one denies that wars continue or that even greater problems still exist with civil war and terrorism; but there are signs of change. For Americans, calculations here may be particularly startling, since the nation has been at war for 14 of 21 years since the Cold War ended. Overall, armed conflict between states has dropped particularly rapidly since 1990, but civil strife is also down – a 60 percent drop for both forms of collective violence, by some calculations. Whereas 30 percent of the world's countries were experiencing some kind of political violence in 1992, that number dropped to 13 percent in 2010, increasing to 16 percent the next year because of the risings in the Middle East.* The questions are, first, are these only temporary trends? – and by definition we cannot know for sure. But also: are there plausible explanations for the changes, and do these explanations offer some hope of durability?

Three transformations in world conditions might suggest some basis for at least modest optimism. First, as we have seen, contemporary weaponry threatens unprecedented damage, possibly even the species itself. A number of states now have the experience of maintaining a nuclear arsenal which, they know, cannot be responsibly deployed in battle. We cannot be sure that this restraint will hold, but it has certainly affected actual political behavior for over half a century; and its implications might extend to other expressions as well, quite apart from the important contemporary precedent of outright demilitarization and the widespread recalculation of military costs.

Second, global changes in political and economic structure might support peace in new ways. The expansion of democracy to most major world regions might be a further deterrent for war. In the flush of excitement at the end of the Cold War, we have seen some pundits argued that democracies would never go

---

* Obviously, estimating rates here is a challenging task, and the figures are debated. It is also worth noting that the same scholars calculate a significant decline in battlefield deaths when war does occur, as a percentage of the population involved, reflecting better medical care but also some of the weapons controls and humanitarian rules that have developed alongside peace efforts.

to war against other democracies – the implication being that ordinary people will push much harder for attention to economic and social issues than for military experiments. The claim is debatable, and of course a number of important states are not democracies in any event. But perhaps popular caution can play some role in promoting greater peace in future, if and as democracy confirms its role as the most common contemporary political form. The move of some newly democratic African and Central American countries to reduce their military forces, in favor of alternative uses of resources, suggests a possible connection in some cases, where responsiveness to voters changes government priorities. If consumerism also supports peace, there may be additional hope for the future.

And third, the rise of explicit peace keeping operations and peace associations surely help explain the recent decline in warfare. Even the proliferation of peace experts, armed with new knowledge and tactics and not simply good intentions (which are not a modern invention), may prove to be a vital innovation in its own right, providing types of practical advice that had not been available before. Here, as with the claims about democracy, there is a chance to test hope against historical experience. Is there enough basic innovation in the substance and influence of contemporary expertise advocacy – compared, for example, to religious guidance in earlier societies – to provide new bases for optimism? Are some of the new groups that both chart peace gains and offer active help in building peace alternatives, like the Alliance for Peacebuilding, capable of wielding even more influence in the future?

The factors of change may of course be combining, gaining force in the process. Consumerism by itself might not convert the world to peace, but if bolstered by new expertise and international organizations the overall accumulation might tip the scales. The basic question involves historical judgment: have contemporary global societies really moved far enough away from the conditions and goals that spoiled peace efforts in the past?

A crucial question involves regional trends, and the interpretation of regional balance. Some key states have converted very little if at all to a new interest in peace, and these include at least one nation with nuclear capacity. As even the optimists recognize, a single nuclear bomb could change current trends in an instant. At least for a time, prospects may depend disproportionately on the United States: is U.S. power a force for peace, or a complication? And is there likely to be any major change in the American equation in the future? Will the number of clear regional trouble spots grow again, or can some existing centers (as with southern Africa in recent decades, or Southeast Asia since the 1970s) be tamed?

Peace has always been a challenge. There is genuine reason to argue that it has become more important than ever before to try to meet the challenge. The historical record offers abundant food for skepticism about the human capacity to manage war. But the same record may also help us figure out what might be open to change, or already be changing, in order to escape some of the failures of the past. And is it just possible, as the optimists argue, that the human species has finally learned from its historical experience, both in terms of the horrors of modern war but also in terms of key innovations that can now be solidified and expanded in order to do better in future – to go beyond former failures? The past offers abundant lessons of aggressive folly, but also a diverse array of precedents for organizing for peace; is the balance changing?

At the very least, awareness of peace is essential. Without an explicit commitment to peace as a goal, a society risks steady military expansion constrained only by resource limits, and sometimes not even by them. And this is a bad result for the society involved and for the world around it. Peace is challenging, its advocacy can seem naïve, but we are better off having it in our active political vocabulary. Here, a fuller sense of human history is a vital part of the process. Peace sometimes results from accident or exhaustion, but more often it follows from explicit goals and actions, and this reliance on intention and effort will surely increase in future.

Further reading

Goldstein, Joshua. *Winning the War on War: The Decline of Armed Conflict Worldwide.* New York: Penguin Group, 2012.

Pinker, Steven. *The Better Angels of Our Nature: Why Violence Has Declined.* New York: Penguin Group, 2011.

Index